The Pleasures of Metamorphosis

SERIES IN FAIRY-TALE STUDIES

General Editor
Donald Haase, Wayne State University

Advisory Editors
Cristina Bacchilega, University of Hawaiʻi, Mānoa
Stephen Benson, University of East Anglia
Nancy L. Canepa, Dartmouth College
Anne E. Duggan, Wayne State University
Pauline Greenhill, University of Winnipeg
Christine A. Jones, University of Utah
Janet Langlois, Wayne State University
Ulrich Marzolph, University of Göttingen
Carolina Fernández Rodríguez, University of Oviedo
Maria Tatar, Harvard University
Jack Zipes, University of Minnesota

*A complete listing of the books in this series
can be found online at wsupress.wayne.edu*

The Pleasures of Metamorphosis

Japanese and English Fairy Tale Transformations of "The Little Mermaid"

LUCY FRASER

Wayne State University Press
Detroit

© 2017 by Wayne State University Press, Detroit, Michigan 48201. All rights reserved. No part of this book may be reproduced without formal permission. Manufactured in the United States of America.

ISBN 978-0-8143-4244-2 (paper) | ISBN 978-0-8143-4245-9 (e-book)
Library of Congress Control Number: 2016959423

Published with the assistance of a fund established by Thelma Gray James of Wayne State University for the publication of folklore and English studies.

Wayne State University Press
Leonard N. Simons Building
4809 Woodward Avenue
Detroit, Michigan 48201-1309

Visit us online at wsupress.wayne.edu

Contents

Acknowledgments vii

Author's Note ix

Introduction 1

1. Fairy Tale Transformations in Japanese and English   5
2. Children's Pleasures in Animated Film Adaptations   39
3. Fairy Tale Architextuality and the Prince's Pleasures   70
4. Mermaids Repeated, Inverted, and Reversed in Women's Fairy Tale Revisions   95
5. Girls Reading and Retelling "The Little Mermaid"   126
6. Beyond Happily Ever After in Women's Post–Fairy Tale Transformations   157

Conclusion   184

Works Cited   191

Index   213

Acknowledgments

I have so many people to thank for their support throughout the long journey of this book—I'll name only a few. I thank my mentors and advisors Tomoko Aoyama, Akiko Uchiyama, Kan Satoko, and Takeuchi Kayo. I am very grateful to Mayako Murai, Rebecca Copeland, and the two anonymous reviewers for their thoughtful and thought-provoking comments. Hong Cai also provided valuable assistance with Chinese titles. I thank Annie Martin, Carrie Teefey, and everyone at Wayne State University Press for their hard work, and for being so understanding and encouraging. I'm lucky to have some wonderful colleagues and friends, and a family who have made this project possible (especially with all their help since August 2016). And of course, my love to Oliver and Theo, who have made life exciting along the way.

Author's Note

Japanese names are given in Japanese order, with family name first and then given name, except for those who adopt the English name order in their publications. Translations are my own unless otherwise indicated.

Introduction

Since the publication of Hans Christian Andersen's fairy tale "The Little Mermaid" in 1837, it has traveled across countries and languages, transforming into an astounding variety of forms. The human-fish hybrid body of Andersen's mermaid and the troubled relationship the story poses between this body and the mermaid's romantic and spiritual desires have inspired critical and creative musings on gender and its intersections with body, sexuality, and social roles. Moreover, the plot of "The Little Mermaid" seems to anticipate the tale's transcultural, translinguistic movement: a nonhuman creature yearns for the human "other," which leads her, first, to change her body and move from the ocean into an alien land where she cannot speak and, second, to move again to another foreign realm as an unseen elemental spirit.

Though Andersen is a beloved figure of the literary fairy tale canon, and his work and life have been thoroughly documented, the current wave of fairy tale studies research has yet to carefully scrutinize the way gender is imagined in retellings of his stories, particularly across different cultures. This book addresses these topics through analyzing Japanese and English transformations of "The Little Mermaid." It especially focuses on the ways transformations respond to and reshape the complex images of gender presented in the tale. This focus in turn facilitates a discussion of the driving forces behind the production of not only fairy tale retellings but also their academic critiques: that is, the pleasures of consuming and transforming fairy tales.

The framework of "pleasure," I argue, can bring together texts that might otherwise be separated by differences in language, background, time period, genre, and medium and by the borders of "high" and "low" cultural forms. In considering the pleasures of reading and writing fairy tale transformations, I focus especially on the pleasure of audiences who enjoy a transformation through their awareness of its relationship with "The Little Mermaid" and with the fairy tale form. The authors of fairy tale transformations themselves, as well as their audiences—including fairy tale studies academics—count among these readers who move between multiple texts and thereby between the ideas of gender that they see in Andersen's tale, in conventional fairy tale gender roles, and in the transformation.

This perspective provides an alternative response to one of the questions at the heart of fairy tale studies, articulated by Jack Zipes, for example, as "why fairy tales stick." Rather than attempting to replicate Zipes's historical investigations into the ideological and social functions of the fairy tale, however, and without eliciting readers' responses, I turn to pleasure as it is presented in fairy tale texts and surrounding "paratexts" (such as prefaces, afterwords, and other commentary). That is, I take up the fairy tale pleasures that the transformations of "The Little Mermaid" invite their readers and audiences to partake in, as well as the pleasures that these stories depict. The texts under consideration transmit a number of metatextual messages about the pleasures of fairy tales and fairy tale transformation. They do so, for example, through images of characters enjoying pleasures that simulate reading or consumption of texts, or images of characters actually reading fairy tales and other texts, or again through authors' commentary. Moreover, the pleasures depicted quite often divide along gender lines, indicating that these pleasures intersect in complex ways with the construction of gender in transformations of Andersen's tale of desire and pain. This consideration of reading pleasure enables the insight that rather than fairy tale audiences—including children and especially girls, who are the objects of particular concern on this topic—being passively influenced by the content they consume, they can enjoy more active and unpredictable interactions with the fairy tale form.

The texts selected here go some way to representing the huge variety of ways in which "The Little Mermaid" has been transformed and the many and nuanced pleasures associated with these transformations. The earliest of the tales I investigate was published in 1891 and the most recent in 2008; they include stories by well-known literary authors, illustrated books for children, young-adult fiction and popular fiction, and animated and live-action television and film productions. All the tales transform across languages, as they are not in the Danish of Andersen's tale but in other languages: English (with some relationship to Danish) and the much more distant Japanese. These languages belong to the "West" and the "East," respectively, two quite artificial and changeable cultural groupings that often imagine themselves in stark opposition. This positioning also entails complex hierarchical relations and shifting ideas of the "exotic" and "other."

The wealth of versions of "The Little Mermaid" in these two languages therefore demands nuanced critical approaches. In exploring gender and pleasure in transformations across English and Japanese, this book takes up

Mayako Murai's project in *From Dog Bridegroom to Wolf Girl: Contemporary Japanese Fairy-Tale Adaptations in Conversation with the West*: it aims to "emphasize the gain, rather than the loss, in adopting a cross-cultural approach" and also to address the "lack of critical, especially feminist, scrutiny of how fairy tales are received and transformed in contemporary Japan" (12). Like Murai, I therefore examine how feminist and other fairy tale studies from the West can be brought to bear on Japanese texts. Like Murai, I am mindful of the risks inherent in such a critical project but also believe that it can in turn enhance Anglophone or Western research. Furthermore, I aim to avoid a Western-centric view by incorporating Japanese theoretical frameworks. One major example is my use of particular literary and cultural studies approaches to girls' culture—*shōjo* (girl) studies. In chapter 5, I argue that because of the cross-cultural roots of *shōjo* studies theories, they can also be effectively used to interpret non-Japanese girls' texts.

In this book's focus on the pleasures of Japanese and English transformations of "The Little Mermaid," then, I hope to offer an open-ended approach toward comparative literary studies, Japanese literary and cultural studies, and gender studies research. In particular, I hope to contribute to the contemporary fairy tale studies enterprise to find ways to approach the bewildering array of texts that emanates from a canonical fairy tale.

1
Fairy Tale Transformations in Japanese and English

> Fairy tales, as the Grimms discovered, have no more sense of nation or native tongue than swifts or butterflies, and have proved stubborn and repeating emigrants, always slipping across the borders (and back again).
>
> —Marina Warner, *Once upon a Time: A Short History of Fairy Tale*

The heroine of Hans Christian Andersen's 1837 Danish fairy tale "The Little Mermaid" becomes, at the end of the tale, a "daughter of the air." Yet even before she is able to fly, she slips across borders: her half-fish form in itself rejects the boundaries of the human body; she changes from mermaid to human and then becomes sea foam so that the border between her body and the sea is removed. Finally she is re-formed as an ethereal air sprite. The mermaid also moves between locations, journeying from the ocean to the land before reaching the sky. Andersen's popular tale itself has shifted between forms, countries, and cultures in similar ways.

The mermaid's movement and metamorphosis are tied to her gendered body in ways that have fascinated retellers of the tale in many different languages. The story is told from the mermaid's perspective, a female "other" to the male, human world. She is portrayed as a desiring, active female subject whose willing abnegation for a man brings her a great deal of suffering. The complexity of Andersen's take on gender, and its occurrence in a genre that is occasionally assumed to be "universal," has offered ample space for interpretation in contexts far removed from the tale's 1830s Danish origins. There is certainly a rich variety of transformations available in the languages of this study, English and Japanese, appearing from the late nineteenth century through to the early twenty-first century.

In engaging with an analysis of cross-cultural reinterpretations of gender in "The Little Mermaid," I respond to Warner's eloquent lines quoted in the epigraph, about the elusive, effusive nature of fairy tales. These words seem to call for scholarship that does not focus on the sense of "nation" of a tale, nor on a hierarchical structure of "influence" that one author receives from another, nor on the authority of any particular version. Rather, such a study should examine the tale's meandering journeys and divergent meanings.

Here I argue for an examination of the "pleasures" of fairy tales and what I term *fairy tale transformations*. This approach provides a means to examine the zigzagging movement of the fairy tale, across national borders as well as between "high" and "low" culture and through different understandings of gender. Through providing a glimpse into Japanese translations, transformations, and theory, I also aim to offer readers some approximation of the mermaid's journey across cultures, enriching the cultural sources of the field of fairy tale studies in English.

This chapter begins with a sketch of the ideas of "pleasure" that are used to analyze the transformations, with a focus on the uses and limitations of these ideas for analyzing gender. I then discuss the use of this approach specifically for the cross-cultural study of one fairy tale in two languages. Setting the scene for the transformations analyzed in the following chapters, the chapter then provides a history of "The Little Mermaid" in Japanese and English, including interpretations of Andersen's tale, and an outline of the paths it has traced since it was translated into these languages.

Fairy Tales, Transformations, and Pleasure

That writers and readers read and retell fairy tales because doing so is pleasurable seems so obvious that it is almost not worth mentioning. Yet theorizing fairy tale texts through the lens of pleasure, I argue, can tell us an enormous amount about individual texts as well as the vitality of the fairy tale form. From a literary studies approach, questions about pleasures are directed at the fairy tale transformations themselves, rather than through a study of reader psychology or reader response, for example. Focusing on the way fairy tale transformations reimagine gender, in this book I ask, how do transformations of "The Little Mermaid" portray pleasure? And what pleasures do the transformations invite the reader to experience? That is, how does pleasure function within these texts? The concept of pleasure becomes most useful where the answers to these questions tend to overlap. That is, many of the transformations portray characters enjoying texts, thereby providing metacommentary on the pleasures we take in absorbing fairy tales and the reasons we continue to transform them.

Transformation is the magic that is built into the fairy tale, which is also known as the "wonder tale." Magic regularly manifests itself in events of metamorphosis, impossible changes in form, as when a fantastical creature such as a mermaid gains human legs or morphs into an air spirit. Transformation also structures the fairy tale genre, in which the fairy tale morphs constantly into new shapes but remains somehow recognizable. *Transformation* is therefore the label I adopt here to describe fairy tale intertextuality. This term is partly a reference to Julia Kristeva, who, working from Mikhail Bakhtin's notion of dialogism, states that "any text is the absorption and transformation of another" (37). The term is also used by Cristina Bacchilega, particularly in her recent work *Fairy Tales Transformed? Twenty-First-Century Adaptations and the Politics of Wonder* (2013). Referring to Jack Zipes's ongoing explorations of the function and power of fairy tales within human society, Bacchilega writes, "Thinking about transformation—within the tales' storyworlds; in the genre's ongoing process of production, reception, reproduction, adaptation and translation; in the fairy-tale's relation to other genres; and more generally as action in the social world—offers a spacious and productive way into that exploration" (*Fairy Tales Transformed?* 3). A specific set of these texts had earlier been described by Bacchilega as "postmodern fairy tales" (*Postmodern Fairy Tales*, 1997), but the term *transformations* proves to be more open-ended. The kind of intertextual practice that Kristeva outlines is not limited to contemporary or postmodern fairy tale retellings: as Walter Ong shows, it was an inherent part of "manuscript" (preprinting) storytelling culture.[1] And the complex mix of literary and oral history of the Japanese fairy tale *otogibanashi*—discussed in this chapter—is a strong example of a similar situation in Japan.

Since the intertextual practice of transformation is vital to the fairy tale genre itself, we might suggest that every fairy tale is also a fairy tale transformation. But the distinction is useful here to emphasize the relationship between Andersen's fairy tale "The Little Mermaid" (which itself absorbs

---

[1] Ong observes that the manuscript culture of medieval Europe "had taken intertextuality for granted. Still tied to the commonplace tradition of the old oral world, it deliberately created texts out of other texts, borrowing, adapting, sharing the common, originally oral, formulas and themes, even though it worked them up into fresh literary forms impossible without writing" (133). In a more specific and fairy tale–related context, Elizabeth Wanning Harries also maintains that self-conscious, transformative, intertextual traditions are not limited to recent texts but were also seen in the literary fairy tales by French women writers in the 1690s.

and transforms other fairy tales and other texts) and subsequent texts that transform Andersen's tale. The umbrella term *fairy tale transformation*, then, is adopted to express a connection to the other genres and the social world that Bacchilega mentions but also because it can incorporate postmodern as well as other types of narratives and because it stretches to describe the quite tenuous ways in which some of these texts retell Andersen's story.

Transformation, as a defining element of the fairy tale's marvelous nature, as well as a description of the fairy tale's tendency to replicate and mutate, is also a source of pleasure in the fairy tale text. Marina Warner ponders on the effects of such fairy tale pleasures, where metamorphosis forms a major part of "all the wonders that create the atmosphere of the fairy tale," which "disrupt the apprehensible world in order to open spaces for dreaming alternatives. The verb 'to wonder' communicates the receptive state of marvelling as well as the active desire to know, to inquire, and as such it defines very well at least two characteristics of the traditional fairy tale: pleasure in the fantastic, curiosity about the real" (*From the Beast* xx). As Warner explains it, the fairy tale's pleasurable engagement with the marvelous means the genre can be both restrictive and potentially liberating. That is, imagining a world where anything can happen allows storytellers to impose limits and boundaries but, at the same time, allows them to "unlock social and public possibilities" (xx).

The conscious transformation of fairy tales—the act of rereading and retelling to create something new—amplifies the "possibilities" that Warner mentions, not least the possibility of questioning restrictive gender norms. Bacchilega articulates the potential for postmodern fairy tales to reimagine notions of gender through Judith Butler's concept of performativity. For Butler, gender identity is constantly produced and reproduced by and on people's bodies, with no "natural" basis: "There is no gender identity behind the expressions of gender; . . . identity is performatively constituted by the very 'expressions' that are said to be its results" (33). This performativity of gender may then be exposed and subverted by more literal performances of gender, such as drag shows: "*In imitating gender, drag implicitly reveals the imitative structure of gender itself*" (Butler 175, original emphasis). In such instances of gender parody that Butler describes, "the parody is *of* the very notion of an original" (175, original emphasis), revealing that gender is not an essential truth but is itself always an imitation. As Bacchilega argues in *Postmodern Fairy Tales*, transformations can similarly exaggerate fairy tale conventions in critical ways that expose their arbitrariness. Traditional fairy tale techniques, such as a disembodied third-person narrator, present gender roles as natural and unquestionable. Postmodern fairy tales can "denaturalize" and question these gender roles by exposing the narrative techniques that entrench them.

One particular pleasure of fairy tale transformations that is especially key to this type of genre/gender parody is laughter. Contagious laughter is portrayed in transformations of "The Little Mermaid"—we see, for example, children and other creatures laughing in the animated film *Gake no ue no Ponyo* (*Ponyo on the Cliff by the Sea*, dir. Miyazaki Hayao, 2008; see chapter 2) and girl readers laughing together (see chapter 5). Many of the texts invite readers to laugh at the gap between Andersen's tale and its transformation, at their inversions of the mermaid—for example, we are invited to laugh at the mermaid's body itself in the fish-headed, human-legged parody in Kurahashi Yumiko's short story (see chapter 4) or at the romance of Andersen's mermaid story as it is juxtaposed against the dystopian realm of the *Dark Angel* television series (see chapter 6). It is easy to imagine how these amusing inversions and juxtapositions are well situated to pose challenges to the constructions of gender proposed in Andersen's story and in broader social contexts.

Laughter in itself is a physical release, a liberating pleasure. The fairy tale's origins in folk culture may make fairy tale transformations especially receptive to the kind of emancipating "folk laughter" that Mikhail Bakhtin argues for. Bakhtin views medieval folk laughter as a complement to the officialdom and serious ceremony of the period, a necessary relief. It is associated with the earthly body, and in this association with the physical, the grotesque, and birth and death, folk laughter becomes a bodily force that disrupts social systems, expressing "an element of victory not only over supernatural awe, over the sacred, over death; it also means the defeat of power, of earthly kings, of the earthly upper classes, of all that oppresses and restricts" (92).

The socially disruptive potential of laughter and other joyful experiences has proven appealing for many who attempt to theorize pleasure. Fairy tale transformations can offer the pleasures of *reading* that Roland Barthes distinguishes: *plaisir* (pleasure) in contenting, "comfortable" reading, and the *jouissance* (bliss) experienced in texts that "discomfort" and "unsettle" the reader (14). We might also discern in some fairy tale transformations the pleasures of *writing* that Hélène Cixous famously described in 1975 in "The Laugh of the Medusa." Using folkloric and mythological imagery and a striking rhetoric of joyful free movement, Cixous calls for women's ecstatic, liberating *jouissance* in *l'écriture féminine*, "writing the body." Laughter, linked to the release of *jouissance*, can disrupt the patriarchal power over/of language; it has the potential "to smash everything, to shatter the framework of institutions, to blow up the law, to break up the 'truth'" (888). In Japan, around the same time of Cixous's writing, the *yamauba*—a "mountain witch" found in folktales, medieval literature, and Noh plays—was being subjected to revisionist writings by women, who used this solitary, frightening female figure to explore the limitations of patriarchal ideas of femininity (Murai, *From Dog Bridegroom* 20–21). In one of several critical considerations of the *yamauba*'s meanings and feminist potential in literature (see Mizuta and Kitada; Wilson; cited by Murai, *From Dog Bridegroom* 148n10), Meera Viswanathan brings *yamauba* short stories by the reviser of fairy tales and folklore Ōba Minako—"The Smile of the Mountain Witch" (1976) and "Candlefish" (1986)—into "imaginary dialogue" (Viswanathan 256) with Cixous's rallying call for women to reclaim their true selves through the pleasure of writing.

In addition to the radical potential of humor and laughter in texts by women in particular, directing the spotlight onto it helps to combat the entrenched stereotype found in both English- and Japanese-speaking cultures that "women are not funny," which has fed into the critical neglect of studies of women's humor in Japan especially.[2] On the other hand, Cixous's potentially essentializing view of a female literary voice—though reclaimed by Bacchilega[3]—should be handled with caution. After all, a different concept of "women's writing" has not been liberating in the Japanese context especially, where so-called women's literature (*joryū bungaku*) has been consistently labeled and marginalized by a male-dominated literary establishment (*bundan*).[4]

Importantly, a pleasure such as laughter—invited by parody and inversion or other comic devices such as exaggeratedly physical bodies—may have the radical potential to overturn the established gender order, but this is not its only possible effect. Laughter may equally be conformist. Humor, as we shall see in relation to the children's animated films in chapter 2, can just as easily utilize audience pleasures to conservative ideological ends.

---

[2] One critique of the lack of studies on women's (literary) humor in Japan is found in Midori McKeon's "Ogino Anna's Gargantuan Play in *Tales of Peaches*."

[3] Bacchilega reads Cixous's "voice" not as "the essentializing expression of what it is to be a woman" but as an idea that displaces the "patriarchal" subject of deconstruction "which privileges speech not only over writing, but over 'voice' as well." Thus a hierarchical system that assigns different values to oral and literary forms of folklore is overturned and, "as Cixous describes it, the feminine 'voice' claims a complex affinity with writing and a material connection with the body, without returning us to the unified subject" (*Postmodern Fairy Tales* 14; see also Bacchilega's "'Writing' and 'Voice': The Articulations of Gender in Folklore and Literature").

[4] The situation of Japanese women's writing is examined in English in Gordon Schalow and Janet A. Walker, eds., *The Woman's Hand: Gender and Theory in Japanese Women's Writing*; and Rebecca Copeland, ed., *Woman Critiqued: Translated Essays on Japanese Women's Writing*.

Indeed, one of the defining features of the disruptive inversions of carnival that Bakhtin describes is its transience. Carnival is a temporary overturning of control and even a kind of venting process that allows order and hierarchy to reign for the rest of year (Bakhtin 75).

The purpose of this book is not to identify and promote those transformations that are the most radical or carnivalesque, nor those that most effectively subvert gender norms. It is rather to demonstrate the usefulness of "pleasure" as a means of approaching a diverse set of fairy tale texts that construct gender in a broad range of ways. Understanding pleasure shows us how children's pleasures can be mobilized to affirm particular notions of gender (as I argue for the Disney and Ghibli animated films in chapter 2) but also how child consumers of texts can take unexpected and critical pleasures (as I argue for the depictions of girl readers I examine in chapter 5). Pleasure is a lens through which to consider and compare the huge variety of transformations that the "The Little Mermaid" has undergone and the notions of gender they produce, whether these texts discomfort or comfort, affirm the status quo, "break up" patriarchal truths, or do something else entirely.

In order to learn more about the fairy tale form through examining pleasure in transformations, the next question to ask is, are the pleasures these texts portray and invite especially allied with the fairy tale? In order to answer this question, we must briefly revisit the nature of the fairy tale itself. As the background to "The Little Mermaid" will show, any single fairy tale has a richly composite history of myth, legend, scholarship, education, translation, genre, and medium. Though this should make the fairy tale extraordinarily difficult to define, a particular notion of the typical or "real" fairy tale seems to remain dominant. In popular definition, the fairy tale continues to be conceptualized in the form of short, simple stories associated with oral storytelling, (in recent centuries) usually targeted at children. Such classic fairy tales are recognizable through features such as verbal formulas (famously, "once upon a time" and *mukashi mukashi*); happy or at least clear-cut, strong endings; their use of repetition and groupings (often of three, seven, or twelve); simple characters sorted into binaries of good and evil; and a third-person voice or a narrator external to the plot. These elements of the recognizable classic fairy tale form are powerful. Although Andersen's literary fairy tale "The Little Mermaid" does not actually reproduce many, they emerge in its transformations anyway. In taking up "The Little Mermaid," transformations thereby consciously engage with the fairy tale form itself.

In fact, the pleasures of playing with the fairy tale seem rooted in this concreteness of form, in the idea that anyone can recognize a fairy tale when they see it. Jessica Tiffin, in *Marvelous Geometry: Narrative and Metafiction in Modern Fairy Tale* (2009), sees the attributes of fairy tales as intersecting to create "*texture* rather than simple form and pattern" (5), the "marvelous geometry" of her title. Tiffin—with reference to famous structural analyses such as Vladimir Propp's—emphasizes the appeal of this palpable texture. As she puts it, "reference to a solid and structurally rigid notion of fairy tale meaning becomes, in the hands of the more self-conscious modern fairy tale writers, essentially oppositional; the somewhat utopian notion of structure is invoked only to be explored and disrupted, either playfully or radically, or both" (2). This observation frames my approach: that the idea that these rules of fairy tales exist is constantly called on and manipulated in fairy tales and fairy tale transformations. Tiffin argues that the fairy tale form, more than others, invites this kind of intertextual manipulation, that there is "a particularly close fit between the base structures of fairy tale and the self-conscious games of postmodern awareness" (22). So perhaps what makes fairy tales amenable to transformation and play—the ritualistic and repetitive nature of the form, its familiar "marvelous geometry"—is often also what makes fairy tale transformations pleasurable.

This specific pleasure in consuming a transformation, then, is offered to audiences who recognize its fairy tale intertextuality. These consumers are what Linda Hutcheon describes in *A Theory of Adaptation* (2006) as "knowing audiences" who are familiar with the source text(s). This is in contrast to "unknowing audiences" who consume and enjoy adaptations without awareness of the source text. Though *adaptation* itself is treated as one specific type of transformation in this book (for film adaptations in chapter 2), Hutcheon's rare attempt to pinpoint the pleasures of transformative texts applies more broadly. One reason it is a useful idea is that the "knowing" audience she envisages may be especially large for fairy tale transformations, due to the ubiquity of the classic fairy tale (or at least the idea of it), which is typically encountered from early childhood.

For "knowing" audiences, adaptations are pleasurable because of their balance of the familiar and the new: they produce "the comfort of ritual combined with the piquancy of surprise" (Hutcheon 4). This produces an "intellectual" and "intertextual pleasure" of "understanding the interplay between works, of opening up a text's possible meanings to intertextual echoing" (Hutcheon 117). Energizing the fairy tale genre, this knowing, intellectual reading pleasure is enjoyed by many different types of readers (and retellers), including, of course, fairy tale studies scholars. This "intertextual pleasure" might also allow the reader to feel membership in an in-group, sharing multiple texts with the author and other readers—such an idea of reading communities emerges in relation to the discussion of "girls' intertextuality" in chapter 5.

As Hutcheon describes it, for knowing audiences, the act of reading an adaptation sets into motion a "constant oscillation" (xv) between the source text and adaptation. This type of doubled, oscillating reading pleasure "is not hierarchical, even if some adaptation theory is" (xv). That is, critiques that judge an adaptation on how closely or successfully it has adapted the source cannot adequately reflect the pleasures of adaptations. Readers do not always encounter texts in chronological order of publication: they do not necessarily read the "original" and then an adaptation. In fact, audience "knowledge" may be initially gained through the adaptation rather than its source: in the Japanese context, Tomoko Aoyama identifies a more "open-ended, decentred, and dispersive" characteristic in Japanese literature from the 1980s onward, with which parody fits especially comfortably ("Love That Poisons" 35). Aoyama notes that parodists such as Kurahashi Yumiko (see chapter 4) do not so much demand that readers share their knowledge of the traditional canon but rather offer readers access to it through their own energetic engagements. In the Western context, also, Bacchilega provides a concrete example of children in the twenty-first century in particular, who may well consume fairy tale transformations before their fairy tale sources—for instance, seeing the *Shrek* film parodies of Disney fairy tales before the Disney films themselves (*Fairy Tales Transformed?* 12). In oscillating between fairy tale source text and transformation, the reading and rereading of each text is informed by the reading and rereading of other related texts, often without concern for which is the "original." This oscillating movement is especially appropriate for the oral, transcription, translation, and literary-based genre of fairy tales, for which the very notion of a single "original" fairy tale available to parody is especially dubious and for which distinctions between fairy tale and transformation are not stable.

Pleasure in transformations, then, is open-ended and nonlinear. Though arguing that a reading experience can be comforting or discomforting, "the pleasure of the text," Barthes writes, "does not prefer one ideology to another" (31). The real value of an analysis focused on pleasure lies in this conclusion that pleasure is not beholden to any particular political stance. The idea of pleasure in the absorption and transformation of texts, in the movement between sources and hypotexts, does not distinguish between subversive and conforming notions of gender, though as we will see, it can be used with either (or neither) purpose. Similarly, despite Barthes's distinctions, we will encounter similar pleasures across a range of "high"- and "low"-culture texts, belying the need for a study of transformations of a specific fairy tale to work from such a distinction. Such ideological and aesthetic assessments are understandably important for fairy tale critics but cannot always capture the ways in which authors and audiences engage with a fairy tale and imagine gender within it.

Critiquing Transformations of "The Little Mermaid" across Cultures

The notion of pleasure brings together a diverse range of texts, making it especially valuable for a cross-cultural study such as this. My aim here is to contribute to broadening the purview of Western fairy tale scholarship, as Mayako Murai has so effectively advocated for (*From Dog Bridegroom*), citing calls made by Cristina Bacchilega (*Fairy Tales Transformed?*) and Donald Haase ("Feminist Fairy-Tale Scholarship"). In Murai's significant exploration of Japanese women writers' and artists' "adaptations in conversation with the West" from the 1990s onward, she notes that criticism of a particular motif or tale type could further her complex cross-cultural project (144). This type of criticism is represented in my exploration of the pleasures of Anglophone and Japanese transformations of "The Little Mermaid."

The examination of these texts does not focus on differences between "the West" and "Japan"; even viewing these two groupings as definable, comparable categories would be problematic. The nebulous term *West* is adopted to describe the cultural histories of mermaid fairy tales and transformations, which extend beyond the English-speaking realm that is examined here. Moreover, the perspective is that of a speaker of English, and for the Anglophone audience of this work, I tend to provide more introductory explanations to Japanese-language sources than to English-language fairy tales and fairy tale studies.

I aim, however, to avoid the kind of Orientalizing construction of Japan that Edward W. Said and others have identified in "Western" interactions with the "East." A variant of this perspective often found in contemporary English sources—especially journalism and popular culture—is the delight in "weird Japan," or what Murai summarizes as a focus on "the bizarre and the cute in Japanese culture" (*From Dog Bridegroom* 36). For this research, texts in English and Japanese are selected and categorized not as representatives of particular cultures, nor as sensational examples of "difference"; rather, they are nominated when, in combination with each other, they have something to say about the reconstruction of gender from Andersen's fairy tale.

Another effort made to avoid Orientalist perspectives is to work from not only Japanese primary texts but also (often untranslated) Japanese scholarship: both on Japanese texts and traditions and on Andersen's Danish fairy tale. This in itself would not be sufficient, as studies of folklore in particular have frequently worked from a paradigm—seen both in Japanese and overseas writings about Japan—that has been critiqued since the 1970s as *Nihonjinron* (literally "theories about Japanese people"; see Mouer and Sugimoto). *Nihonjinron* describes the often nationalist line that argues for what is "unique" about a hegemonic Japanese culture, which is frequently imagined through comparisons with a generalized notion of "the West." It is discernible, for example, in Kawai Hayao's explorations of what Japanese fairy tales reveal about the Japanese disposition in *Mukashibanashi to Nihonjin no kokoro* (1982; translated as *The Japanese Psyche: Major Motifs in the Fairy Tales of Japan*, 1988). One response to this limitation is to turn to adjacent Japanese fields, such as girl studies, which in chapter 5 I find can turn a fresh critical eye not only on Japanese but also Anglophone transformations of "The Little Mermaid."

Fairy tale studies in English, particularly those with an interest in gender, also prove vital to the analysis. Murai has identified in Japanese fairy tale research in the 1980s and early 1990s especially an avoidance or dismissal of feminist fairy tale studies, including seminal works by scholars such as Zipes and Bacchilega. This speaks to the usefulness of applying, with caution, such fairy tale studies to Japanese texts as Murai does. In this case, I find that framing an analysis according to the "pleasures" of "transformations" and their impact on notions of gender encourages a genuinely cross-cultural analysis of texts from two languages. An approach centered on what is pleasurable in fairy tale intertextuality has the advantage of neither universalizing the appeal of the tales nor reducing their cultural contexts to stereotype. Pleasure is subjective and deeply personal and therefore hugely varied, but it is also all-embracing in that it is essential in some form or other for any text to be shared and transformed.

Instead of making a comparison of the essentialized "Western" or uniquely "Japanese" elements of fairy tales, the analysis aims to draw from an interwoven, intertextual "web" of fairy tales (see Bacchilega, *Fairy Tales Transformed?*), and to draw from what I term, with reference to the narratologist Gérard Genette, the fairy tale *architext* (see chapter 3). The examination is undertaken with an eye to the tapestry of mermaid stories that inform both Andersen's tale and its transformations. Because of the importance of these stories within Andersen's tale and in responses to it, a history of mermaids and some of the possible interpretations of "The Little Mermaid" are outlined in the next sections.

"The Little Mermaid" in Japanese and English

Hans Christian Andersen's "The Little Mermaid" incorporates earlier beliefs and tales and, since gaining popularity upon publication, has journeyed into many languages, including Japanese and English. I do not provide a recent chronology of the fairy tale in either Japanese or English—this has already been carried out for the former by Murai (*From Dog Bridegroom*) and for the latter by Zipes, Warner, and several others. Here instead, I trace a prehistory and history of "The Little Mermaid" in Japanese and English. This provides a snapshot of fairy tale history for both languages and a useful basis for the analysis of the transformations, which tend to delve beyond Andersen's tale and into its antecedents and descendants.

Early Western mermaids developed from wiser mythological figures, whereas early Japanese mermaids were less human and more animal, with mysterious medicinal and other properties attributed to their bodies. However, over the centuries, both traditions grew to increasingly centralize and sexualize female mermaids. The voluptuous, temptress mermaid images that developed have not disappeared entirely today. However, from around the time of Andersen's fairy tale, more innocent, tragic heroines emerged, whose struggles center on their own souls. The melding of these different strands of mermaid stories has contributed to the creation of the complex characters and ideas of gender that appear in some of the contemporary transformations discussed in this book.

Prehistory: Mermaids in the West

The great array of fantastical water creatures from around the world includes male "mermen" (see Yolen and Oppenheim); indeed one of the earliest known depictions is the Babylonian Oannes from the eighth century BCE, a bearded half man and half fish. Yet the attractive feminine figure who appears in Andersen's story, with a fish's tale and a female human torso, has come to dominate both Japanese and Western imagery.

The mermaid featured in Andersen's tale descends from the sirens of ancient Greek and Roman mythology, who were earlier depicted as bird-women. In Homer's *Odyssey*, the sirens "bewitch everybody who approaches them" (12.39–40; 158) with their "honey-sweet" voices (12.189;

161). Yet Warner argues that the sirens' allure originally lay less in their physical beauty and enchanting voices and more in their wisdom, their ability as supernatural beings to speak their beyond-human knowledge of past, present, and future (*From the Beast* 399). She shows how this wisdom is intertwined with an association with death, as sirens could hear the words of the dead, and winged sirens were depicted carrying the souls of the dead away from the world of the living. But gradually, Warner observes, as mythologies met, merged, and diverged, sirens "shed their relation to wisdom and retained only their oneness with sex and death" (402). This dark appeal was to dominate imaginings of mermaids over the subsequent centuries.

The increasing attention to the dangerous physical beauty of sirens and then mermaids is reflected in the greatly erotic and attractive visual depictions across the centuries. Mermaids' traditional accouterments, the comb and mirror, were probably inherited from the goddess of love, Aphrodite.[5] Artistic portrayals of the goddess, such as Botticelli's Venus (*Birth of Venus*, 1486), resound with mermaid imagery: Andersen's description of the little mermaid appearing naked from the ocean and "wrap[ping] herself in her thick long hair" (95) is reminiscent of this painting, and mermaids are often portrayed with the same red hair as Venus. Indeed, mermaids with red hair that gorgeously contrasts against the blue-green ocean have continued to appear, from Pre-Raphaelite paintings such as John William Waterhouse's *A Mermaid* (1900) to recent animated mermaid protagonists in the films discussed in chapter 2. The artistic possibilities presented by a mermaid mythology that combines delicate human beauty with animal otherness has lent strength and staying power to folktales and literary stories.

The powerfully erotic, worldly imagery of sirens and mermaids steered the Christian church, in the Middle Ages, to adopt the pagan mermaid into its own symbolry. Though the mermaid may be at times a pitiable, godless creature seeking her own eternal soul, she is also an Eve-like image of the fatal dangers of the flesh. Images of these deadly fish-women seem to have decorated medieval and early-modern churches to remind congregations of the risks of animalistic physical temptation. Accordingly, in the sixteenth and seventeenth centuries, *mermaid* was a slang word for a prostitute ("Mermaid"). The word *siren* is now often used alongside *femme fatale*, a nineteenth-century incarnation of these same frightening, titillating characteristics. Such fleshly, womanly figures evince a powerfully self-interested

---

[5] As noted by Warner (*From the Beast* 406) and others. In a cross-cultural comparison of mermaid legends and fairy tales, Nishimoto Keisuke points out another parallel between Aphrodite and Andersen's little mermaid: Aphrodite is born of foam on the sea, while Andersen's mermaid turns to foam (4).

eroticism and sexuality that is divorced from the socially acceptable aims of producing children to form families (see V. Allen 4; Finley).

However, this disconnection from reproduction does not always hold; in some stories, mermaids do have children. Images of mermaids with (semi) split tails that would allow this reproductive act are seen in paintings such as Isobel Lilian Gloag's *The Kiss of the Enchantress* (1850; see fig. 1.1) and Arnold Böcklin's *Naiad* (1887).[6] Other mermaid figures are sea creatures such as seals or fish-tailed women in water but fully human on land, sometimes marrying and bearing children to human husbands. The seal women "selkies" can be taken as wives by men who get hold of their seal skins when the selkies have shed them and appear in human form, seen in "The Seal Skin" from Iceland, "The Mermaid Wife" from Shetland Islands, and others catalogued as "The Mermaid Wife" (Ashliman). Remarkably similar tales are found around the world; in one story from the Gurindji Aboriginal Australian people of the Victoria River District in the Northern Territory, for example, a young man finds a *karukany* (mermaid) and takes her for his wife by smoking off her fish tail to reveal human legs underneath, but like the seal wives, the *karukany* escapes back into the water at the first opportunity (Wavehill).

Whether these mermaids are self-serving femme fatales or reluctant wives and mothers, all of them seem to be drawn to relationships with human men. This is indeed the common factor for the separate strands of mermaid stories discernible around the beginning of the nineteenth century. At this point, the Romantic mermaid can be distinguished from the cruel temptresses (see Donder). Romantic mermaids can be traced to European tales of Melusine water sprites, appearing in literary form from the medieval period, famously in the fourteenth-century tale by Jean d'Arras. However, their epitome is found in Friedrich de la Motte Fouqué's *Undine* (1811). This quintessential German Romantic fairy tale, which is an important source for Andersen's story, portrays a charmingly girlish, naïve water sprite. As an elemental creature, Undine, like many other mermaids, has no soul of her own but gains one through marrying a human man. Though some mermaid figures remained hungry destroyers of men's souls, other, purer, more vulnerable, girlish versions yearned in this way for their own souls instead. A similar differentiation of mermaid types continued into the later fin-de-siècle culture, which depicts desirable *ondine* (undines) alongside dangerous, animal sirens (Dijkstra 258).

---

[6]This depiction seems to have come to be considered inappropriate, as seen in the changes to the Starbucks coffee-chain logo, which had from 1971 featured a shapely mermaid encircled by her split tail but in 1987 concealed her breasts with long, wavy tresses and from 1992 zoomed in to exclude the tail and feature only her torso (Works Design Group).

Figure 1.1. Isobel Lilian Gloag's *The Kiss of the Enchantress* (1850).

All these types of mermaids, despite their differences, become involved in romances with humans. And whether the mermaids are innocent girls or cold temptresses, whether they are calculating seducers or somewhat unwilling mothers, their love affairs tend to end badly, often with one partner's tragic demise. (As we shall see, this connection of mermaids with death may be tied to the associations of their watery homes.) On the whole, it seems that while some tales feature children of mermaid-human marriages, the European mythology—especially as it is taken up by Andersen in "The Little Mermaid"—has centered on a sexualized, nonreproductive figure and her romantic, usually tragic, liaisons with human men.

Prehistory: Mermaids in Japan

China and Japan have long histories of their own mermaid mythologies that have carried through to current-day Japan, describing creatures that seem further distanced from the human world than Western mermaids. In the modern and contemporary transformations examined in this book, these ideas have mingled with the Western stories, which were introduced into Japan more recently.

The main Japanese word for mermaid, 人魚 (*ningyo*), is technically gender neutral, comprising the Chinese characters for "human" and "fish." One of the earliest appearances of the word in Japan was in the first Chinese-to-Japanese dictionary, published in the Heian period (794–1185), in 937 (Tanabe 22).[7] Previously, the word is seen as early as the Warring States period (476–221 BCE) in China. These *ningyo* are characterized as strange beasts rather than beautiful half-human creatures (Tanabe 17). Their bodies appear to have been prized for their practical uses: some Chinese sources state that they could be used to produce oil that will burn and never go out[8] or to make waterproof cloth.[9]

A popular belief in Japan told that one could gain eternal youth and incredible longevity through eating this mysteriously powerful mermaid flesh. The best-known story on this theme is "Yao bikuni" (or "Happyaku bikuni"), with one version recorded as early as 26 May 1449. In the story,

---

[7] The dictionary, *Wamyōruijujō*, was put together by Minamoto Shitagō (Kuzumi, "Edo-jidai izen" 52).

[8] From 異物誌 *Yiwù zhì* (Chinese) or *Ibutsushi* (Japanese), 800 BCE–200 CE (cited in Tanabe 31), an account of unusual geography, people, animals, and so on translated as "Record of Foreign Matters" or "Record of Rarities." Estimations of the publication dates for these texts are taken from the source that quotes them.

[9] 述異記 *Shùyì jì* (Chinese) or *Shu(/Ju)tsuiki* (Japanese), 460–508 CE (cited in Tanabe 33–34), an example of early supernatural fiction or "tales of the strange."

a girl eats mermaid meat and lives for some eight hundred years, eternally youthful and long outliving her father and husband(s) (Shida 964), eventually becoming a Buddhist nun. Though distributed quite widely across Japan (Tanabe 83), the tale is classified as a legend (*densetsu*; Shida 964), tied as it is to particular locations and supposed historical figures. A cave in which the eponymous long-lived nun is said to have dwelled remains a tourist attraction today, at the Kūin temple in Fukui Prefecture. The association of mermaids with eternal youth and longevity—also seen in Abe Kōbō's story examined in chapter 3—was reinforced in the contemporary imagination by Takahashi Rumiko's popular manga series and animated adaptations on this theme, *Ningyo shirīzu* (serialized in *Shōnen Sunday* periodical for boys, 1984–94, translated as *Mermaid Saga*).

Edible animals and monstrous *ningyo* seem quite different from Western mermaids, who, although alien and often animal-like representatives of the natural world, do not appear to be viewed as consumable by humans as food, medicine, or other products.[10] However, even before Japan had much cultural exchange with the West, Japanese mermaid figures came to have similar erotic associations. As early as the eighth century, *ningyo* are described as resembling beautiful white-skinned women (Sasama 23). One account from around the eleventh or twelfth century remarks that mermaids are often caught by single male fishermen,[11] and several texts mention naked mermaids and men having sexual relationships with them.[12] By the Edo period (1603–1868), *ningyo* were often imagined as naked, white-skinned, long-haired female beauties (Sasama 23) and were associated with prostitution (Kabat 49–51).

Apart from these accounts and encyclopedia-type texts, tales classified as *mukashibanashi*—literally "tale of long ago," often translated as "folktale"—also feature mermaids. Many of these folktales involve male human contact with beautiful female mermaids. Tanabe notes that there are *ningyo* stories on the theme of *ongaeshi*, returning a favor or repaying a debt. "Grateful animals" appear frequently in Japanese fairy tales, exemplified in the canonized story "The Crane Wife" (see Murai, *From Dog Bridegroom* 44–48). In the mermaid tales of this type, most commonly a fisherman or

---

[10] One comparison summarizes that in contrast to Western mermaids, *ningyo* are extremely nonhuman, strange, and discomforting, and they rarely speak; although they sometimes cry tears, they are more likely to be monsters with voices of skylarks or deer (Nishimoto 9).
[11] 徂異記 *Cúyì jì* (Chinese) or *Soiki* (Japanese), 1000–1129 (cited in Tanabe 33).
[12] For example, in the Chinese official Zhou Daguan's writing on Cambodia, 真臘風土記 *Zhēnlà fēngtǔ jì* (Chinese) or *Shinrō fudoki* (Japanese) from 1295 (cited in Tanabe 36), translated as *The Customs of Cambodia* or *A Record of Cambodia: The Land and Its People* (Harris).

Figure 1.2. "Hako-iri musume men'ya ningyō" (The mermaid, a treasured daughter of a doll-maker's, 1791). From a playful Edo-period parody about a mermaid born to a female carp mother and fathered by the fairy tale fisherman Urashimatarō. By Santō Kyōden and illustrated by Utagawa Toyokuni. Courtesy of National Diet Library digital collection.

other man helps a mermaid or is kind when he catches her, and she rewards him with a magical gift or by offering herself as a bride (Tanabe 79).

The stories of mermaid brides follow a standard pattern of non-human spouse stories, which are especially prolific within Japanese fairy tales (Ozawa 26; Kobayashi 1). Usually, supernatural beings or animals—famously the crane but also fish and other creatures—take human form and marry. Though animal husbands do appear, animal wives seem to be more common and to vary across a broader spectrum of tale types.[13] Animal husband and wife tales do differ (see Murai, *From Dog Bridegroom*; Kobayashi; Ozawa), but in either case, as the Jungian psychologist Kawai Hayao points out in a prominent analysis, in Japanese tales, "animals transformed into human figures . . . try to marry humans and cannot achieve a happy union," usually because the animal is killed or simply leaves (117). Kawai claims that such unhappy endings are less common in Western

---

[13] Fumihiko Kobayashi (24, 123–36) discusses the eight "animal wife" tale types ascribed by Inada Kōji in *Nihon mukashibanashi tsūkan* (General survey and analysis of Japanese folktales) and the seven designated by Seki Keigo in *Nihon mukashibanashi taisei* (Corpora of Japanese folktales, 1987–90), as opposed to the three "animal husband" tale types.

fairy tales (105), which tend not to feature actual animals (transformed into humans) but rather humans transformed into animals. Several folklore scholars highlight cross-cultural differences between Japanese animal wives and selkie or Melusine tales; the latter share with Japanese animal wife stories a taboo on the husband looking at his wife in her animal form, which taboo he inevitably breaks, necessitating their separation.[14] Though these cultural differences are significant, Japanese stories that end with the separation of the romantic partners certainly resonate with tragic mermaid tales such as Andersen's and seem likely to be readily assimilated by readers familiar with tales of water women who leave their human lovers and sometimes their children.

Japan encountered Western mermaids well before modernization, with illustrations of mermaids from Holland appearing in a 1786 Japanese text, *Rokubutsu shinshi* (Record of six new things; Tanabe 45). The most significant flow of mermaid culture in the opposite direction—Japanese mermaid culture reaching the West—occurred from the mid-1800s. So-called mermaid mummies (*ningyo no miira*), which were actually monkey torsos sewn onto fish tails, were often displayed in *misemono*, sideshow-style exhibits during Edo-period Japan (Tanabe 218). One such mummy journeyed from Nagasaki to London in 1822 and there became the notorious "Feejee mermaid." From the 1840s onward, it was exhibited in sideshows across the United States, inspiring many similar mermaid curiosities (Markus 528). Some of these mummies are still exhibited in Japan today (Tanabe 226–55).

In a thought-provoking comparison of Andersen's story and "Yao bikuni," the scholar and translator of English children's and fantasy literature Waki Akiko stipulates that the Japanese mermaid mummies—bodies preserved into a deathless condition—were probably born of the "Yao bikuni"–type stories of the mysterious preservative powers of mermaid meat (188). This brings together the close associations of mermaids with death, afterlife, and eternal life that are also seen in Western stories and taken up, of course, by Andersen in his fairy tale.

Andersen's Mermaid

Andersen's imaginative tale of "The Little Mermaid" works with the plentiful European source material, incorporating a number of elements from

---

[14] See Kawai; Ozawa; Seki, *Nihon no mukashibanashi*, which is also cited in Kobayashi Fumiko's comparison. While insightful, at times these comparisons of "Western" and Japanese tales tend to be used to bolster claims about the uniqueness of Japanese tales within the world folklore treasury, evincing the aforementioned *Nihonjinron* attitude.

Figure 1.3. Vilhelm Pedersen's illustrations for "The Little Mermaid" (Denmark, 1849).

mermaid folklore, as well as from literary texts such as Friedrich de la Motte Fouqué's *Undine* (1811). These provide the foundations for a complex mediation on individual identity, explored through notions of gender, belonging, growing up, and self-expression. The rich possibilities for interpretation that the tale offers have invigorated an afterlife of replication, translation, transformation, and criticism.[15] While recent readings often focus on the way the mermaid's wishes are thwarted and view the tale's tragic ending as entirely unhappy, Andersen's powerful imagery of female desire has been equally important for its transformations.

Hans Christian Andersen (1805–75) had published short stories, poetry, and a novel in his native Danish from the late 1820s, but it was his fairy tale collections in the 1830s that established his long international career. "Den lille havfrue" (The little mermaid) was first published in Denmark in 1837 in a third installment of the popular *Eventyr, fortalte for Børn* (Fairy tales, told for children), three booklets published 1835–37. Andersen's work was facing mixed reviews and some stringent criticism in Denmark around this time, but the fairy tales were received comparatively positively and were reportedly especially well appreciated by their intended audience of children (Bredsdorff 124–25). Greatly reliant on patronage up to that point,

---

[15] The wealth of analyses is neatly exemplified in Pil Dahlerup's article "Splash! Six Views of 'The Little Mermaid,'" which compiles perspectives on the tale by different authors, from structuralist to psychoanalytical to "folktale/Disney" approaches.

Andersen's career was much supported by a royal annual allowance granted in 1838 (Bredsdorff 131–32) and then by good sales for his *Nye Eventyr* (New fairy tales), published in 1843 (Bredsdorff 165).

"The Little Mermaid" seems to have appealed to readers from early on: Andersen himself mentions it in a letter as one of the most popular (Bredsdorff 165). The story begins in the fantastical underwater mermaid kingdom. The eponymous mermaid princess is different from her five older sisters because she yearns for the human world and wants an eternal soul such as humans possess. When the mermaid turns fifteen, she is permitted to swim to the ocean surface. There, she falls in love with a human prince she sees on a ship and rescues him from drowning when the ship is wrecked in a storm. After returning to her ocean home, the mermaid cannot forget the prince. She goes to the sea witch, giving her voice in exchange for a pair of human legs so that she can go to meet the prince on land. Part of the price is that she feels incredible pain with every step she takes. As another condition of the bargain, the mermaid can gain an eternal soul only if she "wins[s] the prince's love" (94) and marries him. On land, the mermaid dances and smiles for her beloved despite her pain. The prince takes a liking to her, but eventually he marries another woman, whom he mistakenly believes is the one who rescued him from drowning; because the mermaid has no voice, she cannot convey her love or correct his misapprehension. The mermaid is now fated to turn to foam on the waves. Her sisters buy her the chance to return to the ocean if she kills the prince, but rejecting this option, the mermaid chooses instead to throw herself into the water. She turns to sea foam but then becomes a kind of spirit, a "daughter of the air" (101) who may gain a soul after three hundred years "by doing good deeds" (102).

"The Little Mermaid" is, then, a tale structured around conflicts and oppositions ranging from physical (fish versus human) and geographical (ocean, land, and sky), to spiritual (soulless versus ensouled) and emotional (desire versus self-denial) (see Dahlerup; Thomsen). These conflicts shape the central drive of the story, the mermaid's desires for what she does not have: the prince and an eternal soul. Her desires motivate her to become something she is not—human—and to move between different physical realms and change between different physical states. Ultimately, this means that the mermaid is constantly isolated, not belonging fully to any place or state (see Easterlin; Johansen 350). Through this constant otherness and not-belonging caused by the mermaid's hybrid body,[16] Andersen's tale

---

[16] See also Pedersen's monograph on the mermaid as a means to examine identity in early-modern Britain.

mediates and indeed complicates the biological, gendered, emotional, and spiritual boundaries of the self.

The sense of not-belonging and the yearning that pervades the story is also what informs its powerful imagery of girlhood and growing up. This aspect particularly develops on the girlish "Romantic" water sprite figure of Friedrich de la Motte Fouqué's *Undine*, which distances the mermaid from the more deathly, womanly allure of the siren. In Andersen's tale, the girlish figure's growing-up narrative, her mermaid body, and her watery home are all closely linked. The links are articulated by the childhood studies scholar Honda Masuko, who explores the deep-rooted cultural associations of water, death, and *shōjo* (girls) in both Japanese and Western texts in *Ofīria no keifu: Aruiwa, shi to otome no tawamure* (The genealogy of Ophelia; or, Death and the maiden playing, 1989), a work that admirably crosses cultural, temporal, and disciplinary borders. The *shōjo* that Honda discusses, explored further in chapter 5, resonates with mermaid imagery. Honda speculates that societies define womanhood by the ability to give birth, so that "femininity" becomes synonymous with "motherhood." The *shōjo*, however, is a liminal figure who refuses maturity and removes her body from any symbols of fertility (*Ofīria no keifu* 16). Both the *shōjo* and Andersen's fish-tailed mermaid, who in her current form seemingly cannot engage in reproductive sexual intercourse, are sexualized nonreproductive figures associated with death and water rather than the fecund earth.

The little mermaid's movement from ocean to land may in this way be interpreted as a gendered process of growing up. When the mermaid drinks the potion that transforms her into a human, it feels "like a double-edged sword going through her delicate body" (Andersen 95). Responding in part to this image of penetration, psychoanalytic readings of this fairy tale focus on the mermaid's metamorphosis to human as a loss of virginal innocence and a difficult taking on of adult sexuality (for example, Dinnerstein 105). Certainly, if the mermaid is identified as Honda's *shōjo*, alienated from the fertile earth that symbolizes sexual maturity and reproduction, then we may say when her tail is split open into legs—and she presumably gains genitalia—and walks on the earth, she leaves the timeless world of the girl and enters the adult system.

The other significant physical change that the mermaid experiences is the loss of her voice: the witch cuts her tongue out, a kind of symbolic castration (Soracco 149) that also deprives her of her siren art of singing as well as of the power of language itself. The mermaid's surrender of language can be interpreted via Jacques Lacan's theorizing of identity (see Johansen 353; Tseëlon), in which the child must undergo castration to separate from the "imaginary, pleasurable, erotic, symbiotic, mother/child relation" (Grosz 70). In Andersen's tale, the mermaid's having her tongue severed allows her to leave her feminized ocean family. However, as a result, she cannot progress into the human-adult-male realm of the symbolic. To do this, she would have to acquire the language and accept the law that is represented by the figure of the Father (Lacan 688). From this viewpoint, then, the mermaid's movement to land is a failed attempt to grow up, and her voluntary muteness is paradoxically necessary for her to enter the patriarchal systems of adulthood but also prevents it.

Alongside these images of the mermaid's first metamorphosis, the means of her death also aligns with girlhood and growing-up narratives. Again, the significance of this imagery is explicated by Honda. Honda develops on this theme through her use of the philosopher Gaston Bachelard's understanding of the literary associations of water, death, and femininity, which resonate with Andersen's depiction of the little mermaid's demise. Bachelard writes that in literature water is "the element of a death with neither pride nor vengeance—of masochistic suicide" (82)—and "the true matter for a very feminine death" (81). Honda narrows Bachelard's discussion to the figure of the girl. Drawing on figures such as Shakespeare's Ophelia, she adds that it is the girl's unavoidable fate to die young; water is the necessary element to enhance the "beauty" of that death (14), and when this beautiful death is achieved, the girl is able to become the *eien no shōjo*, or "eternal girl" (14). In Andersen's tale, despite the little mermaid's willing metamorphosis, she is thwarted in her attempt to grow up, seemingly dragged back by this storytelling need to maintain the mermaid's unearthly, elemental beauty.

These close associations with girlhood seem to have contributed to the current special popularity of mermaids in stories for girls, but Andersen's "The Little Mermaid" retains interest for other audiences. The mermaid's loss of her tongue has important resonances for feminist fairy tale studies examining girls' and women's voice and silence in their roles as characters, narrators, and tellers of tales.[17] The mermaid's journey from ocean to land, where she is unable to communicate with the prince, also paints a vivid portrait of cross-cultural experience. She becomes a lost outsider in a foreign space whose fate is decided by other people's failure to understand her: a princess

---

[17]See Warner's thoughtful discussion in *From the Beast to the Blonde*, especially in "The Silence of the Daughters" (387–408); Ruth Bottigheimer's observations on the editing of women's voices in the Grimms' fairy tales (*Grimms' Bad Girls and Bold Boys*); Karen E. Rowe's "To Spin a Yarn"; and Mizuta Noriko on the "discourse of silence" in women's literature ("Chinmoku—josei hyōgen no shinsō" [Silence—the layers of women's expression], in *Feminizumu no kanata* 66–102).

in her own world, she is viewed as a "foundling" by the human prince, who never recognizes her as his rescuer or shares her intention to marry.

Then again, the mermaid's loss of her voice and singing and her dancing on her painful legs also present powerful imagery of the difficult experience of artistic creation. Biographical readings note Andersen's struggles to gain patronage and publishing opportunities from his impoverished beginnings in the lower social classes within the town of Odense.[18] Some scholars, then, interpret the mermaid as an artist whose loss of voice represents the passionate struggles of poetry or unappreciative audiences or painful compromises made for the sake of artistic success and patronage (see Fass; Kanai, "Anderusen no shitsū"; Zipes, *Hans Christian Andersen*). The mermaid's graceful dancing for the prince, despite her physical agony, might be seen as the artist enduring pain in order to produce and perform a work of beauty.

These interpretations can be developed to take into account one aspect of Andersen's story that perhaps has yet to be fully explored: that is, the prince's lack of subjectivity and dimensionality and the way the mermaid turns an objectifying gaze on him. There is a sense of the sculptor Pygmalion to Andersen's young female, who adores a statue of a boy in her garden before she sees the prince. In fact, Fouqué's *Undine* does mention the Pygmalion story: in the tradition of male as artist and animator of passive female, Fouqué describes the "prince" figure as happier than Pygmalion with his water-sprite bride (86). But in Andersen's tale, the female mermaid is the active artist figure. When the prince appears, it is as if the object of the mermaid's desire has been made flesh; she kisses his sleeping body on the beach and thinks "that he looked like the marble statue in her own little garden" (86).

This episode highlights the way the mermaid's powerful desires drive the story; yet perhaps even more important than her desire for the prince is her spiritual yearning for an immortal soul. The mermaid's religious motivations move the plot as much as or even more than her romantic wishes do (see Ingwersen and Ingwersen; Ōsawa; Mylius, "Voice of Nature"). Significantly, she successfully gains the immortal soul she seeks without the prince's help. Andersen wrote in a letter to his friend, the novelist Bernhard Severin Ingemann, "I have not, like de la Motte Fouquet in *Undine*, let the mermaid's gaining an immortal soul depend on a stranger, on the love of

---

[18] The narrative of Andersen's own origins and success tend to be confused by the romanticized view he presents in his own autobiographical writings, vividly represented, as Zipes notes, by one title, *Mit Livs Eventyr* (1855), translated as *The Fairy Tale of My Life* (1868) (Zipes, *Hans Christian Andersen* 2–3).

another person. It is definitely the wrong thing to do. It would make it a matter of chance and I'm not going to accept *that* in this world. I have let my mermaid take a more natural, divine path" (qtd. in Andersen 104n101). The tale's resolution glorifies the mermaid's self-sacrifice, but her ascendance toward heaven is clearly a happy ending in Andersen's eyes. Certainly the story's conclusion brings the little mermaid one step closer to attaining the soul that she ambitiously set out to gain. In this way, the depiction of a young girl as the active, desiring, controlling artist figure is quite radical. In any case, this sentimental, heartrending tale proved appealing not only in Andersen's native Denmark but also overseas. Its impact and the interpretive possibilities it presents ensure that it continues to be translated and transformed.

The Afterlife of Andersen's Tale: Mermaids from the Nineteenth to the Twenty-First Centuries

The emotional impact and the wealth of meaning that "The Little Mermaid" offers has ensured the story's continued success, seen first in its popularity and translation and then in its continued transformation. In both the English-language and the Japanese contexts, the tale was introduced at points when it could meet the current needs of children's literature. In each context, also, its introduction as a children's story ensured its reach to generations of readers who went on to transform the tale in their own work, enriching the afterlife of the "The Little Mermaid."

In the English-language context, Andersen's stories arrived exactly at the period 1830–1900, when the growing middle and upper classes generated a demand for entertaining and edifying stories for children in Britain and the United States (Zipes, *Why Fairy Tales Stick* 86). Andersen's insistence on the immortal soul at the heart of his story brought a didactic Christian bent to the body of existing mermaid myths and folktales. The sentimental ending—if morbid from today's view—was well suited to British, Victorian sensibilities. Upon early success for Andersen's *eventyr* in Denmark (and early translations into German and Swedish), some of the tales were first translated into English in Britain in 1846, in Mary Howitt's *Wonderful Stories for Children*; a pirate copy is said to have been published in New York in the same year (Mylius, "Life"). "The Little Mermaid" appeared in the same year in the periodical *Bentley's Miscellany*, translated by Lady Duff-Gordon, as well as in a collection titled *Danish Fairy Tales and Legends*, translated by Caroline Peachey.

The stories became beloved favorites, with "The Little Mermaid" established as one of Andersen's classic and most published works. But critics deplore Victorian and indeed many of the English translations of Andersen (see Banerjee; Bredsdorff; Briggs; Frank and Frank). Recent translators describe the difficulty of conveying his style, which they describe as childlike, vernacular, an "invented... form of expression that could ignore conventional literary forms and language" (Frank and Frank 157), "vivid, lively, and engaged" with a "happy use of non sequiturs, merry truisms, puns and rhymes" (Frank and Frank 159), and sprinkled with "topical and historical references, local color and cultural associations" (Zipes, *Hans Christian Andersen* 30). The tendency for poor renditions continued until better-quality English translations of Andersen's work became available from about the 1950s onward (Bredsdorff 336, 366; Zipes, *Hans Christian Andersen* 30).

As in Denmark and then in European and Anglophone countries, Andersen's tales appeared in Japan at a time when there was a particular appetite for children's literature that could be adopted for educational purposes. After a long history of cultural exchange with China and Korea especially, followed by a period of relative international isolation from the seventeenth to the nineteenth centuries, Japan was pressured by the United States from the 1850s to open to international trade. This led to the Meiji period (1868–1912), a time of massive economic, technological, and social change, which saw an influx of Western ideas. As part of the Meiji project of modernization and nation-building, compulsory education was implemented in stages from the 1870s, and student numbers increased rapidly. The period saw a new concept of childhood arise alongside the emergence of a new middle class. By 1930, the middle class had come to be defined around the family, which was characterized by a dedicated zeal for educating children (M. Jones 2). Such educational aspirations saw a prolonged growth in children's literature and periodicals for children. Stories included reworkings of Japanese folktales and sometimes Western tales, with Iwaya Sazanami's translations of Western fairy tales as well as his own children's stories, published from the 1890s, among the most famous. Maeda Ai notes in his essays on texts and urban modernity that literature at this time aimed to shape boy readers into ideal citizens of the Meiji state (*Text* 110–11), so that histories and biographies were favored over fairy tales (112). Nevertheless, the Grimm brothers' tales, introduced in regular succession in magazines for children from 1891 onward, came to be well known across Japan (Yamada 64), as did other Western fairy tales and children's stories.

One of the first of Andersen's stories to be translated into Japanese was "The Emperor's New Clothes," which was published midway through the

Meiji period in 1888.[19] Such early Andersen stories in Japan were generally not translated directly from Danish but rather from the oft-criticized English translations.[20] This aligns early Japanese translations and transformations more closely with Anglophone versions of "The Little Mermaid," creating another point of comparability for fairy tale transformations in these two languages. Also similar to the situation in English, in Japan, in line with the purposes of children's education, early translations of Andersen's fairy tales were closer to adaptations, tending to reshape the text to suit national moral outlooks and traditions (Yamada 61). Andersen's stories were admired for their messages ("Anderusen hen" 56), and translations of his tales were often undertaken by prominent literary men (Hirabayashi 56). In addition to Andersen's fairy tales, between 1892 and 1901 the well-known author Mori Ōgai, following his sister Koganei Kimiko's (less acknowledged) translation of some of Andersen's work, translated a German translation of Andersen's 1835 breakthrough travel novel written for adults, *The Improvisatore* (see Nagashima; Yamamuro 17; Hirabayashi 56). Ōgai's translation is said to have influenced Japanese literary romanticism (Hirabayashi 56).[21]

The first Japanese translation of "The Little Mermaid," published in 1904, was completed by Takasu Baikei, a journalist and literary critic known for his research into classical Japanese literature. Another was made in 1911 by a pioneer of Japanese linguistics, Ueda Kazutoshi. Thirty-two more translations were then published in the subsequent period up to 1925 (Kawato and Sakakibara), and more continued to appear regularly after that. Andersen's writing thus seems to have enjoyed a relatively privileged status from early on, his longer fiction having been established in the male-dominated mainstream literary spheres and his fairy tales having been approved as suitable educational material for children. Existing literary and fairy tale tropes of tragedy and separation and a contemporary official line of striving for the greater good may have facilitated the popularity of "The Little Mermaid."

---

[19] Fukawa Gen'ichirō notes in his article on fairy tale translation that a limited section of the population, those studying English, were exposed to Andersen's stories in English translation as early as 1875, when the British textbooks *Chambers's Narrative Series of Standard Reading Books*—featuring English translations of tales such as the "The Ugly Duckling" —were used in a Tokyo language school (Fukawa 146).

[20] An overview of translations of Andersen's work in Japan is found in the chapter "Anderusen hen" (cited under this title) in the illustrated encyclopedia of translated children's literature *Zusetsu jidōbungaku hon'yaku daijiten*.

[21] And as the scholar of Meiji-period translation Kawato Michiaki remarks, the use of Andersen's stories in educational texts for the young generations who were to direct the future of the "New Japan" meant that Andersen's influence on modern Japanese literature should not be ignored (Kawato 243).

Most Japanese readers today seem to recall the mermaid's choice to disintegrate into foam as the end of the story. The subsequent event of the mermaid becoming a "daughter of the air" in search of an eternal soul, and the Christian moralizing it entails, is often erased from Japanese translations and adaptations.[22]

Subsequent transformations of Andersen's tale in Japanese and English similarly reflect shifts in the uses of fairy tales and in the role of children's literature in each period. In English, a trend for what Zipes describes as "utopian" fairy tales, often imaginative children's literature, developed from the 1850s (*Why Fairy Tales Stick* 87–88). Among these number Oscar Wilde's fairy tales, which include his opulent transformation of "The Little Mermaid," titled "The Fisherman and His Soul," which was published in 1891 (see chapter 3). Wilde's fairy tales also gained admiration in Japan, appearing in translation from the 1910s.

In Japan, images of Western types of mermaids (and other fairy tale creatures) began appearing more often in illustrations for magazines and books for children and adults, especially from the Taishō "romantic" period (1912–26) onward. These ranged from dramatic, ornate images by Takabatake Kashō and Tachibana Sayume to Nakahara Jun'ichi's colorful, flower-bedecked book illustrations.

Work by all of these illustrators appeared in periodicals for girls, and *shōjo* genres remain powerfully influenced by fantastical fairy tale illustration and children's literature such as Lewis Carroll's *Alice's Adventures in Wonderland*. In Japan, "The Little Mermaid" is particularly associated with girlhood, and while earlier translations of the title varied, the standard has become "Ningyo-hime"; this roughly translates as "Princess Mermaid," incorporating the little mermaid into a company of fairy tale girls known as *hime*, ranging from the Japanese Kaguya-hime to the translated Snow White (Shirayuki-hime).[23] In girls' culture, the *shōjo manga* (girls comics) that grew out of periodicals also evince a fairy tale aesthetic. Manga featuring mermaids range in style from the more realistically drawn human figures in the romance/drama by Shimizu Reiko *Tsuki no ko* (Moon child, serialized 1988–92) to the sparkly eyed, hypercute aesthetic of *Māmeido merodī pichi pichi pitchi* (Mermaid melody pichi pichi pitch, by Yokote

---

[22] These observations about "The Little Mermaid" in Japan are all also made by Adam Kabat in his 2004 article comparing Japanese and Western mermaid stories (47).

[23] The suffix *hime*, meaning "princess," "young woman of noble birth," or "beautiful woman," is often used to refer to female fairy tale protagonists, whether in imported or local stories. Other examples include Oyayubi-hime (Thumb princess, for Thumbelina) and Uguisu-hime (Bush warbler).

Fig. 1.4 "Umi no gensō" (Ocean Fantasy 1930) by Tachibana Sayume. Courtesy of Katō Chizu.

Michiko and Hanamori Pinku, serialized 2002–5, adapted to a brightly colored television anime aired in 2004, dir. Fujimoto Yoshitaka).

Just prior to the advent of Taishō romanticism, from the close of the Meiji period, the modern field of Japanese folklore was emerging. This endeavor was to shape much of the transmission and reproduction of fairy tale texts in Japan. From 1910, the founding scholar of the field, Yanagita Kunio, was recording and analyzing a huge volume of oral folklore from different areas of the country; his work continues to be used as the basis for folktale collections and classifications.[24] Yanagita's influential definition in *Kōshō bungeishi kō* (On the history of oral literature; 1947) describes *mukashibanashi* (folktales; lit. stories of long ago) as one type of story that children hear from adults or that is recorded in the memories of elderly people, marked by set opening phrases such as *mukashi mukashi* (lit. long ago long ago) and its regional variants; these opening phrases signal to listeners that the story does not represent the current reality (59). He also notes that *mukashibanashi* use set closing phrases, for example, *medetashi medetashi* (it went well, it went well; 61), and set sentence-ending formulas such as *to sa*, *gena*, *sōna*, and *to iu* (63), which all denote hearsay or reporting the words of others.

Mukashibanashi was used to describe folktales, but the early translations of Andersen's work for children, like other children's stories, were often published under another heading, *otogibanashi*. The term, introduced by the aforementioned fairy tale translator and writer Iwaya Sazanami (Murai, *From Dog Bridegroom* 14), might be translated as "fairy tales," whereas *mukashibanashi* would be "folktales." *Otogibanashi* is believed to have previously described the stories told by professional storytellers to entertain powerful figures such as *daimyō* (feudal lords) from the Sengoku period (from the late 1400s) and through the Edo period (1603–1868); they were technically polished versions of popular folk tales (Nakagawa 160; Namekawa 135). A related genre is *otogizōshi*: medieval written short prose narratives, mostly from the fifteenth and sixteenth centuries. *Otogizōshi* are featured in *Naraehon*, illustrated books and scrolls produced from about the fourteenth to the eighteenth centuries (Araki 1). As such, the *otogibanashi* label entails a complex history of oral, literary, and visual storytelling that engages with folk

---

[24]Seki Keigo, a student of Yanagita's, later built on his efforts and published an index of folktales titled *Nihon mukashibanashi shūsei* (Anthology of Japanese folktales, 1950–61), dividing *mukashibanashi* into three broad types: animal folktales (*dōbutsu mukashibanashi*), genuine folktales (*honkaku mukashibanashi*), and funny tales (*waraibanashi*). Another of Yanagita's students and of Stith Thompson's, Hiroko Ikeda, published in English *A Type and Motif Index of Japanese Folk-Literature* (1971). Based on the Aarne-Thompson index, Ikeda's work cross-references both Yanagita's and Seki's data, as well as other sources.

culture. Its importance in fairy tale history is cemented by the fact that some of the *otogizōshi* are recognizable precursors to members of the modern fairy tale canon (Murai, *From Dog Bridegroom* 11).

From the Taishō period, the "uses" of fairy tales (of both *mukashibanashi* and *otogibanashi*) and the nationalistic messages of Meiji literature were being challenged. Writers for the *Akai tori* (Red bird) children's magazine (1918–36), especially Ogawa Mimei (whose famous mermaid tale is mentioned in chapter 2), began instead to propound a romantic image of innocent and pure childhood. Ogawa positioned *otogibanashi* in the past in his essays and instead advocated *dōwa*, literally "children's stories,"[25] which he argued should be "beautiful dreams born from people's lives today" ("Shin dōwa ron"; On the new *dōwa*). Despite the idealistic and critical leanings of this romantic image of the "childlike child," it grew popularly and commercially successful, co-opted by the same privileged classes and media that had previously supported the ideals of the child as contributing citizen and "superior student" (M. Jones 301–3). While Ogawa sees *dōwa* as a contemporary form, in more general definitions, the term can refer to "richly fantastical imaginative works" but also to "traditional stories" (Inada, "Dōwa" 642). Currently, it is most often used for books aimed at the lower grades at primary school (Fukuda 512), especially compilations familiarizing students with the local and overseas fairy tale and children's literature canon. The title *dōwashū* (*dōwa* collections) is used for compilations of tales containing anything from Perrault, the Grimms, Andersen, and Andrew Lang, or Aesop's fables, to the Japanese children's literature authors Ogawa Mimei and Miyazawa Kenji and world folklore collections.

In addition to this large audience of children, mermaid tales, as noted, have a long adult history in Japan. A prominent example from the modern period is found in Tanizaki Jun'ichirō's sensual foreign siren representing the allure of the West in "Ningyo no nageki" (The mermaid's lament, 1917), discussed in chapter 3 alongside "The Fisherman and His Soul" (1891) by Oscar Wilde, an author Tanizaki had complicated feelings for. Later decades saw the avant-garde novelist, poet, playwright, and photographer Abe Kōbō's humorous prince-centered story "Ningyo-den" (Legend of a mermaid, 1962; see chapter 3), as well as the writer, filmmaker, and photographer Terayama Shūji's tragic puppet-play retelling of "The Little Mermaid" ("Ningyo-hime," 1968). Kurahashi Yumiko's darkly funny retelling,

---

[25] The broader term *jidō bungaku* (children's literature) was also established around the end of the Taishō period. While the category is associated with *dōwa*, it is not as closely associated with fairy tales but covers all types of fiction for children up to about twelve years old.

"Ningyo no namida" (The mermaid's tears; see chapter 4), appeared in her best-selling and provocatively titled *Otona no tame no zankoku dōwa* (Cruel [children's] fairy tales for adults, 1984).

Disney's hugely successful 1989 animated adaptation *The Little Mermaid* (dir. Ron Clements and John Musker), released in Japan with the loanword title *Ritoru māmeido* (1991), has left its mark on subsequent transformations, including Miyazaki Hayao's animation *Ponyo on the Cliff by the Sea* (2008). As noted in chapter 2, Disney seems to have cemented and attempted to update Andersen's mermaid as a figure for girlhood and growing up. This is further evidenced by the examination of girls' mermaid stories in chapter 5, from *Utakata* (Bubbles), a 1988 novella by the famed "girl" author Yoshimoto Banana, to the more recent film *Aquamarine* (dir. Elizabeth Allen, 2006). A kind of romantic enthusiasm for the girlish mermaid now coexists with ambivalent and cynical responses to Disney's version, present in the girls' tales and demonstrated especially lucidly in the postfeminist television series episode of *Dark Angel* and novels by Nonaka Hiiragi and the author known as D[diː], discussed in chapter 6.

Disney's dominance over the fairy tale in the twentieth century has affected expectations for happy endings; this is where popular definitions of fairy tales may differ most between Japanese and Anglophone understandings. In contemporary usage in English, the term *fairy tale* is closely tied to the happy ending,[26] which now often specifically denotes the marriage or union of the male and female protagonists. As Tiffin observes, in fairy tales, "unequivocally defined forces confront one another before proceeding to an unambiguous resolution, an artificial and often perfect closure," but this closure has not always necessarily been happy (14). Conversely, though a kind of localized process of Disneyfication has been especially strong in Japan (see Yoshimi; M. Yoshimoto), happy endings do not seem to have as strong a grip on the fairy tale in Japanese as they do in English. Animal wife and husband fairy tales in particular tend to end with the spouses parting ways, and the famous "Taketori monogatari" (Tale of the bamboo cutter) closes with the moon-child Princess Kaguya leaving the earth and her beloved companions. Other popular tales are presented to children with some cruelty intact, especially the well-known "Kachi-kachi-yama" (Crackling mountain), a comic tale of the violent revenge a rabbit takes on a raccoon dog who has tricked and murdered an elderly human woman.

---

[26] *The Oxford English Dictionary* notes in its second definition for *fairy tale* that the term can refer to "Something . . . having an idealized happy ending" ("Fairy tale").

Any Japanese fascination with unhappy endings and the dark side of fairy tales was bolstered by the *Gurimu būmu*—Grimm boom—of the late 1990s. As Murai delineates (*From Dog Bridegroom* 29–34), these were highly popular works that purportedly "uncovered" (but often inflated) violent and sexual content of fairy tales such as the Grimms'. These transformations tend to attribute a deep psychological symbolism to the tales they retell, indebted to psychoanalytic approaches such as Shibusawa Tatsuhiko's (the writer, scholar, and translator of French literature; see Murai, *From Dog Bridegroom* 19–20) and fairy tale scholarship by Maria Tatar and others. The "Grimm boom" label is somewhat deceptive, as works in this wave, such as Matsumoto Yūko's revision of Andersen's "The Little Mermaid" (1996; see chapter 4), often include fairy tales other than the Grimms'. Ogawa Yōko's later collection of *Otogibanashi no wasuremono* (Lost property fairy tales, 2006) may also appear to follow this trend of "uncovering" the hidden darkness of "original" fairy tales, albeit in quite different ways (chapter 4).

In Japan, "The Little Mermaid" is now a regular inclusion in compilations of world folk and fairy tales targeted at primary-school-age readers. Though versions continue to appear in English too, this tragic tale of Andersen's may well be more popular now in Japan than in the West, because Japanese readers are not so demanding of a Disney-style happy ending. As we shall see, the dark and painful aspects of Andersen's tale can indeed play important roles in the pleasures of transforming it.

The transformations examined in chapter 2, however, tend to elide much of Andersen's tragedy because they are directed at child audiences. The two animated adaptations, Disney's *The Little Mermaid* (dir. Ron Clements and John Musker, 1989) and Studio Ghibli's *Ponyo on the Cliff by the Sea* (dir. Miyazaki Hayao, 2008), are examples of pleasures directed at more "unknowing" audiences. Rather than working from familiarity with Andersen's story or the fairy tale form, they seem to aim to delight child viewers by using animation's tools of music and voice and visual effects of movement and metamorphosis to simulate pleasurable physical experiences. Through such experiences, these films' young protagonists are socialized into strict, though quite different, gender hierarchies, making these films significant texts within debates about the influences of fairy tales on child audiences.

The remaining chapters, however, take up texts that are far more self-consciously and deeply engaged with the pleasures of the fairy tale as a form. In chapter 3, literary stories by the canonical male authors Oscar Wilde, Tanizaki Jun'ichirō, and Abe Kōbō and a more recent short story by the woman author Kawakami Hiromi invoke familiar fairy tale conventions and delineate some of the pleasures of what can be painful enchantment with a mermaid or with the fairy tale itself. Wilde's and Tanizaki's transformations especially embed differing Orientalist aesthetics into their fairy tale landscapes, reveling in the genre's ability to fantasize and wonder but in doing so objectifying the mermaid herself into another wondrous, art-like object.

This kind of objectification and devaluing of fairy tale women—of mermaids—is the subject of quite varied feminist reevaluations in the three literary short stories examined in chapter 4, by Matsumoto Yūko, Kurahashi Yumiko, and Ogawa Yōko. These women authors use parody to invite laughter at the gender systems they perceive in Andersen's tale, or they disrupt the mermaid's body with comic and thoughtful inversions and reversals, inviting intellectual and "knowing" pleasures through their sustained engagement with familiar fairy tales, reference to fairy tale research, and reflections on the immersive experience of reading.

The transformations in chapter 5 project equally engaged and critical approaches to fairy tales on the part of girl readers. Contemporary novels, short stories, and a film are shown to portray girl protagonists' pleasures in practices of community reading and layered interpretation, which is viewed through the lens of Japanese *shōjo* (girl) studies as "girls' intertextuality." The field of *shōjo* studies enables the argument that, contrary to assumptions made about fairy tale texts for children, girls' pleasures in mermaid stories and fairy tale transformations can be multiple, critical, and self-conscious.

The women characters and authors taken up in chapter 6 are also hyperaware of the possible meanings of Andersen's "The Little Mermaid" and of the fairy tale itself. In Nonaka Hiiragi's novel *Ningyo-hime no kutsu* (The little mermaid's shoes, 1994) and D[di:]'s novel *Sentō no ningyo-hime to majo no mori* (The little mermaid of the public bath and the witch's forest, 2008), as well as an episode of the science-fiction television series *Dark Angel* (dir. Bryan Spicer, writ. Marjorie David, 2001), the protagonists experience the ambivalent pleasures of reading and retelling fairy tales, consciously using them to frame and interpret their lives. All three works explore further afield than Andersen's story, using it to undertake postmodern and open-ended engagements with the broader fairy tale form.

Commentary on Andersen's "The Little Mermaid" positions it as more of a tale of desire and pain than one of pleasure. Yet I endeavor to show that approaching transformations of the tale from the viewpoint of pleasure is a particularly effective means to investigate and analyze the diverse ways in which they interpret and reimagine Andersen's ideas of gender. The pleasures of fairy tale transformations in this way offer tools to analyze and compare a body of texts that are intriguingly varied.

2
Children's Pleasures in Animated Film Adaptations

> Literature that centers on children must be drawn from the child within ourselves, developing the child's world, living it, observing it, and considering it. Some part of the child's psychology is shared by us all, and it is from here that we reflect, become self-aware, and critique. As such, this kind of literature enlightens readers not through conceptual guidance, nor through heavy-handed morals; rather, through experience, readers take responsibility for their own learning and understanding.
> —Ogawa Mimei, "Shin dōwa ron"
> (On the new children's stories, 1934)

Animated adaptations of "The Little Mermaid" often express desire and pleasure through motion. In the famous Disney adaptation of Andersen's fairy tale, *The Little Mermaid* (dir. Ron Clements and John Musker, 1989), the mermaid heroine Ariel sings of her desire to walk and run on land, spiralling upward through the ocean water toward the sun. A few decades later, in *Gake no ue no Ponyo* (*Ponyo on the Cliff by the Sea*, dir. Miyazaki Hayao, 2008), Studio Ghibli launched its fish-girl Ponyo into an uninhibited dash over the waves to her prince. These scenes capture some of the possibilities that animation brings to fairy tale transformation; they also capture the intense energy of the teenage and childhood desires and pleasures that these particular films offer to their audiences. Focused as they are on a kind of sympathetic immersion and audiovisual spectacle, these animated films are set apart from the other transformations examined in this book: unlike the other works, the films generally offer pleasures that do not demand an audience with knowledge of the fairy tale context. They are not particularly tied to conscious play with the fairy tale and its possibilities, nor do they require familiarity with Andersen's fairy tale or any sustained engagement with the patterns of the fairy tale form. However, they do relate to some issues that are at the heart of contemporary engagement with the fairy tale: the genre's relationship with gender, especially the use of the genre to socialize children into gender roles.

The issue of gendered roles and gendered imagery in fairy tales is vital to current debates around the uses of the genre. Debates become especially vexed when stories are directed at child audiences, who are perceived to be particularly sensitive to the ideas a tale presents. As indicated by Ogawa's 1934 essay quoted in the epigraph, discussions of the currency and potential of the fairy tale form have long concerned its role as a pleasurable pedagogical tool for children. And though many transformations of "The Little Mermaid" examined in this book target adult readers, Hans Christian Andersen's source text itself was closely associated with children. The huge popularity of Andersen's *Eventyr, fortalte for Børn* (Fairy tales, told for children) from the time of publication in the 1830s is attributed to the tales' lively creativity but also to their appearance at a point when the emerging middle classes in Europe and beyond welcomed such accessibly packaged Christian moralizing.[1] The ground for Andersen's success had been prepared by the Grimms' popular collections of tales, which were redirected toward young audiences in the 1819 second edition of *Children's and Household Tales*. These processes repeated themselves somewhat when, from the end of the nineteenth century, Andersen's tales began to reach Japan, where they were used in educational settings directed toward modernization and the growth of the new Japanese nation.

Despite changes in the way children's entertainment is understood, the purpose of providing some kind of spiritual and social education for child audiences has not been entirely rejected in the two more recent animated film adaptations of "The Little Mermaid" examined here. In this chapter, I unpack the varying pleasures that two contemporary fairy tale films offer to their child and adult audiences, showing the extent to which the pleasures are tied to the animated medium. Further, I underscore the socializing drive of these pleasures, especially in the context of the gender roles that the stories appear to construct and reinforce. This is not to claim that these films achieve their didactic goals; the way actual viewers—children especially—might take pleasure in these films is quite a different matter from the mode of viewing that the texts encourage, as we shall see in discussions of portrayals of girl readers in chapter 5.

---

[1] Though, in fact, Andersen's early fairy tales themselves were also criticized by some people for their lack of suitability and moral instruction for child readers; see Bredsdorff 123–24.

Many scholars observe shifts in the history of the Western fairy tale form, from earthy oral and written folktales of the Middle Ages to sophisticated stories for adults, such as those of the seventeenth-century French salons, to moralizing literary fairy tales for children in the nineteenth century. Histories of the subsequent ages of children's literature often describe a movement from educational and instructional texts to more child-centered and pleasurable stories from the middle to late nineteenth century.[2] In contrast, in *Off with Their Heads: Fairy Tales and the Culture of Childhood* (1992), Maria Tatar argues strongly for the socializing efforts made by literary fairy tales for children, making an especially perceptive point about what is seen as the modern swing toward "pleasure." In contrast to earlier figures, more recent authors of children's literature, she writes, "often see themselves as conspiring with children." However, "they are unable to escape creating new behavioral models and programs for them. In empathizing with children, for example, they are often at pains to help them work through problems by providing cathartic pleasures that, in the end, will turn them into 'well-adjusted' (read: 'socialized and productive') adults" (xvi–xvii). As Tatar notes, children's actual responses to reading are complex and unpredictable. Nevertheless, "cathartic pleasures" and their possible socializing functions are clearly discernible in the two recent fairy tale films examined here. The child protagonists and child and adult audiences are offered depictions of gratifying physical activities including eating tempting dishes and free movement such as swimming and running. Audiences are invited to participate in joyful and playful acts, the carnival release of singing and laughing. We shall see that these pleasurable experiences are linked closely to the power structures presented and supported by the films; in Disney, this means the stable continuation of patriarchal family arrangements, while Ghibli pushes for a matriarchal world order in greater harmony with Mother Nature.

Socialization, though, is not identical to psychological growth. In Tatar's discussion of the "uses" and "abuses" of fairy tales for children, she is of course alluding to Bruno Bettelheim's claim in his influential work *The Uses of Enchantment: The Meaning and Importance of Fairy Tales* (1976) that fairy tales can play a significant and positive role in children's "evolution from immaturity to maturity" (309). Certainly, the wealth of research into Disney and Ghibli films attests to their openness to psychoanalytical interpretation.

---

[2] William F. Touponce cites titles such as *From Primer to Pleasure in Reading*, by Mary F. Thwaite (1972), and *From Instruction to Delight: An Anthology of Children's Literature to 1850*, ed. Patricia Demers and Gordon Moyles (1982).

But while the films do, as claimed earlier, seem to attempt to socialize children into gender hierarchies through offering them pleasurable viewing experiences, it is less clear whether this may assist child viewers on journeys toward moral and mental maturity of the kind Bettelheim describes. In fact, on closer view, psychological growth seems to be experienced more by adult characters and more geared toward the adult segment of the films' audiences. This growth is especially focused on parental anxiety over children's choices and growing up, a major topic of both films.

Much of this theorization of fairy tales, however, works from children's literature or literary fairy tale texts. Yet the medium and type of transformation of these new versions of "The Little Mermaid" have a huge effect on the pleasures that are offered to child and adult audiences and on the ways in which these films transform gendered roles. The films must therefore be understood specifically through the medium of animation, as well as through *adaptation* as their approach to transforming "The Little Mermaid." As outlined in the following section, they must also be considered in the specific contexts of the animation studios from which they emerged. An understanding of animated adaptation proves a vital foundation for the analysis that follows here, which examines the transforming body of the mermaid daughter, the role of her prince in her education, and the significance of her mermaid mothers and fathers in the patriarchal and matriarchal systems that the films seem to espouse.

Animation Architexts

In considering these animated fairy tale films, the storytelling medium and the mode of retelling emerge as significant dimensions of transformations of "The Little Mermaid." Approaching the films as animations and as "adaptations" in Linda Hutcheon's sense of the term therefore provides special insight into the pleasures of these texts and the intended functions of these pleasures.

Rather than interrogating an adaptation's "fidelity" to its source text, studies now often focus on the way movement into a different medium necessarily and significantly affects an adaptation. In *A Theory of Adaptation*, Hutcheon describes adaptations as "translations in the form of intersemiotic transpositions from one sign system . . . to another" that involve "necessarily a recoding into a new set of conventions as well as signs" (16). Like the feminist short stories examined in chapter 4, *The Little Mermaid* and *Ponyo on the Cliff by the Sea* might be labeled "fairy tale revisions" in that they focus on a single, named hypotext. However, the "adaptation" label enables a closer focus on transformation *across media*. The pleasures that are invited and depicted by Disney's and Ghibli's transformations are driven by the possibilities and patterns of animated children's film, the "new set of conventions as well as signs" into which the films "transcode" Andersen's "The Little Mermaid."

The animated medium is thought to be particularly well matched to fairy tales. Paul Wells argues that though there has been relatively little critical discussion of literary texts adapted into animated films (199), animation is the form best suited to this process because of its ability to "incorporate the hybridity, instability and mutability of the perception of textual allusion" (201). Wells's point that "the mechanism of metamorphosis" (201) is the best example to illustrate the possibilities of animation in adapting literary texts rings especially true for the frequency of magical transformation in fairy tales and particularly for the number of physical changes Andersen's mermaid undergoes. As we shall see, a comparison of the depiction of metamorphosis in these works underlines important differences between the two films' interpretations of Andersen's tale and their presentation of pleasure.

The film adaptations of "The Little Mermaid" are shaped not only by the conventions of the animation format and by their target child audiences but also by the genres of their respective film studios. Disney and Studio Ghibli are both extremely well-known and powerful producers of animation, so that their body of work in each case has effectively become its own genre. These adaptations of Andersen's tale therefore build on each studio's reputation and body of work, what we might term its own *architext* (see chapter 3). The films' position within each studio's oeuvre is an important aspect of what Hutcheon delineates as the "audience's 'palimpsestuous' intertextuality," in which "our intertextual expectations about medium and genre, as well as about this specific work, are brought to the forefront of our attention" (*Theory of Adaptation* 21). For these transformations, in fact, the studios' architexts are far more influential than any broader fairy tale architext is, a notion that is taken up further in chapter 3.

The significance of the Disney architext is captured by the music composer for *The Little Mermaid*, Alan Menken, who states that in developing the film, "We were adapting Hans Christian Andersen's fairy tale in the style of Disney. And so in a sense we were pastiching Disney" ("Special Features"). Menken might be referring to Disney's stock fairy tale format, usually replete with comic animal characters, campy musical numbers, and colorful, increasingly realistic renderings of motion and scenery. He may also imply a pastiche of the values associated worldwide with the Disney brand, which according to an international survey of students include "happiness, friendliness, honesty, innocence, industriousness, cleanliness"; apparently "most respondents agreed that Disney did not approve of sex, violence, greed, laziness, un-American activities and left politics" (Wasko 14). Disney also enjoys great success in Japan. Despite the company's U.S.-centrism, critics argue that Disney products are not viewed as an exotic "other" in Japan but rather have been internalized and function as part of the local culture (see, for example, Yoshimi; M. Yoshimoto). This kind of appropriation of the North American brand in Japan resembles the way that Andersen's fairy tales have been absorbed into the local corpus of children's literature where they are read.[3]

Disney has maintained a strong and commercially successful association with the classic fairy tales and has participated in their ongoing canonization. *The Little Mermaid* (1989) premiered in the United States around fifty years after Disney's first feature animation, *Snow White and the Seven Dwarves* (dir. David Hand, 1937), and was subsequently released in Australia in 1990 and Japan in 1991. Disney's choice to transform Andersen's classic story thus continued a long tradition of fairy tale adaptations that seem to indicate an increasing sense of ownership of the genre. Indeed, many critics feel that rather than contributing to a diverse and ever-growing body of fairy tale adaptations, Disney films dominate the form in such a way that their renditions take over and rewrite the source text and any other versions.[4] There seem to have been several reasons for Disney's choice to adapt Andersen's "The Little Mermaid" in particular: its firm place in the classic fairy tale canon; the appeal of its active, desiring heroine for the cultural context at the time; and also, more pragmatically, the great success of a mermaid film that Disney had just enjoyed via its Touchstone Pictures studio, the live-action romantic comedy for adults *Splash* (dir. Ron Howard, 1984).

Credited with a renewed popularity for the studio known as the "Disney Renaissance," *The Little Mermaid* was a huge hit, scoring nominations

---

[3] As the Andersen scholar Mylius puts it, "[Andersen] is so renowned that many have no idea from which country he comes.... He has become an international writer absorbed in each country, so that he has lost his national identity in quite a few cases" ("Voice of Nature" 23). Of course, on the other hand, the Danish tourism industry commemorates and commodifies Andersen through sites such as his childhood home in Odense and Edvard Eriksen's oft-photographed statue *The Little Mermaid* in Copenhagen.

[4] See, for example, Brockus on Disney as a "memory taker." For Andersen's fairy tale, Emily Collins demonstrates one example of the impact of Disney's dominance in her work on allusions to "The Little Mermaid" in Vladimir Nabokov's novel *Lolita* (1955). Collins argues that readers' familiarity with the Disney version rather than Andersen's story may substantially affect their understanding of the text through its allusions. Furthermore, in this case, lack of knowledge of Andersen's tale could encourage a sympathetic reading of the pedophile narrator Humbert's narrative rather than a critical reading of Nabokov's text.

and wins at the Academy Awards and many other prizes. The corporation has continued to capitalize on this popularity: the film fed into a sequel, a prequel, and a television series. It was adapted into a Broadway musical and was merchandized in many forms, from video games to cake tins. In Japan, the mermaid protagonist and her companions continue to endure in the public imagination through merchandise as well as the "Mermaid Lagoon" section of the immensely popular Tokyo DisneySea theme park.[5] The film's popularity may have also motivated Disney's profitable return to Andersen as a source in recent years: the 2013 animation *Frozen* (dir. Chris Buck and Jennifer Lee), loosely adapted from Andersen's longer story "The Snow Queen," enjoyed huge domestic and international success, especially in Japan (see Sudo). While the claim that through such success Disney comes to own and define fairy tales such as "The Little Mermaid" is debatable, the company's significance in the genre is certainly massive. Many contemporary writers and readers may be transforming or recalling the Disney film when they consume and produce transformations of Andersen's "The Little Mermaid." This is made clear in the example of the television series *Dark Angel* (see chapter 6), in which characters explicitly compare Andersen's story with the Disney adaptation and discuss their preferences.

Like Disney, the Japanese animation giant Studio Ghibli has long enjoyed domestic and international success, demonstrated by both box-office figures and film prizes.[6] One clear marker of this global success is that Disney has taken on distribution of Studio Ghibli films outside Japan since 1996. Studio Ghibli has also grown to form its own recognizable architext. With the studio founder Miyazaki Hayao's (1941–) inventive hand at the helm, the films incorporate imaginative mixtures of Japanese and Western folklore, fairy tale, and myth, especially imagery of metamorphosis and flying. Some Ghibli films are adaptations of single texts, including Japanese manga or Western children's and young-adult fiction, such as Diana Wynne Jones's fairy tale novel *Howl's Moving Castle*. The films tend to display concern for the environment and the natural world and a fascinated but critical view of technology and human civilization; these issues are frequently negotiated through interesting female protagonists. Conclusions of these stories are often indefinite and subtle, not

---

[5] DisneySea and Disneyland combined have attracted over twenty-two million visitors each year since DisneySea opened in 2001, with numbers rising to over thirty-one million in 2014. From 2007 to 2014, over 90 percent have been domestic visitors, and over 70 percent of all visitors have been female (Oriental Land Group).

[6] *Sen to Chihiro no kamikakushi* (*Spirited Away*, dir. Miyazaki Hayao, 2001) remains the highest grossing film in Japan and is to date the only film made in a non-English-speaking country to win the Academy Award for Best Animated Feature.

following the classic fairy tale pattern of definitive, closed endings in the same style as Disney's happy narrative resolutions.

Andersen's fairy tale certainly matches Studio Ghibli's penchant for imaginative children's literature and stories with complex, ambivalent endings. The commercial success of Disney's adaptation may well have been another factor in Studio Ghibli's choice to adapt "The Little Mermaid"—as will be noted, Ghibli's mermaid film takes up several elements from Disney's. *Ponyo on the Cliff by the Sea* (hereafter *Ponyo*) was not the studio's most popular film, but it was certainly a hit.[7] Part of its success may be attributed to the names attached to it. Whereas the creators of Disney's *The Little Mermaid* insist that making the film "was a collective process; no one person can claim ownership" (Peter Schneider, in "Special Features"), Miyazaki Hayao's name as auteur on a Ghibli product is paramount. Production of *Ponyo* involved several well-known figures, such as the composer Hisaishi Jō and celebrity voice actors, but Miyazaki is widely known for his central role in creating and directing and, in this film, for returning to older techniques of hand-drawn animation. These studio architexts are vital foundations for the transformations both adaptations make to gender and pleasure in Andersen's fairy tale.

Studio Ghibli's Otherworldly Fish-Girl

The way the mermaids' bodies in these texts are *animated*—brought to life—is telling of the films' approaches to children's pleasures. Child viewers are invited to take joy in the movement and metamorphosis of the mermaids' and other characters' bodies. These dynamics closely reflect their adult creators' visions of the child and childhood pleasure and in turn their notions of desirable gender norms. One major difference between the two films that affects these portraits of children and the lessons they should learn is that while Disney's mermaid, Ariel, is sixteen years old, around the same age as Andersen's mermaid, Ghibli's mermaid protagonist, Ponyo, is reimagined as a girl of preschool age, about five years old. Though characters run the gamut of ages, and a recurring setting is a seniors' center next door to a preschool, *Ponyo* especially excels in its evocative portrayal of young children's mannerisms, moods, and interactions.

---

[7] It topped the Japanese box office in 2008 and stayed in that position for six consecutive weeks, the longest for a film in that year ("Japan Box Office Index"). In the United States, it was dubbed with voices from an all-star Hollywood cast and ranked ninth on box-office charts on its opening weekend.

Ponyo might not be immediately recognizable as an adaptation of Andersen's tale. However, the relationship is confirmed in promotional material: the official Studio Ghibli website describes the story as "Andersen's 'The Little Mermaid' transferred into the setting of Japan today, with the Christian coloring wiped away" (Studio Ghibli). The film itself makes some oblique reference to "The Little Mermaid," for example, when we learn that the mermaid will turn to sea foam if she does not win the affections of her beloved. But generally, in plot and characterization, it departs quite drastically from Andersen's tale. The mermaid is a small, bright-red fish with a human face. She escapes from an underwater castle and encounters a human boy, Sōsuke, who puts her in a bucket of water and names her Ponyo. The two develop a bond, but Ponyo's ocean-dwelling "ex-human" magician father, Fujimoto, recaptures her and takes her back underwater. Ponyo then steals and drinks Fujimoto's magic potions and uses them to change herself into a human girl. She runs along the waves to find Sōsuke, creating a tsunami that floods his seaside town. Her reckless use of magic threatens the world's natural balance. After the two children are united, they ride a boat in search of Sōsuke's mother, Risa, who had left them at home. When they find her, Risa and Ponyo's ocean-goddess mother, Gran Mamare, have consulted. Sōsuke's true love for Ponyo is tested, and when he passes the test, Ponyo is allowed to remain as a girl and live with Sōsuke. She loses her magic and is fixed permanently into human form; as a result, the world's balance is restored. Fujimoto apologizes for his actions, and Ponyo kisses Sōsuke to seal the transformation.

According to critical views that Disney controls and dominates fairy tales, Andersen's source text would be eclipsed by the Disney version, and the Disney story has become the point of reference for all future audiences of transformations of "The Little Mermaid." In fact, the Studio Ghibli adaptation—along with a number of the post-Disney mermaid stories—demonstrates a concurrent consciousness of both Andersen's and Disney's texts. On top of the paratextual citation of Andersen's story, the Ghibli film references the Disney adaptation in several ways. First, while the protagonist mermaid does not resemble traditional mermaids or Disney's Ariel in her body shape, she has the same vivid red hair color as Ariel and other mermaid predecessors. Second, as in the Disney film, a wizardly father figure is added into Andersen's story.

Ponyo's lowered age, combined with the film's use of more animal-like Japanese mermaid figures, distances her from the erotic associations of the traditional Western mermaid and the sexual dimension of Andersen's mermaid's metamorphosis. Ponyo's human head is joined directly to a squishy body that looks like a soft toy, so that she has neither breasts nor a slender waist. She swims with pulses and wiggles rather than the sinuous movements of mermaids such as Disney's Ariel. In fact, a Ghibli research group notes that Ponyo was criticized on online forums and other venues for being "weird/disgusting" (Jiburi kenkyūkai 43). And although the word "mermaid" (*ningyo*) is used for Ponyo in the promotional text quoted earlier, it is never mentioned in the film. Rather, she is described by characters in the film as *osakana* (fish) and *kingyo* (goldfish) and in the theme song as *sakana no ko* (child of a fish or fish-child). She is also referred to as *jinmengyo* (lit. person-faced fish), an ill-omened fish with a face that is eerily human,[8] and as *hangyojin* (lit. half-fish person), often imagined as a human-like two-legged beast with gills and scales. Finally, Ponyo is described as *ningen ni bakete iru* (taking human form), as many animals do in Japanese folk tales about cross-species marriages (see chapter 1).

Where Andersen's adolescent mermaid is described as attractive, experiences romantic longing, and undergoes changes that resemble a first sexual experience, Ponyo's younger body is rendered cute and at times adorably grotesque. As such, her desire for the prince, and the metamorphosis that this desire leads to, is also adjusted to suit her young age. One substitute it finds is an appetite—often carnivorous—for human food. When Ponyo first meets Sōsuke in her fish form, she licks blood from a cut on his finger, then later rejects bread from his proffered sandwich, choosing to gobble down the ham instead. Miyazaki's films often present tantalizing visions of food, such as the steamy hot noodles in broth that Risa serves Ponyo in the cozy cliff-side house on the stormy night, leaving Ponyo comfortably warm and drowsy. Ponyo's hunger for ham and fascination with human foods—reiterated throughout the film—expresses her mermaid-like desire for the human world. Her hungry desire weaves seamlessly with her five-year-old's curious and demanding disposition, captured so vividly in the film.

The second change in the nature of desire in Ghibli's animated adaptation is the film's more girl-like rendering of the romantic longing of Andersen's mermaid. Ponyo's doubled desire for her prince reflects the "girl consciousness" that the novelist and literary critic Takahara Eiri identifies with the *shōjo*, a particular Japanese figure of the girl taken up in detail in chapter 5. Though the typical *shōjo* is older than Ponyo, Takahara's theorization of the "consciousness of the girl" proves insightful here. This girl

---

[8] When an old woman at a seniors' center sees Ponyo, she tells Sōsuke to return her to the ocean because *jinmengyo* (person-faced fish) bring storms. As Kuzumi notes, the superstition of mermaids as omens of storms existed in Japan up until the Meiji period ("Taishō" 51).

consciousness, Takahara notes, is formed through two key attitudes of "freedom" and "arrogance" (192). On the former, Takahara explains that the girl "has no actual power" (193); freedom refers to "freedom as it functions in the imagined text" (192). "Arrogance," on the other hand, is "the self-satisfaction associated with intense narcissism" (192). Ponyo's free physical movement and unshakeable belief in her own desires meet the former, and her childlike self-absorption is seen in her desire to both be with and imitate Sōsuke: as Takahara puts is, "Rather than longing to possess the desired object, the girl seeks to become like it. Girl consciousness is contemptuous of the naked desire that demands complete ownership, positing against this a desire that longs to emulate the desired" (193). After Ponyo first meets Sōsuke, she is then recaptured by her father, Fujimoto, who traps her into a bubble in his underwater home. Ponyo rebels, shouting, "I want arms! . . . I want legs like Sōsuke!" and "Wanna see Sōsuke!"

Reducing the age of Andersen's mermaid affects, thirdly, her physical metamorphosis: the Ghibli film avoids the sexual connotations of Andersen's tale. Ponyo acts on her girlish desire to see and be like Sōsuke, bursting the bubble that imprisons her with the help of her smaller fish sisters. She holds her breath and wills limbs to grow from her body, gleefully announcing "Hands!" and "Legs!" that sprout with a *pop!* In other words, her mermaid's tail is not penetrated or painfully split open. Instead, viewers are offered an image of a creature with the enviable ability to change her body with the power of concentration. Having modified her body to suit her purpose, Ponyo then begins a journey toward the ocean surface in some of the film's most memorable and evocative scenes of childish power. She floods the underwater lair of her father, Fujimoto, imbibing his potions and then surging upward in a golden jet, slowly morphing as she goes from a creature with bird-like legs[9] to a more human form.

On the ocean surface, Ponyo runs and leaps with joyful abandon along dark, anthropomorphic waves. Her movement is not restricted by her small child's body, nor is her access to the ocean prohibited. A powerful storm rages above her, and the ocean swells over the cliffs and roads of the human world, but the mermaid remains oblivious to the danger she visits on the human world she wants to join. On the musical score by the well-known composer Hisaishi Jō, the soundtrack for Ponyo's journey is titled "Ponyo no hikō" (Flight of Ponyo), a direct homophonic reference to "Warukyūre no hikō," what is known in English as "Ride of the Valkyries." The music

---

[9]This transformation is perhaps a throwback to the origins of the Greek sirens, who in the works of Homer and Ovid have bird bodies (see Warner, *From the Beast* 399–402).

itself borrows from this piece in Richard Wagner's opera *Die Walküre* (The Valkyrie), in *Der Ring des Nibelungen* (The Ring of the Nibelung); the stirring arrangement reinforces the impressive animation of this scene and adds a dimension of strength and passion to Ponyo's joyful run toward Sōsuke. In fact, this implicit allusion is taken further: the name that Ponyo's father gives her is Brunhilde, also the name of the chief of the powerful Valkyries in Wagner's opera. Ponyo, like her namesake, is imprisoned by her father into a magical sleep. Again, another time when she has fallen asleep, like Brunhilde, Ponyo is awoken by the male who is to become her love interest.[10]

The tsunami in "The Flight of Ponyo" also links the film to another mermaid tale that is deeply concerned with the roles and possibilities that children can represent: Ogawa Mimei's famous story for children *Akai rōsoku to ningyo* (The red candles and the mermaid, 1921). Ogawa, whose essay on children's literature is quoted in the epigraph to this chapter, is a celebrated "romantic" writer of *dōwa* (children's stories) whose work began to be published in the Taishō period (1912–26; see chapter 1). The influential literary critic Karatani Kōjin attributes Ogawa with the discovery and creation of the modern notions of "the child" and childhood.[11] Ogawa's imaginative romanticism heralded a shift from the more didactic Meiji-period fairy tales, including imported and adapted stories by Andersen, that were intended to mold future subjects of the nation.

The Red Candles and the Mermaid is one of Ogawa's best known stories. It begins with a mermaid mother who does not want to raise her daughter in the "cold, dark, depressing" ocean (3). Instead, the mother abandons her daughter on the doorstep of a human couple who live near a temple. The mermaid grows up working with them, selling candles to passing templegoers, becoming famous for her beautifully decorated candles. Eventually, a

---

[10] Another Japanese transformation of Andersen's tale that possibly references Wagner is Terayama Shūji's puppet-play adaptation, "The Little Mermaid" ("Ningyo-hime" 1968). Shimizu Yoshikazu writes that Terayama's prince figure is named Siegfried, probably with reference to *Der Ring des Nibelungen*—which Terayama translated—in which Siegfried wakes Brunhilde from her hundred-year sleep and marries her (54).

[11] Karatani, in his seminal work *Nihon kindai bungaku no kigen* (1980; translated as *Origins of Modern Japanese Literature*, 1993), argues that the current idea of the child developed in tandem with the new concept of "literature" in modern Japan, so that "although the objective existence of children seems self-evident, the 'child' we see today was discovered and constituted only recently" (115). This discovery, he contends, was prefaced by the Meiji period (1868–1912) idea of children as prospective citizens who would actively contribute to the nation and the future Japanese empire. Karatani states (134) that at the time of writing, he was not familiar with the similar assertion about the invention of the child made about the European context by Philippe Ariès in *Centuries of Childhood* (1960).

Figure 2.1. Ponyo's joyful run toward Sōsuke in *Ponyo on the Cliff by the Sea*.

peddler offers to buy her, planning to sell her as a novelty; the adoptive parents, driven by greed, agree. After the mermaid is sold, her mother visits the human parents in the night. Then a huge wave rises, and the town below the temple gradually perishes and disappears. This tsunami may be interpreted as a chaotic force of childhood or feminized nature encroaching on a cynical adult world.[12]

The Ghibli film revisits the final event of the devastating wave in Mimei's tale, endowing the sense of power and possibility with more optimism. Whereas the water in *The Red Candles and the Mermaid* wipes out the village, in the Ghibli film, Ponyo's tsunami brings an ocean of wonderful sea creatures. Ponyo and Sōsuke venture out on a magically enhanced toy boat, admiring the prehistoric ocean creatures swimming in what was Sōsuke's seaside suburb. The unharmed residents enjoy boating around and cooperating in their search and rescue efforts. The meaning of this kind of optimism is captured in a schema of three symbolic figures of the child in literature, as proposed by the literary critic Maeda Ai, who critiques and expands on Karatani's claims for Ogawa Mimei's "discovery" of the child:

> Firstly, there is the child's existence as something that will "become something": the figure of the child who encapsulates the process of

---

[12]Kimura Sayo notes that the ocean in Ogawa's work has been interpreted as the "illogical, illusive world infested with the imagination" (Nakamura Miharu, qtd. in Kimura 259) and adds that whereas the ocean appears as a dream world from the land, the land itself is "merciless reality" (258).

becoming an adult. Secondly, there is the concept of the "innocent/pure child": the child's world is a utopia for adults, that adults can "return home" to.

Finally, there is the child who is neither something who will "become something" nor a destination to "return home" to. This figure is the child as child, encapsulating a range of possibilities that adults do not have, or again, an attempt to discover creation. ("Kodomo-tachi" 32–33)

The first pattern, the child who will "become something," then represents the Meiji expectations for future representatives of the Japanese empire. Ogawa and other Taishō-period romantic writers, however, shifted toward the "innocent/pure" child figure; it is this as well as the figure of the child as "possibility" that we find most prominent in Miyazaki's film.

The role of representing the alien, illogical, and natural world has often been accorded to children in this way. The scholar of children's cultures Honda Masuko, in her important work *Ibunka to shite no kodomo* (The child as another culture, 1982), examines this role through the practice of children playing with mud, which involves mixing two very different substances—sand and water—to create something entirely new. She explains, "As the paved streets of large cities show, 'mud' should be eliminated and covered up by civilizations" (27–28), but children are allowed to play with it in defined spaces such as the kindergarten. In their play with mud, children—and child characters such as Ponyo—function as retainers and symbols of the human connection with nature and wildness. In *Ponyo*, then, Miyazaki uses the figure of a child human-fish hybrid, and the water she brings to the land, to break the confines of the child's symbolic function that Honda describes and to imagine the possibility of closer links between the natural world, the childish imagination, and human adult civilization.

Throughout the film, Ponyo undergoes a whirlwind of shifts back and forth between different shapes. At the peak of her magic, she is a human girl, but as her powers begin to fade, we see her melt through in-between phases; her legs become more bird-like and her eyes more bulging and fish-like. The ever-changing hand-drawn form of Ponyo makes a striking departure from the realism found in other animated works such as Disney's. As such, *Ponyo* seems to represent the "utopian" drive that Zipes identifies as present in fairy tales but not in Disney films. *Ponyo* is, in Zipes's terms, "utopian" in its themes of "mutual trust and acceptance of difference" (*Enchanted* 109). As the fluid, childlike animation style expresses, the film ultimately values the process of change. However, Disney films, Zipes argues, "set limits on the possibilities of utopia that laid out a prescribed way of ordering the world and curbing the imagination" (*Enchanted* 25). This prescriptive limiting is certainly discernible in the body of Disney's little mermaid, Ariel, which is animated in a more realistic style.

Disney's Rebellious Teenage Daughter

Unlike Ghibli's more oblique adaptation, the Disney film signals its relationship with Andersen's tale in both the title (a common English translation of Andersen's title) and through crediting the fairy tale as a source text. In the "Disney version," the little mermaid, named Ariel, is obsessed with collecting relics from the human world. Her father, King Triton, is a powerful gray-bearded merman with crown and trident, attended by his court musician and general drudge, a hermit crab named Sebastian. A feisty teenage daughter, Ariel defies her father's ban on contact with humans and swims to the ocean surface, where she falls in love with the human Prince Eric. She then seeks out the sea witch Ursula, a voluptuous black-and-purple squid-hybrid whose role has been much developed from Andersen's hag. They strike their bargain: to become human, Ariel must exchange her voice and receive a "kiss of true love" from the prince within three days, or she will return to mermaid form and her soul will belong to Ursula. Rather than simply disappearing, the mermaid's voice leaves her body and is stored in a shell by the witch. Ursula has evil designs on Triton's throne and tries to use Ariel in her plot, but Prince Eric helps the mermaids to foil the sea witch and destroy her. Triton then relents on his hatred for humans and helps Ariel regain her human form. The film closes on Ariel and Prince Eric's wedding.

Like the Ghibli film, Disney deems the incredible pain experienced by Andersen's mermaid inappropriate for young audiences. However, the films differ in their approaches to Andersen's romantic heterosexual longing; while this drive is decentered by a younger child's hunger and desire for movement in *Ponyo*, it seems to be the *only* permissible desire for Disney's sixteen-year-old protagonist. This is linked to the common contemporary need for mermaid stories to, in Studio Ghibli's words, "wipe away" not only the mermaid's pain but also its meaning in Andersen's tale as suffering and sacrifice for the sake of the Christian soul. Andersen's mermaid has a series of overlapping desires: she wants to become human, and she desires the prince himself; these wishes are partly an expression of her desire to gain an immortal soul. In order to achieve these desires, she undergoes a painful metamorphosis and suffering and ultimately a selfless sacrifice. Like Ghibli's adaptation, the Disney film erases the pain from Andersen's story and downplays Christian ideology. However, unlike Ghibli's, the Disney film retains the adolescent protagonist. This has the result of amplifying the mermaid's other desires, focusing on puberty and sexual development.

Clearly an attempt at a new type of heroine for the studio, Ariel is seemingly more demanding and rebellious than Disney's earlier princesses. As Warner shrewdly points out, drawing from Andersen's fairy tale, "the issue of female desire dominates the film, and may account for its tremendous popularity among little girls: the verb 'want' falls from the lips of Ariel, the Little Mermaid, more often than any other" (*From the Beast* 403). At the beginning, this female desire reaches further than Ariel's attraction to the prince: whereas Ponyo desires to be human to match Sōsuke, Disney's mermaid dreams of becoming human before she encounters the prince. In Ariel's signature piece, she frames her desire as a need for more freedom of movement:

> I want to be where the people are
> I want to see, want to see them dancing
> . . . .
> Flipping your fins you don't get too far
> Legs are required for jumping, dancing
> . . . .
> Up where they walk, up where they run
> Up where they stay all day in the sun
> Wish I could be wandering free, part of that world.

Laura Sells sees this song as representing the mermaid's desire for "access, autonomy and mobility," noting that Ariel "yearns for subjecthood and for the ability to participate in public (human) life. She is figuratively and literally an upwardly mobile mermaid" (179). It is worth noting, though, that the mermaid's desire for free movement and freedom on land might hold less appeal for actual viewers than the vivid animation of the mermaid swimming lithely through the colorful, musical ocean kingdom. The movie at the time likely encouraged a great deal of children's water play as mermaids, and years later, at the time of writing (2016), "mermaid schools" are budding up in Australia, the United States, Japan, the Philippines, and elsewhere. They offer customers the opportunity to learn how to swim in a sparkling mermaid tail, complete with fin.

Ariel's obsession with the land is demonstrated through her fanatic collecting of human artifacts. But in her signature tune, the mermaid sings that

Figure 2.2. Ariel dreams of the human world from among her collection in *The Little Mermaid*.

her ambition to explore the human world eclipses even her desire for collectibles, her unquenchable hunger for "stuff."[13] However, Ariel's wide-reaching desires are narrowed over the course of the film. This narrowing process manifests itself in the changes Disney makes to the statue of a handsome boy that the mermaid keeps in her garden. While in Andersen's story the statue signifies the mermaid's curiosity about humans and belongs to her before she meets the prince, in the Disney film it becomes a statue of Prince Eric that falls from his ship after Ariel first sees him. Through personalizing the statue, Disney narrows the focus of the mermaid's desire to one particular man, denying the more general ambition and (sexual) curiosity that Ariel first expressed (see also Sells 180) and removing any creative role for her in the Pygmalion plot that Andersen's statue implies (see chapter 1). As in *Ponyo*, the heroine's desire-driven free movement is stilled on her union with the prince, the endgame or reward of classic fairy tale quests.

Despite an apparent focus on the mermaid's desire for the prince, the Disney mermaid is relegated to a more passive role in the scene from Andersen's tale in which she rescues the unconscious prince and kisses him.

---

[13]Nevertheless, Ariel's consumerist habits are convenient for the Disney corporation, which gains enormous revenue from products associated with its films: the little mermaid remains even now, as the sea witch describes her, "a precious commodity." Boria Sax argues that such consumerist culture is prefigured in the soulless, vain mermaid of mythology: "The mermaid has been absorbed into the kitsch of modern [and postmodern] culture with remarkable ease. . . . The traditional depiction of a mermaid, gazing in the mirror and combing her hair, anticipates the self-absorption that is characteristic of consumer society" (53).

After Ariel drags the unconscious Prince Eric onto the beach, the audience sees her face framed on the screen by the prince's fluttering eyelids as he begins to wake. Subsequently, according to the bargain she makes with the sea witch, Ariel, unlike Ponyo, must wait for "the kiss of true love" *from* Prince Eric. Later, in the happy ending on the same beach, we are treated to Eric's view of Ariel rising from the water with the sun shining from behind her. While the bulk of the narrative skews toward Ariel's viewpoint, in these key scenes of attraction, the viewer experiences not the mermaid's but the prince's desire: literally through his eyes.

This focus in the Disney film on heterosexual romantic union is clearly manifested in the mermaid's body. Whereas Ponyo shifts between cute human preschool-age girl and grotesque fish creature, Ariel is a sexualized, objectified teenager in any of her forms. As mentioned, *The Little Mermaid* film took advantage of the popularity of the sexy adult mermaid heroine of the romantic comedy *Splash*. Ariel's long, lustrous red hair—partly chosen to differentiate her from the *Splash* actress Daryl Hannah's blond mermaid (Mark Henn, in "Special Features")—is set off by her slender body and tiny waist; underwater she wears a seashell bikini top over developed breasts. The final scene on the beach shows her rise from the ocean wearing a sparkling, slinky purple dress with a long slit up the side and a scooped cowl neck.

The restrictions on Ariel's body are reflected particularly in her scenes of metamorphosis, which never seem to take full advantage of the animation technology that Wells sees as so suited to visualizing physical transformation. We might recall that Ghibli's Ponyo undergoes a whirlwind of shifts back and forth between different shapes. In fact, Miyazaki's more fanciful, childlike approach and hand-drawn animation allows him greater exploration of the medium, and metamorphosis is a major visual feature of femininity in his film. Ponyo's hundreds of fish sisters transform into other forms, such as huge fish, a tsunami, and for a moment young women. Ponyo's mother, Gran Mamare, to be discussed in more detail, moves gracefully on the screen in an ever-changing, fluid shape. Other figures of change are the elderly women residents at the seniors' center where Sōsuke's mother, Risa, works. These women function as a kind of "Greek chorus to the action" (Schilling), but they also represent desire for freedom of movement: they are limited by their stiffened, wheelchair-bound bodies. Toward the end of the film, seemingly as a result of their contact with Gran Mamare and the magical ocean, their limbs magically start to function again. Like elderly mermaids who have gained human legs, they bound about in delight. Through the constant portrayal of females of different ages in different stages of metamorphosis, the Ghibli film develops an audiovisual continuum of "natural" feminine powers.

In sharp contrast, in the Disney adaptation, Ariel's first metamorphosis from mermaid to human takes only about ten seconds of screen time. Her tail, shown in close-up so that her torso is not visible, splits at the center of the fin into two shapely legs. The scene then zooms out to show her whole body; in a flash of light, Ariel loses her ability to breathe underwater, and her friends drag her to the surface. Later, when Ariel reverts from human to mermaid, she falls to the deck of a ship, the change from legs back to tail concealed by her long dress. Then at the end, her final, permanent change is shown only through a glow emanating around the mermaid's body, before she simply rises out of the water with legs and the aforementioned sexy purple getup. Other transformations are to be feared and reversed rather than celebrated: mainly, when Ursula claims Triton's magic trident and uses it to change him into an abject gray worm, then to transform herself into a terrifying giant. The Disney film's comparative lack of interest in metamorphosis may also be explained by Wells's suggestion that the studio's concern with developing animation technology into the "photorealist mode" (206) limits its possibilities for depicting the fantastic.

These distinctive approaches to mermaid metamorphosis by Studio Ghibli and Disney offer their child viewers different pleasures and ultimately different gender norms and hierarchies. Ghibli's hand-drawn, ever-changing animation values nature as part of a feminized, cooperative world, where female characters seem to transform and sometimes meld with the ocean around them. The Disney film, on the other hand, uses cartoon techniques of exaggeration but generally presents more realistic imagery of bodies that are delineated from their surrounds, and it likewise delineates clear gender roles and clear-cut narrative conclusions. These different approaches to gender become even more noticeable when we examine the use of animation, voice, and music for the paternal and maternal figures in the films.

Language, Laughter, and Desire: The Name of the Mermaid's Father

Both these mermaids are disobedient in their pursuit of their romantic objectives, and their rebelliousness is specifically framed in terms of their conflicts with their fathers. Just as *Ponyo* was lauded for its immersion in a child's world, the creators of the Disney film claim to have portrayed "a real teenager, with genuine teenaged angst about 'I'm still a little girl but

I want to be a big girl'" (Mark Henn, in "Special Features"). Both texts, in Tatar's words, "see themselves as conspiring with children" in this way but offer pleasurable experiences to child viewers who watch these characters socialized (xvi). Specifically, both Ariel and Ponyo learn their positions as girl protagonists in these gender systems through language. In line with Andersen's muted mermaid, their acculturation is almost a literal playing out of Lacan's theorization of development: entry into "the symbolic"/society is marked by taking on the name of the (fatherly) prince, accepting a place within the patriarchal rule of his world. At the same time, depictions of this process seem to offer a means of mental evolution for adult audiences, rehearsing a way for parents—especially fathers—to accept the "loss" of their daughter to a romantic relationship. The particular pleasures that makes these processes enjoyable for viewers are vital elements of children's animations: comedy and laughter.

One of the main points that the film adaptations have in common is their increased emphasis on patriarchs and their reimagining of maternal figures. In Andersen's story, the little mermaid's father is mentioned but plays no major role. The mermaid learns of the human world from her grandmother, who also initiates her into society; the sea witch, though grotesque, is not malevolent and warns the mermaid of the dangers of her quest. In Disney's and Ghibli's adaptations, on the other hand, the father plays a major role, and the female figures become literally enlarged representatives of nature and femininity. The transition of the mermaid protagonists in these films, from the magical realm of childhood into adult gender systems, is marked by the girl's desire being problematized by her father but then achieved with his help through marriage or pseudomarriage to her prince.

Ponyo is packed with strong female characters and ultimately values an idealized mother-nature supernatural force over individual men. Accordingly, father figures still possess power but are somewhat lacking: Sōsuke's father, Kōichi, is absent for most of the film, and his ship is helplessly caught up in the storm Ponyo creates, requiring rescue by Ponyo's goddess mother. Ponyo's father, Fujimoto, is a wizard who has quit the human race. He is powerful and grand but also a little ridiculous, with a gangly body, a wild mane of hair, and a harried look about him. In contrast, whereas *Ponyo* communicates a sense of change to a more natural, playful world, *The Little Mermaid* follows a pattern of crisis and restoration. The ocean kingdom is ruled by the kindly yet fearsome King Triton: the realm is threatened by a dark female power, but she is defeated by the young human prince, the future patriarch. The balance is restored, and the world remains relatively unchanged.

The mermaid daughter's induction into a gendered identity in the human realm in these films is enacted through humorous patriarchal figures rather than these actual powerful fathers. These figures—whom I label *minipatriarchs*—provide comic relief even as they reinforce the role of language in establishing patriarchal authority. In a twist on Lacan's model, in order to become human, then, the mermaid is named by the prince and learns to speak the language of his world. The minipatriarch renders this process funny and unthreatening.

First, in *The Little Mermaid*, there is one of Disney's trademark amusing animal sidekicks, Scuttle the seagull. Scuttle, a parody of the experienced human sailors on Prince Eric's ship, lives in the middle of the ocean on a nest that is built in the protruding mast of a sunken ship, complete with its own anchor. He is a self-styled teacher: Ariel brings him her treasured salvaged human objects to learn their names and functions. Scuttle tells Ariel with certainty that her silver dinner fork is a "dinglehopper" used for combing hair or that a tobacco pipe is a "banded bulbous snarfblatt" that makes fine music. Their interaction invites the audience to enjoy knowing laughter at Scuttle's confidence in spouting these nonsense pronouncements about everyday objects, as well as at Ariel's wide-eyed delight in his lessons. Only later, when she has given her voice in payment to the sea witch—having been castrated and lost language—does Ariel step onto land to meet the real patriarch, the avid sailor prince, who in his palace is master of forks and other such objects and their names.

The minipatriarch in *Ponyo* is Sōsuke, whose father is a ship's captain. Like Scuttle the seagull, Sōsuke playacts at being a sailor, with his sailor's cap and toy boat. Ponyo, although she never gives up her voice, is young and newly human: she is learning to speak and does not have full command of language. She metamorphoses into a human girl the same age as Sōsuke; but her speech is more infantile in its grammar and pronunciation than his, and she lacks the vocabulary of the human world. Accordingly, he authoritatively educates her in its ways. He teaches the hungry and delighted Ponyo the names and functions of things like instant noodles, gas burners, and even breastfeeding. Sōsuke is also a fluent user of the adult, military language of Morse code, using a lamp to communicate with his father at sea.

Certainly, unlike Andersen's prince, Sōsuke recognizes the mermaid when she comes to him in human form and is attentive to her. In Andersen's text, the tragedy of the mermaid's silence is underscored when she, who knows "a lot more than anyone about the bottom of the sea" (98), must listen to the prince tell her about the ocean. In contrast, in the Ghibli film, Sōsuke avidly listens to Ponyo rattle off the difficult names of the creatures swimming below them. However, Sōsuke still has a much firmer grasp of language and ability to instruct. In fact, we learn that it is his blood (which Ponyo licks from a wound) that has imbued Ponyo with powers of metamorphosis. In Andersen's story, the little mermaid will win a soul if she and the prince let "the pastor put [their] hands together so that [they] become man and wife" (94). In Miyazaki's version, the soul may not be transmitted from man to woman via Christian marriage, but male blood—combined with the magic that Ponyo steals from her father—animates and empowers the girl.

These minipatriarchs humorously reinforce the relationship between language and authority. While Cixous and others explicate the feminist potential of women's laughter and subversive humor, laughter here "affirms" the status quo (Pailer et al.). The filmmakers and audience gently ridicule Ponyo's, Ariel's, and Scuttle's misunderstanding and misuse of objects. Laughter is directed not at the rules of the society—the proper uses of forks and instant noodles—but at the characters who contravene them. The gender order is cemented in this way: "laughing *at* someone who transgresses a norm always requires the implicit acceptance of and identification with the norm" (Horlacher 27).

Lacanian entry into the patriarchal system of values also occurs in a much more concrete way when each of the daughter-heroines is "named" in some way by her prince. In the Disney film, the muted Ariel cannot tell the prince her name. In a pseudonaming scene, Sebastian whispers Ariel's name into Prince Eric's ear, and the prince triumphantly says it out loud, believing he has correctly guessed it himself. In the Ghibli film, Sōsuke actually bequeaths the name Ponyo, his invented onomatopoeic word for the mermaid's squishy body. In other words, Sōsuke instructs Ponyo on her own name and nature. From then on, Ponyo refuses her father's name for her, Brunhilde, and adopts Sōsuke's choice. Her mother approves, saying, "ii na moratta no ne" (what a lovely name you received). This change in names foreshadows Ponyo's transfer from the father's to the husband's home. At the end of the film, Ponyo's wish to stay human and live with Sōsuke is granted when he passes the test by saying that he loves her no matter what shape she is. Fujimoto then shakes hands with Sōsuke and asks the little boy to take care of her. Significantly, however, this takes place only after Ponyo's and Sōsuke's mothers have conferred and apparently discussed the arrangement. This maternal approval, combined with Sōsuke's ability to appreciate nature and recognize Ponyo in all her shapes, predicts that Sōsuke will be more nurturing and successful than his father, the absent Kōichi, or Ponyo's father, the misguided Fujimoto. In this sense, Sōsuke resembles Maeda's figure of the child who represents new possibilities for adults but also, to an extent, the Meiji-period *shōnen* (boy) who is set to become a responsible and contributing citizen, albeit in a very different type of nation from the Meiji ideal.

The Disney film also closes with a similar exchange: after Prince Eric kills the evil Ursula, King Triton acknowledges his daughter's love for Eric and magically restores her human legs so that she can marry the prince. In the closing scene, Ariel regains her affection for her father, and her previous words of rebellion—"But Daddy, I love him!"—become "I love you, Daddy." The men acknowledge each other with a bow and a nod.[14] In fact, although Ariel is the eponymous heroine of the film, the words of one of its writer-directors are telling: "The movie, in essence, *is about the king* realizing that he can't control his daughter and that she has to follow her heart" (Clements, in "Special Features," emphasis added). The mermaid may achieve her desire, but it is her father who traces a path of learning and growth. Thus, these transformations of "The Little Mermaid" present in comic scenes a Bettelheim-style conflict and resolution that allows the father a means to confront and accept his waning power and the "loss" of his daughter. And they invite laughter and pleasure in the girl's initiation into a gendered adult order through language.

The Voice of Disney's Dark Mermaid Mother

If laughter is one central feature of animated fairy tale films for children, then music, voice, and sound effects are also vital elements of the "new set of conventions" of animation into which these films "transcode" "The Little Mermaid" (Hutcheon, *Adaptation* 16). Animation's ability to transmit music and voice makes the medium peculiarly apt for Andersen's tale of a mute mermaid. In these transformations, whereas the Disney movie is a typical musical film, the Ghibli story does not pause for songs but nevertheless makes complex use of music. Both films also make broad use of animation conventions of funny voices and speech styles, evocative sound effects and

---

[14] As such, Joseph Zornado places the film in the context of the adult-child relationship that he insistently argues is "the story of hierarchy, buried rage, domination, subjugation, violence, and an all-consuming desire for power" (xiii). Zornado shrewdly points out that Ariel is not allowed the upward mobility she aspires to: "In re-establishing the father's rule, Prince Eric wins the right to marry Ariel because he has revealed himself to be a benevolent father/king in his own right. And so after Ursula's death Ariel returns to the role of subjugated daughter, moving from her father's castle under the sea to her husband/father's castle above the sea. This is no hierarchical climb up the ladder for Ariel; rather her move is a lateral one" (164).

emotive background scores. They also effectively employ the soundscape to create pleasurable audience experiences that reflect the particular gender hierarchies valued by each text. The expression of these hierarchies can be considered through a look at the maternal figures in each film.

Both the Ghibli and Disney films make significant changes to the witch and (grand)mother figures from Andersen's story. Following a long fairy tale tradition of absent mothers, Andersen's mermaid is motherless but has a father and a grandmother. In the animated adaptations, Disney (as in many of its films) maintains the absent-mother tradition, whereas Ghibli (also true to form) adds many new female figures. In both, maternal figures are transformed in ways that are closely involved with the medium of animation and clearly reflect broader attitudes to gender and gender roles. Visually, maternal bodies are blown up larger than surrounding characters, signaling their increased influence in the stories. The two main maternal characters in these two films fall neatly on either side of the Jungian archetypal "great" mother: Gran Mamare in *Ponyo* represents the positive aspect who has "maternal solicitude and sympathy; the magic authority of the female; . . . all that cherishes and sustains, that fosters growth and fertility," and Ursula in the Disney film is the "negative side" who "may connote anything secret, hidden, dark; the abyss, the world of the dead, anything that devours, seduces, and poisons" (Jung 82).

The Disney film is a musical, and interestingly, the soundtrack was written before the final character animations were completed ("Special Features"), so that the music strongly influenced the visual characterizations. Moreover, even beyond the "dark mother," each character's singing and voice reflects the deep-rooted gender hierarchies of the film. There are two important songs by Sebastian the crab, the court musician who conducts a concert performed by Triton's daughters at the opening of the film. First, "Under the Sea" is a calypso number that Sebastian starts up with the sea creatures in order to convince Ariel that it is "better where it is wetter": that is, it is his entertaining attempt to staunch her curiosity about the human world and convince her to stay close to home. Second, in "Kiss the Girl," Sebastian conducts a choir of frogs, birds, and other lagoon creatures in his song to "create the mood" for Prince Eric to kiss Ariel. The mermaid's song, on the other hand, is neither deliberately arranged nor self-consciously directed at the world around her. As Ariel's voice actor, Jodi Benson, points out, in the film, "the characters actually run out of words, can't express themselves any more, and it has to come out in song"; Ariel's signature song, "Part of Your World," in particular "comes right out of the dialogue that she has, and then it begins this monologue that just happens to be put to music" (Benson, in

"Special Features"). That is, whereas Sebastian's numbers are arranged, self-aware compositions, performed with specific desired effects, Ariel's music is a natural outpouring of her overflowing desires, stemmed when she voluntarily mutes herself in order to achieve them.

Sandra Gilbert and Susan Gubar trace a similar gendered pattern of voice in fairy tales and mythology. They argue that "the male child's progress toward adulthood is a growth toward both self-assertion and self-articulation, . . . a development of the *powers* of speech," whereas "the girl child must learn the arts of silence either as herself a silent image invented and defined by the magic looking glass of the male-authored text, or as a silent dancer of her own woes, a dancer who enacts rather than articulates" (*Madwoman* 43).[15] The latter image is certainly evocative of Andersen's mermaid, dancing silently on torturously painful feet for her beloved prince. The Disney film's soundtrack also plays out a degree of (female) inarticulate passion against (male) conscious artistic composition.

Voice and speech also index identity in the film, and comic characters are othered and even ridiculed via their speech. Scuttle (played by the comedian Buddy Hackett) is a know-it-all New Yorker (who knows nothing), Grimm is the classic English butler, and Eric's staff all chat in the homey tones of Anglo-American servants, with the exception of the violent, mustachioed chef, who is the quintessential stereotype of a Frenchman. Finally, although Sebastian is a vocal maestro with music at his command, he is also a central figure of comedy and fun. This role is tied uncomfortably closely to the cultural associations of his Caribbean accent and large lower lip and his subservience to the white merman king (see Zuk 171; Murphy 132). On a side note, these connotations tend to be lost in the Japanese dubbing of the film, in which accents are translated into quirky individual speech styles rather than regional dialects or foreign pronunciation.

The two powerful male characters, King Triton and Prince Eric, are differentiated through their voices and speech styles. Triton's growling voice projects like a stage actor's; he speaks with the rich, beard-muffled enunciation of the powerful aging hero in Hollywood film. Eric is fairly flat and undeveloped—unlike Wilde's and Tanizaki's prince-centered versions discussed in chapter 3, Disney does not invest much into this character. Eric was voiced by Christopher Daniel Barnes, himself only about sixteen or seventeen years old at the time of recording. As Regina Bendix points out,

---

[15]Gilbert and Gubar are here comparing the murdered boy in the Grimms' "The Juniper Tree," who becomes a bird and sings the song of his murder to achieve revenge, with different versions of Philomel of Greek mythology, who is changed into a nightingale and "speaks with an unintelligible bird's voice" (*Madwoman* 43).

the prince is mainly distinguished by his speech and clothes: he "speaks like the stereotypical American 'good kid,' his 1980s style in sharp contrast with the Baroque dress and wigs of Chancellor Grimm and his staff" (287). Eric and Ariel, the representatives of the new human generation, approximate Standard American English accents (and Flounder, Ariel's fish friend, speaks like her cute younger brother) and youthful language. Ariel, then, moves from her frightening, old-fashioned father to a modern-day nice guy (see also Zuk 171), and the significance of this transfer is underlined by the two men's distinct speech styles.

Interestingly, neither the patriarch nor the patriarch-to-be sings his own song. King Triton, duly serious and regal, looks forward to his daughters' singing performances but never sings himself. Prince Eric plays the pipes and enjoys a hearty sea shanty but does not have his own solo. The male monarchs in sea and on land do not need to sing but employ their inferiors to do so. So while Sebastian may be an accomplished composer and performer, he is merely an entertainer, both for Triton and for the film's audience. The more developed human world can only faintly hear his frivolous songs. Against this backdrop, the sea witch Ursula's relationship to voice is significant.

Ursula is not a conventional mermaid but has black squid tentacles that join to become a bodice for her voluptuous human torso and large breasts. Ursula also has long predatory fingernails and coiffed short gray hair and wears bright-blue eye shadow. A classic witch figure, she resides alone in shadowy, dangerous waters with her animal familiars, some distance from the bright royal palace, in a dark, womb-like cave. The Disney version, like Andersen's, has no mother figure, but Disney goes even further, also erasing the little mermaid's grandmother. The only character close to a maternal figure for Ariel, then, is Ursula—who, according to cut scenes in the DVD extras, is Ariel's paternal aunt ("Special Features"). Wolfgang Lederer suggests that the witch in Andersen's story is a "double" or "shadow" of the grandmother (172); the Disney film leaves us with only the shadowy double, with only the dark side of the great mother figure.

Ursula is hungry for more power in Triton's kingdom. In contrast to Andersen's sea witch, who warns the little mermaid that her quest will end badly, Ursula uses the mermaid's desire and her voice to her own ends. She calls Ariel a "precious commodity," explicitly describing her as an exchangeable item in a way that Triton and Eric (despite their formal exchange of her) do not. This dynamic between the young princess/daughter and the middle-age witch/mother is common in classic fairy tales and is central to the Disney fairy tale film architext (see Bell 108). In this pairing,

Ursula embodies the queen in "Snow White" as Gilbert and Gubar capture her: out to destroy the angelic daughter, she is "a plotter, a plot-maker, a schemer, a witch, an artist, an impersonator, a woman of almost infinite creative energy, witty, wily, and self-absorbed as all artists traditionally are" (*Madwoman* 38–39).

Ursula convinces Ariel to give up her voice by posing with good intentions in her signature song, "Poor Unfortunate Souls." Like Sebastian's pieces, then, Ursula's song is not a natural outpouring of emotion but a deliberate, calculated seduction. Ariel is persuaded to give up her voice, which Ursula stores away, later using it to seduce Prince Eric to further her evil plan. The sea witch is articulate, with by far the most sophisticated vocabulary of all the characters. Her voice actor, Pat Carroll, states that she played Ursula as "a has-been Shakespearean actress" ("Special Features"). Whereas foreign or lower-class accents are used in the film for comic characters, Ursula is the disturbingly educated and eloquent villain.

While Ursula's voice mimicked that of a Shakespearean actress, her figure and movement was modeled on the outrageous drag queen Divine ("Special Features"), highlighting again her role as performer and artist and literal (woman) "impersonator." The deliciously frightening Ursula has been read convincingly as a subversive element within the film who "threatens to dethrone the Disney patriarchy" (Zornado 164). Adapting the sea witch's advice in Andersen's tale, Ursula tells Ariel that a girl does not need her voice to win the prince's love because "there's always body language." Sells sketches the subversive nature of the visual story accompanying Ursula's advice:

> Ursula stages a camp drag show about being a woman in the white male system, beginning "backstage" with hair mousse and lipstick. She shimmies and wiggles in an exaggerated style while her eels swirl around her, forming a feather boa. This performance is a masquerade, a drag show starring Ursula as an ironic figure. . . . Ursula is a multiple cross-dresser; she destabilizes gender. . . .
>
> In Ursula's drag scene, Ariel learns that gender is performance; Ursula doesn't simply symbolize woman, she *performs* woman. . . . Ariel learns gender, not as a natural category, but a performed construct. (182–83)

Actually, male characters reiterate Ursula's lesson on performing femininity: Scuttle tells the newly muted Ariel, "If you want to be a human, the first thing you've got to do is dress like one." And Sebastian advises her what she must do to attract the prince: "You gotta look your best. You gotta bat your eyes like this. You gotta pucker up your lips like this," demonstrating correct eyelash fluttering and lip pouting as he speaks. At Ursula's behest, then, Ariel's period of voicelessness offers the carnivalesque pleasures of "dressing up"—she impersonates the humans she aspires to be by wearing human clothes, and she enjoys gorgeous princess gowns as part of her conscious performance of attractive femininity.

Impersonation performances threaten the concept of stable gender, Judith Butler argues, because "gender parody" or imitation reveals that the notion of an "original" fixed gender itself is only an imitation (138). However, the film attempts to reinforce the notion of fixed gender identity. When Ursula later changes into a beautiful human maiden and tries to use Ariel's captive voice to enchant Eric into marrying her, loyal animal sidekicks see through the disguise and attack her. The evil, sexual mother figure cannot "pass" as a virginal young woman. During the battle, Ariel's voice is set free from its seashell prison and flies back into her throat. Ursula returns to her grotesque form, and at the same time, Ariel's enchanted human shape reaches its time limit and is transformed back to her mermaid body. It is as if Ursula's dangerous, feminine magic of performance and impersonation cannot hold for either herself or Ariel. Ariel can become permanently human only through her approving father's legitimate powers.

Ursula's hunger for power and her obsession with voice is an image of feminine envy of male-controlled language. The witch tricks Ariel into signing her soul away and later forces King Triton to sign a similar agreement. Whereas Triton sears his name on this Faustian contract[16] with a straightforward stab of his trident, Ariel does not have her own writing implement but scrawls her name with a fishbone that Ursula conjures up, which disappears when she has finished writing. Neither Ursula nor Ariel, then, is in possession of her own pen. While innocent Ariel is apparently content with the body language that Ursula has prescribed to her (and makes no attempt to communicate with Prince Eric through writing), the sea witch has other ideas. Ursula is motivated by pen/penis envy, attempting with her artistry what Gilbert and Gubar outline as "the escape that the female pen offers from the prison of the male text" (*Madwoman* 44). In this largely male-authored collaborative text,[17] she nearly succeeds, but

---

[16] Disney erases the mermaid's desire for immortality, but other Christian imagery remains. Ursula's hunger for power is tied up in her Satanic desire to possess souls, and she poses as "a saint" to trick Ariel into signing herself over when she sings about "Poor Unfortunate Souls."

[17] The section of the DVD that introduces the mostly male writers, directors, producers, and other figures involved in making the film is titled "Renaissance Men."

her momentary seizure of Triton's crown and trident/pen is a nightmarish vision of a motherly body unnaturally possessing male power. The "great mother" Ursula grows enormous and towers out of the ocean, whipping up a dark storm; her face, belly, and breasts are heavily shadowed, while the trident glows gold and shoots lightning bolts at the young lovers. Prince Eric, however, uses his sailing skills to steer a broken ship's mast through Ursula's gut, killing her. Several critics point out the strongly phallic imagery of the impalement (Murphy 133; Whitley 43; Zuk 172). The storm subsides, and the sun comes out; the seductive song of the dark mother has been silenced.

The Music of Mother Nature in *Ponyo*

While the Ghibli adaptation is not a musical, music played a key role in its storytelling and promotion. Music and sound are important elements of the film's vision of a different kind of "great mother" as well as its focus on early childhood. The key role of music, in fact, manifested itself when the theme song was released in 2007, before the film itself: the song became incredibly popular and increased public recognition of the film and the protagonist's invented name.[18] It was performed by an eight-year-old girl, Ōhashi Nozomi (a different child provided Ponyo's voice) with an adult-male folk duo, Fujioka Fujimaki.[19] When it was dubbed into English, the children used to voice the two protagonists and sing the theme song were both members of pop-star dynasties and Disney Channel television actors.[20] The Japanese lyrics include energetic onomatopoeia such as *petapeta* (for feet slapping the ground) and *pyonpyon* (for hopping and skipping). These words are extremely closely tied to the figure of the child, as evidenced in *Ibunka to shite no kodomo*, in which Honda uses such onomatopoeia for sounds, feelings, and physical sensations to capture cultural ideas of childhood. Ponyo's name itself, in fact, is an onomatopoeic word invented by Sōsuke to describe the way she bobs (in fish form) in the water.

---

[18]The song played incessantly on television and radio and was performed on the favorite New Year's Eve television event, the singing contest *Kōhaku uta gassen*. Later, the film's soundtrack won the Japan Gold Disc Award for the best-selling soundtrack of 2009.
[19]The duo's name combines the names of both members, Fujioka Taka'aki and Fujimaki Naoya, and sounds similar to the name of the character of Ponyo's father, Fujimoto. The word *Fuji* is somewhat reminiscent of the famous mountain of the same name, which is a strong symbol of Japan. However, these names are not written in the same *kanji* character as the mountain.
[20]Ponyo was voiced by the child actor Noah Cyrus, the younger sister of the then-teen pop singer and Disney Channel actor Miley Cyrus and the daughter of the country singer Billy Ray Cyrus. Sōsuke was voiced by the child actor Frankie Jonas, whose older brothers belonged to a Disney Channel boy band, the Jonas Brothers.

Within the film, musical intertextuality is utilized to appeal to both child and adult audiences; alongside the reference to the classical "Ride of the Valkyries" during Ponyo's joyful journey on the ocean waves, there is a more self-referential moment. Sōsuke's mother, Risa, comforts Sōsuke by singing to him, "Watashi wa genki" (translated as "I'm as happy as I can be"). This line is from a song in another of Miyazaki's most childlike films, *Tonari no Totoro* (*My Neighbor Totoro*, 1988), and its use firmly reinstates the film's place within the Studio Ghibli architext. In this way, *Ponyo* mixes children's and adult's musical genres, inviting the audience to derive "intertextual pleasure" from recognizing these other texts and experiencing the added level of meaning that they bring to the film (Hutcheon, *Adaptation* 117).

Risa is a somewhat surprising mother figure for a children's animation. Very unusually, Sōsuke addresses her using her first name rather than "mommy" or something similar. And she is neither a villain nor a perfect mother silenced into invisibility. When Risa's husband tells her that he cannot come home from his ship, she becomes angry and slams open the refrigerator to grab herself a can of beer. She is dynamic and energetic, enjoying some determined, madcap driving when she forces her tiny car up mountain roads to escape from Ponyo's storm. Yet she is also nurturing, looking after Ponyo and mothering the visitors to the seniors' center where she works. Risa speaks in a competent and confident way, modeling polite language for her well-mannered son and making appropriate use of motherly language in her kindly yet authoritative interactions with the children (see J. Smith). Importantly, Risa is not the only mother figure: like the Disney film, *Ponyo* expands both the mother's body and her role from Andersen's tale. In this case, a number of maternal figures are added into the plot.

Unlike the quite three-dimensional Risa, Ponyo's mother, Gran Mamare, is literally a "great ocean mother": her name plays on the French *grand* (great), *ma* (my), and *mère* (mother), the French *mer* or Spanish *mare* (ocean), and *mama* (used by many Japanese children for "mommy"); her body is giant and ever changing, and when her fluid, wavering form glides through the water, her blue dress resembles a mermaid's tail in some moments. Like other mermaids and like Oscar Wilde's passionate Witch (see chapter 3), Gran Mamare has long, flowing red hair. Sparkling waters and golden fish announce her approach, and she is bedecked in jewelry. The fairytale appearance of the jewels is compounded by the music that accompanies Gran Mamare, awe-inspiring notes overlaid with the tinkling bell-like sound effect usually associated with magic. Gran Mamare's voice is light and serene, and she uses highly feminine sentence endings such as *na no ne* and *no yo*, which are associated with refined women's speech styles that are perhaps more frequently encountered in fictional texts than everyday interactions (see Inoue). Her "great mother" status is reconfirmed when she rescues Kōichi's ship from a mysterious ship graveyard, and the sailors worship her as Kannon-sama, the bodhisattva of compassion or Goddess of Mercy. In contrast to Triton's decision to grant Ariel her wish to become human, Ponyo is allowed to become human after Sōsuke's very human mother, Risa, and her own goddess mother, Gran Mamare, consult over the decision. The mothers' consultation is only shown from afar. The women exude a sense of calm earnest against background sounds of reverent, wordless, choral harmonies interspersed with the giggles and excited shouts of the elderly ladies from the seniors' center, who have gained use of their legs in the underwater bubble around the center.

In this way, the Ghibli film presents a new gender system in which females are more valued for their spiritual connection to nature and their ability to change, yet it is one in which males maintain symbolic control over language and females voluntarily subdue their powers in order to participate in heterosexual relationships. The Disney film, on the other hand, introduces and then vanquishes an unruly feminine threat, perpetuating the patriarchy when the mermaid's father authorizes her marriage to the prince and move to his land. Importantly, these gender hierarchies are discernible through a focus on the various pleasures that are depicted and invited by these films. Audiences—especially child viewers—are offered pleasurable experiences of song, sound, movement, and laughter, experiences that are enabled by the medium of animation.

Children's fairy tale reading and viewing pleasures have a long history of educational and socializing functions. It may be easy to believe that the "cathartic pleasures" presented here do effectively socialize child audiences into the hierarchies that the films portray. However, as chapter 5 argues, some mermaid stories for girls offer a more complex understanding of the way readers and viewers themselves might enjoy and consume fairy tale transformations. First, though, to develop an understanding of the complexity of this kind of reading pleasure, chapters 3 and 4 explore textual pleasures related to a more "knowing" interaction with the fairy tale form and with Andersen's "The Little Mermaid" especially.

3
Fairy Tale Architextuality and the Prince's Pleasures

[The fairy tale] is fond of gold and silver, and iron and crystal, if for no other reason than it prefers everything solid and clearly formed....

The tendency toward extremes and contrasts, toward metals and minerals, cities, castles, rooms, boxes, rings, and swords, and the tendency to make feelings and relationships congeal into objects, so to speak, and thus become outwardly visible—all these things give the fairy tale definiteness, firmness, clarity.
—Max Lüthi, *Once upon a Time: On the Nature of Fairy Tales*

Animated adaptations of "The Little Mermaid" bring the fairy tale to life in brilliant color, sound, and movement, but of course, literary texts had endeavored to capture the striking aesthetic impact of the mermaid in the centuries before these films. In doing so, the transformations I take up here evince a particularly suggestive fondness for gold and silver and other precious objects, as Lüthi describes in the epigraph. Their dialogues with Andersen's story engage the "clarity" of the fairy tale form to their own stylized, art-obsessed ends, delving into the pleasures of a deep knowledge of the structures and patterns of the fairy tale form.

More practical changes to the plot of Hans Christian Andersen's "The Little Mermaid" also shape the imagining of gender and pleasure in these transformations. Andersen's tale foregrounds the mermaid protagonist and endows her beloved prince with little voice or personality. This has left openings for subsequent writers to flesh out the prince and retell the tale from his perspective. In the literary short stories I examine, male authors and established members of their respective canons transform Andersen's tale by installing the prince figure as its protagonist: Oscar Wilde's "The Fisherman and His Soul" (1891), Tanizaki Jun'ichirō's "Ningyo no nageki"

(The mermaid's lament, 1917), and Abe Kōbō's "Ningyo-den" (Legend of a mermaid, 1962). More recently, the contemporary woman author Kawakami Hiromi has offered a female prince figure who falls under a frightening mermaid's spell in her short story "Hanasanai" (I won't let go, 1998). Regardless of the shift in perspective from female to male protagonist, each of these texts inherits and cultivates the themes of longing for and identifying with the other found in "The Little Mermaid." Like Andersen's tale, they wallow in the pain and suffering of the yearning protagonist, enjoying a kind of deep satisfaction in abandoning themselves to emotion and, often, in expressing this emotional recklessness through intense physical pain. Just as Andersen's mermaid aspires to the land and a human soul, these protagonists dream of different realms and seek the completion and continuance of the self. But the switch to the prince's viewpoint is, seemingly, a switch from a narrative sympathy with the hybrid mermaid as "other" to the more hegemonic perspective of the male human. In these stories, this shift results in an objectification of the mermaid as a feminine figure for the seductive unknowable, the foreign, the animal, and the marvelous supernatural.

This figure of the mermaid, then, also expresses the fairy tale's own enchantments of wonder and difference. Here, these fairy tale enchantments include the way the transformations solidify ideas and relationships into objects and take pleasure in treasure and precious things; the transformations also appeal in their adoption of "once upon a time" style formulas and their emphasis on enchantment. Altogether, they form relationships less through direct transformation of "The Little Mermaid" and more through their pleasure in the fairy tale genre itself. That is, they engage with the fairy tale genre as an "architext," what the narratologist Gérard Genette describes as "the entire set of general or transcendent categories—types of discourse, modes of enunciation, literary genres—from which emerges each singular text" (*Palimpsests* 1). This interaction with the fairy tale form generates pleasures quite different from those of the animated films, which do not demand conscious engagement with Andersen's tale or the fairy tale genre but offer immersion in an enjoyable childlike world, also encouraging a childlike assimilation of particular social structures.

The fairy tale architext that is so central to these prince's stories is, in Genette's words, "everywhere—above, beneath, around the text, which spins its web only by hooking it here and there onto that network of architexture" (*Architext* 83). In this understanding, the transformation is part of a network, fastened at certain points onto what Cristina Bacchilega calls the "fairy-tale web" (*Fairy Tales Transformed?* 18). This image enables us to examine the ways in which these transformations not only emulate but also actively reject the conventions of the fairy tale. The relationship of architextuality is the adoption of but also "the blending or scorning of genres" (Genette, *Architext* 83). It is through such a dynamic that Wilde's and Tanizaki's tales especially invite readers to share in their fairy tale pleasure in enchantment with beautiful objects and with the exotic setting removed from the mundane world. Abe's tale uses the narrative norms of the fairy tale form to ridicule the narrator who is caught up in them, mesmerized by story as much as he is by the mermaid he captures. Like Abe, Kawakami tells of the lure and the danger of being bewitched, emphasizing the impossibility of connection and communication through an absolutely alien mermaid. These transformations, although their connections to Andersen's tale are among the most tenuous of all those identified in this book, are therefore an important starting point for a contemplation of the "knowing" fairy tale pleasures of transforming ideas of gender in "The Little Mermaid."

The Prince's Lament

Oscar Wilde's loving reversal of Andersen's "The Little Mermaid," titled "The Fisherman and His Soul," appears in *A House of Pomegranates* (1891), the second of his fairy tale collections, following *The Happy Prince and Other Tales* (1888). "The Fisherman and His Soul" intersects with the fairy tale genre through its wondrous imagery; it also has relationships with a number of mermaid texts and with other stories by Andersen. Indeed, Wilde (1854–1900) had an especially solid grounding in wonder tales. "The Fisherman and His Soul" shares links with *Ancient Legends, Mystic Charms, and Superstitions of Ireland* (1887), the tales collected by Wilde's father, the folklorist Sir William Wilde, and compiled after Sir William's death by his wife (Oscar Wilde's mother), Lady Jane Wilde (see Killeen 148). Oscar Wilde would have also read stories of water spirits such as "A Warning," "Undine," and "The Fisherman" in his mother's poetry translations of Scandinavian legends (Killeen 154), published as Jane Wilde's *Poems by Speranza*.[1]

The eponymous protagonist of Wilde's story is a fisherman who catches a mermaid and falls in love with her and her seductive song. He courts her,

---

[1] Acknowledging these mermaid histories, Christopher Nassar directs our attention to another of Andersen's fairy tales, "The Shadow," which he claims has "by far the deeper influence" on "The Fisherman and His Soul" (218). Another possible hypotext for both Andersen's "The Shadow" and Wilde's "The Fisherman and His Soul" is Adalbert von Chamisso's *Peter Schlemihls wundersame Geschichte* (Peter Schlemihl's wondrous history, 1814; see Hoban 26–27), about a man who sells his shadow to the devil.

but he cannot marry her because the sea folk do not have souls. The Fisherman therefore sets out to rid himself of his Soul. His struggles occur in the fairy tale groupings of sets of three and in what Max Lüthi describes as "stylized intensification," where "the last adventure is the most dangerous, the youngest princess the most beautiful, the youngest son is the fairy-tale hero" (54). First, the Fisherman asks the unforgiving local Priest how to rid himself of his soul, but the Priest angrily casts the Fisherman out. The Fisherman then tries to sell his Soul to merchants, but they tell him it has no value. Third, then, he visits a Witch, who tells him that she can detach his soul for the price of a dance with her. The Fisherman performs this dance, which is observed by the Devil, the Witch's master. In return, the Witch tells the Fisherman how to cut off his own soul—his shadow—which he does; then he goes into the ocean to marry the Mermaid. The ejected Soul leaves the Fisherman but comes back once a year to tell of its independent journeys. The Soul, left without a heart, performs awful deeds. It tempts the Fisherman to leave the Mermaid and travel with it; the Fisherman finally succumbs to the third temptation, a promise of dancing girls in faraway countries. On their journey, the Soul convinces the Fisherman to perform acts of evil. The Fisherman finally refuses the Soul and returns to the seashore to wait for the Mermaid, but she has died. When he finds her body, the Fisherman's heart breaks, which gives the Soul an entrance back into the Fisherman's body, and they are joined again. The Fisherman dies with the Mermaid's corpse in his arms. The Priest is mysteriously moved by the flowers that grow on their unmarked grave and begins to preach love instead of hate.

Though Wilde's rhythmic and lyrical writing has often been compared to his captivating speech (Murray 1), his lavish prose does not match the simple oral style often emulated by fairy tales. Nor does Wilde use Andersen's intimate narrative techniques—which may not have been communicated in the translations of Andersen that Wilde had access to—of childlike and vernacular language. No narrator addresses the reader in the way Andersen's does. No insight into the mermaid's perspective is provided, though we have a glimpse of the Witch's feelings when the Fisherman is out of sight. Wilde's tale remains in the third person, narrated nearly entirely from the Fisherman's viewpoint, with a good part of the story taken up by the detached Soul recounting its journeys in direct speech.

Although these are rather adult-oriented storytelling techniques, Wilde's tales seem to be dogged by a debate about their intended audience that has perhaps affected the critical attention paid to them. Despite their popularity, they have been the subject of comparatively little discussion (Murray 1). Some critics argue that the tales were not meant for children or *only* for children, sometimes seeming to imply that unlike stories for children, the tales are serious literature worthy of research. This may be tied to a need to position Wilde as a "subversive writer," a need that is at odds with the impression that children's literature socializes children into conforming to the existing inequitable hierarchy (see Killen 9–10, 13–15). Such concerns about children's stories in general, which are by no means uncommon, come to the fore in the analysis in this book of children's animated films (see chapter 2) and girls' mermaid stories (see chapter 5). In the case of Wilde, scholars resolve this contradiction by assigning a more "subversive" and perhaps adult stance to his stories (for example, see Zipes, *Fairy Tales and the Art* 121). But Wilde, for his own part, seems less concerned with age and more with the fairy tale affiliation with pleasure in the marvelous. In a frequently quoted letter on the subject, he writes that the tales in *The Happy Prince* are "studies in prose . . . meant partly for children and partly for those who have kept the childlike faculties of wonder and joy." Somewhat contradictorily, he adds that the tales are "not for children, but for childlike people from eighteen to eighty!" (qtd. in Tattersall 135).

On the other hand, the Japanese mermaid tale that I argue takes up Wilde's, titled "Ningyo no nageki," is unquestionably written for adults. It was published in the general monthly periodical *Chūō kōron* and uses difficult language and script. The story, moreover, contains adult scenes of erotic desire and opium smoking. The tale's author, Tanizaki Jun'ichirō (1886–1965), enjoyed a long and celebrated literary career that began in the final years of the Meiji period (1868–1912) and spanned the relatively liberal Taishō period (1912–26), then an increasingly militarized Japan and its involvement in World War II, followed by the Allied occupation after the war (1945–52) and finally the subsequent rapid economic growth. Writing against the vein of the naturalist (*shizen-shugi*) literature that prevailed at the time, Tanizaki debuted in 1910 to critical acclaim, including praise from the established author and so-called antinaturalist Nagai Kafū (Chiba, "Tanizaki" 331). Tanizaki is known for his education in classical Chinese and Japanese literature, as well as his early-career fascination with Western literature and the modernization of Japan. Many of his works have erotic or sadomasochistic themes; they were subjected to censorship a number of times for this reason but also more broadly because of his lack of support for war efforts (Rubin 234).

Tanizaki discusses his reading of the work of Oscar Wilde and was quite likely to have read Andersen's work also. By the time "Ningyo no nageki" was first published in January 1917, Andersen's "The Little Mermaid" had been translated into Japanese over a decade earlier (1904), and "The Fisherman and His Soul" had recently been translated into Japanese in 1914.² In any case, Tanizaki was able to read and translate literature from English; he may have encountered Andersen's mermaid tale and certainly would have known Wilde's, as he demonstrated a great interest in Wilde's work in his early years of writing. However, most commentary on this textual relationship focuses on Tanizaki's response to Wilde's aestheticism and on Tanizaki's preface to his translation of Wilde's play *Lady Windermere's Fan* (1893; trans. Tanizaki, 1918). Here Tanizaki writes that though he was an ardent admirer of works such as *Salome* and *The Picture of Dorian Gray* when he was younger, he is now repelled by Wilde's vulgar attitude (Preface 157–58). Another mark of Tanizaki's concern with Wilde is the illustrations to "Ningyo no nageki" by Mizushima Niou,³ which resemble Aubrey Beardsley's illustrations for Wilde's *Salome*; as we shall see, Tanizaki actually names one of Beardsley's illustrations for *Salome* in "Ningyo no nageki." Thus, Tanizaki's mermaid tale is more often compared with *Salome* and Wilde's portrayal of the femme fatale. A more detailed comparison with "The Fisherman and His Soul," then, is long overdue.

"Ningyo no nageki" is set in late eighteenth-century Nanjing, China, during the Qing dynasty. It tells of a wealthy, intelligent, learned young Chinese nobleman named Mō Seichū (Meng Shidao). The tale presents a one-sided emphasis on the hero's good looks and talent in typical fairy tale style, though he is also a "typical Decadent hero," a handsome and clever youth who in Wildean style is "assailed by a typically *fin-de-siècle* ennui" (Pinnington 83). By the age of twenty-four, Meng Shidao has already tired of the best women, wine, song, and even opium that his riches can buy him and seeks some greater pleasure. As in Andersen's tale, the story is dominated by the protagonist's yearning. His desires seem to be met when a Dutch merchant, who has heard of this nobleman's quest, sells him a captured mermaid. Meng Shidao is fascinated by the foreign man and then immediately entranced by the mermaid. The mermaid, when she finally speaks, convinces him to take her back to her native Mediterranean waters and release her. The mermaid transforms herself into a snake, and Meng Shidao, carrying her in a jar, boards a boat to Europe. When he releases her as promised, she shows

---

²Horiguchi Kumaji's translation in *Osukā Wairudo no kessaku* (Oscar Wilde's masterpieces). New translations were published each year for the following three years ("Wairudo hen" 877).
³Mizushima's illustrations for "Ningyo no nageki" are often reported to have been censored for their eroticism. Chiba Shunji asserts that, in fact, the subjects of censorship were illustrations to two other stories by Tanizaki that were published together with "Ningyo no nageki" by Shun'yōdō in April 1917: Nagoshi Kunisaburō's illustrations to "Majutsushi" (The magician) and "Uguisu-hime" (The bush warbler princess) (Chiba, "Ningyo" 145).

herself in her mermaid form for him one last time; then he sails on toward Europe. Whatever her significance for the nobleman, then, Tanizaki's mermaid does achieve her unfaltering aim to return to her native waters—a reversal of Andersen's mermaid's desire to leave the ocean for the land.

The author very consciously marks his story as a fairy tale. It begins with the *mukashi mukashi* (once upon a time) formula, and it is narrated in the third person using verb endings (*desu/-masu*) that are more associated with speech than literature.[4] This fairy tale style departs from literary norms of the time; the Meiji period had seen a strong push for the *genbun itchi* (unified writing and speech) colloquial literary style, which included the use of *de aru* rather than *desu/-masu* verb forms. This style distinguished the Japanese modern novel (*shōsetsu*) from predecessors such as the Heian-period (794–1185) *monogatari* (usually translated as "tale").

Tanizaki's fairy tale narrative voice seems to have somewhat different effects from the voice of the fairy tale narrator in English. Atsuko Sakaki argues that in the modern novel the new *genbun itchi* colloquial style greatly "neutralized markers of class, gender, and social status of the narrator and created the illusion that he or she is omniscient and omnipresent, free of any position and relation to others" (*Recontextualizing Texts* 16). This kind of modern style, as opposed to that of the traditional fairy tale, seems to reflect what Bacchilega describes as the "external or impersonal narrator whose straightforward statements carry no explicit mark of human perspective—gender, class, or individuality" (*Postmodern Fairy Tales* 34)—and who helps the fairy tale to "silently assume" (35) and "naturalize" (34) a given set of social conventions and constructions of gender. Conversely, the more oral fairy tale feel of the *desu/-masu* style that Tanizaki uses might lend a sense of subjectivity to the voice of this disembodied narrator (see Chiba, "Ningyo" 149). To an extent, when Tanizaki invokes the orality of *mukashibanashi* (folk tales), he implies a storytelling narrator and draws attention to the act of narration, eschewing a sense of universality—at least more so than the grandiose third-person voice of Wilde's tale does.

Fairy Tale Treasures

The fairy tale, as Lüthi observes in the epigraph to this chapter, "is fond of gold and silver, and iron and crystal, if for no other reason than it prefers

---

[4] The Tanizaki scholar Chiba Shunji demonstrates that this was a conscious choice: an early draft shows that Tanizaki altered the first line to add the *mukashi mukashi* formula and also shifted from the written *de aru* verb form to the more oral *-masu* form (Chiba, "Ningyo").

everything solid and clearly formed"; fairy tales have "the tendency toward extremes and contrasts, toward metals and minerals, cities, castles, rooms, boxes, rings, and swords, and the tendency to make feelings and relationships congeal into objects" (51). Wilde's and Tanizaki's stories share this fairy tale fascination with precious objects and indeed cultivate it into a pleasure in the artifice of literary language and pleasure in the marvelous object of the fairy tale itself.

Examples of the tales' obsession with precious objects are abundant. "The Fisherman and His Soul" is laden with gorgeously described exotic treasures, from "an idol seated on a throne of jasper bordered with great orient pearls" (61) to "silver bracelets embossed all over with creamy blue turquoise stones" (64). Tanizaki takes up this pleasure in "Ningyo no nageki," especially in his use of many difficult *kanji* and unusual words to both describe and evoke the historical Chinese setting. As the tale's translator, Thomas LaMarre, puts it, "line after line of rare and dazzling characters adorn the text, strings of exotic, beautiful, and sometimes unreadable characters" (56). These difficult characters tend to describe physical objects, as in a litany of the rare and valuable wines the nobleman collects:

甜くて強い山西の潞安酒、淡くて柔らかい常州の恵泉酒、その外蘇州の福珍酒だの、湖州の烏程潯酒だの、北方の葡萄酒、馬奶酒、梨酒、棗酒から、南方の椰漿酒、樹汁酒、蜜酒。

(Tanizaki, *Ningyo* 13)

a strong, sweet Luan wine from Shanxi, and a light, mild, Huiquan wine from Changzhou, then a Fuzhen wine from Suzhou, a Wuchengxun wine from Huzhou, and an entire range of wines, from the grape wines, fermented mare's milk, pear wines, and date wines of the North, to southern varieties like coconut wines, resin wines, and honey wines. (trans. LaMarre 35–36; all subsequent translations are LaMarre's)

Tanizaki—no stranger to literary fetishism in other forms—takes a fetishistic fairy tale joy in beautiful objects and converts the rare and beautiful words themselves that describe these objects into items of pleasure (see also Sakaki, *Obsessions* 85). This kind of fetishizing of the words themselves is aptly described by Roland Barthes, who muses that in "a typology of the pleasures of reading—or of the readers of pleasure . . . the fetishist would be matched with the divided-up text, the singling out of quotations, formulae, turns of phrase, with the pleasure of the word" (63).

As well as using these elaborate Chinese characters, Tanizaki inserts exotic Roman script into the text, as in the use of the word "umlaut" among the Japanese here:

> 南洋の旅人の口から、「人魚」という支那語が、一種特有なUmlaut を以て発音されると、それに一段の神秘な色が籠っているように思われたのです。(25)

> issued in Chinese from the mouth of the south-seas traveler, pronounced with a peculiar inflection like foreign umlaut, the word "siren" seemed to possess a singularly mysterious and sensuous coloration. (trans. LaMarre 41)

A glance shows the visual effect of the conspicuous single German word within the Japanese scripts. While sophisticated contemporaries of Tanizaki would have understood its meaning, the foreign expression underscores the exotic, "mysterious" image of the foreigner even for readers unfamiliar with the term. Similarly, later the mermaid gives the nobleman

> ビアズレエの描いた、"The Dancer's Reward" という画題の中にあるサロメのような、悽惨な苦笑い。(42)

> a smile as poignant and bitter as that of Salome drawn by Beardsley in "The Dancer's Reward." (trans. LaMarre 49)

In this case, the English illustration title is separated even more markedly from the Japanese script by the use of quotation marks. Some readers would have access to the intertextual pleasure of familiarity with Beardsley's illustration, which would enrich their reading of Tanizaki's tale. They might enjoy the nod to the conscious similarity of Mizushima's illustrations to Beardsley's and then the implicit allusion to Wilde's work. But even for readers unaware of these elements, the English illustration title lends an exotic and esoteric atmosphere. In one of the doubled Orientalizing moves enacted by the story, Tanizaki makes an exoticizing use of the English title for an illustration by a British artist who was in turn influenced by Orientalized Japanese aesthetics.

Beautiful words and the tales themselves become artifacts similar to the gleaming treasures that the narratives describe. These pleasures are granted concrete form by the physical presence of the text itself. Given the

Figure 3.1. Mizushima Niou illustration of the Dutch merchant with the mermaid in "Ningyo no nageki" (*Ningyo no nageki / Majutsushi*, Tokyo: Chūō bunko, 1978).

significance of the illustrations for Tanizaki's story and the history of beautiful editions of Wilde's tales,[5] as well as Wilde's collaborations with Beardsley, the physical book in the hands of the reader becomes another treasure. Fairy tale books are often collectors' items, for which the illustrations, the font and arrangement of the words, and the covers and book binding of the volumes can all be significant factors in the reading pleasure they invite.

This fairy tale pleasure in words and tales as objects extends to the depiction of female figures. Wilde's and Tanizaki's beautiful, hyperfeminine, othered mermaids are, as Sandra Gilbert and Susan Gubar put it for the sleeping Snow White, "killed . . . into art" (*Madwoman* 41). In Wilde's story, while the Witch is a captivating and somewhat complex character, the Mermaid has no active role, undergoes no transformation, makes no movement from one sphere to another, and is imagined in terms of precious materials from the earth and the ocean. Her lack of transformation is apparent in the

---

[5]Killeen notes that "while *The Happy Prince and Other Tales* was published to appeal to a large and popular market, *A House of Pomegranates* was a much more expensive volume and was clearly designed only to tempt connoisseurs" (12).

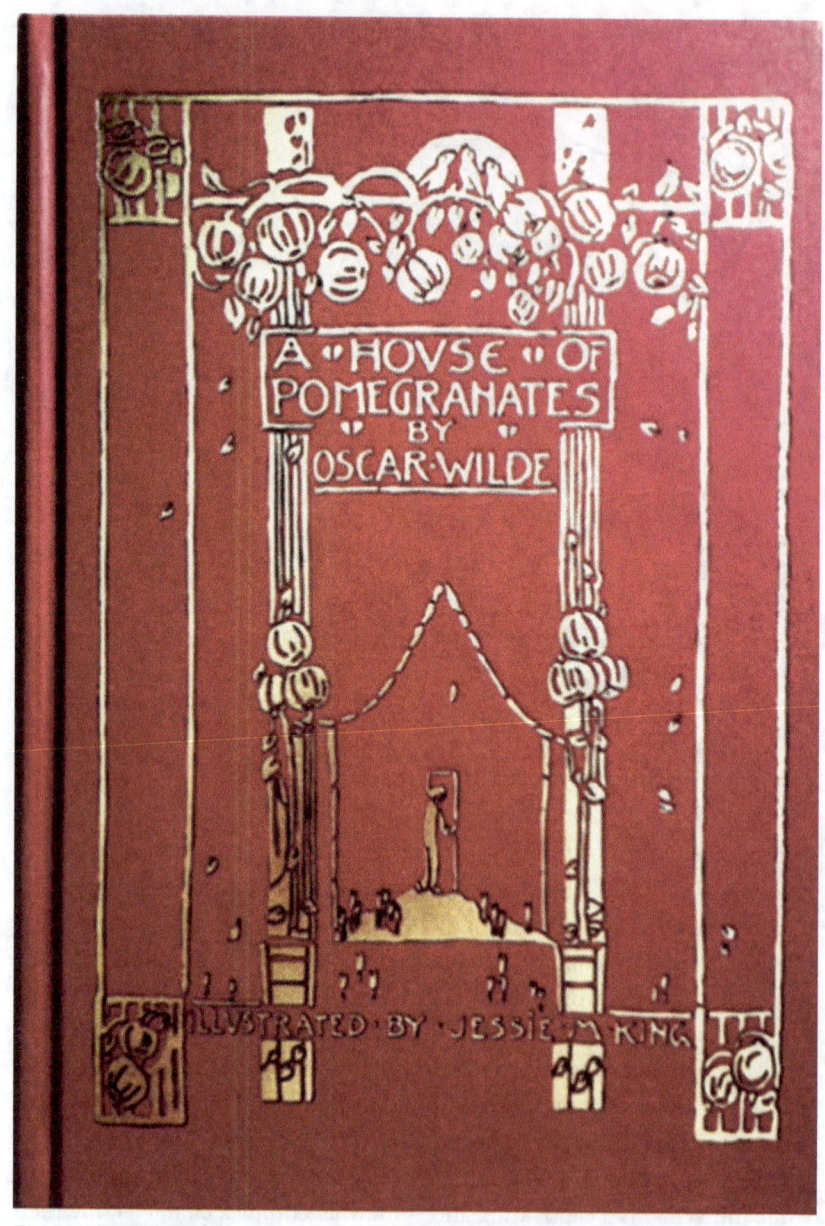

Figure 3.2. Cover of the 1915 edition of *A House of Pomegranates*, illustrated by Jessie M. King (Methuen).

similarity between the description of her living body when the Fisherman and the reader first encounter her and the description of her corpse at the end of the story. At the beginning, "Her hair was a wet fleece of gold, and each separate hair as a thread of fine gold in a cup of glass. Her body was as white ivory, and her tail was of silver and pearl. Silver and pearl was her tail, and the green weeds of the sea coiled round it; and like sea-shells were her ears, and her lips were like sea-coral. The cold waves dashed over her cold breasts, and the salt glistened upon her eyelids" (Wilde 43). Later, when the Fisherman sees her corpse, "the black waves came hurrying to the shore, bearing with them a burden that was whiter than silver. White as the surf it was, and like a flower it tossed on the waves.... Lying at his feet the young Fisherman saw the body of the little Mermaid.... He kissed the cold red of the mouth, and toyed with the wet amber of the hair.... Cold were the lips.... Salt was the honey of her hair.... And to the dead thing... into the shells of its ears he poured the harsh wine of his tale" (78–79). Dead or alive, the mermaid is associated with metals and other cold, precious materials.

Women are also numbered among the dazzling treasures catalogued in Tanizaki's tale. In one line, the nobleman takes "the seven most beautiful and talented women" as wives; then the next sentence goes on to list his acquisition of "the rarest wines" (trans. LaMarre 35). Elsewhere, when a merchant tells the nobleman about a "beautiful gem of a girl" (37), the nobleman coldly compares her value with that of his own wives. Admittedly, for Meng Shidao, the wives, as possessions, contribute to his emptiness and dissatisfaction, while the mermaid is a more "true" woman worthy of his affections. Indeed Tanizaki's mermaid is drawn with more life and movement than Wilde's: she is a beguiling combination of "voluptuous flesh,... the elasticity of a fish, the vitality of a beast, and the charm of a goddess" (45). Yet she too is compared to gemstones and other precious objects, which are used to exclaim her superiority. The merchant tells the nobleman that the mermaid is "far more precious and lovely than any pearl" (41), and the nobleman purchases her with "seventy Arabian diamonds, eighty Indochina rubies, ninety Aman peacocks, and one hundred Siamese ivories" (42). The mermaid may be fleshy and alive, but this only contributes to her value as a kind of collector's item.

Enchanting Orients

The objectifying eroticism of words and women in these tales is tied up in the invocation of the exotic that the fairy tale architext enables. Though Wilde's and Tanizaki's stories may "kill" Andersen's desiring, active mermaid "into art," they undertake intimate explorations of Andersen's motifs of yearning and identification with the "other." This is achieved largely through the tales' depictions of different Orients and of a sense of longing for the faraway exotic. In Wilde's case, the Fisherman feels the pull of the othered mermaid and then the mysterious Orient, which mirrors the fairy tale's pleasurable ability to eroticize and exoticize the world for the reader. In Tanizaki's tale, the fairy tale's fantasy is used to build a complicated, gendered layering of othering, identification, and yearning between characters, cultures, and geographic locations.

"The Fisherman and His Soul" reflects the opulent fin de siècle aesthetic of exoticism that developed against a backdrop of well-established British imperialism. The fairy tale's fondness for treasures and solid objects dovetails with this aesthetic in which, as Ania Loomba observes in her account of European imperialism, "images of 'the Orient' cluster around riches, splendour, and plenty" (152). Orientalist depictions of the Far East would have held appeal for Wilde and his interest in Japonisme. Andersen's Orientalist depictions of China in tales such as "The Nightingale" may have also informed Wilde's Orientalist mode.[6] However, "The Fisherman and His Soul" imagines not so much East Asia but rather a Middle East of the translated *Arabian Nights*—this is an important intertext in fairy tale history, the role of which has perhaps yet to be fully acknowledged (see, for example, Warner, *Once upon a Time* 49). On the Soul's first journey, it encounters Tatars and Muslims; on the second journey, it meets Bedouins and goes to a bazaar; its third destination seems to be Turkey, where it eats bay leaves and fish and sees a veiled dancing girl.

Wilde's Fisherman character reflects an almost standard Orientalist attitude for the time, whereby faraway places provide a kind of blank page onto which European readers and writers could project sexual fantasy and anxiety (McClintock 22, cited in Loomba 154). Accordingly, the Soul finally manages to tempt the Fisherman away from the ocean-bound Mermaid with the image of an Oriental dancing girl:

> "Her face was veiled with a veil of gauze, but her feet were naked. Naked were her feet, and they moved over the carpet like little white pigeons...."
>
> Now when the young Fisherman heard the words of his Soul, he remembered the little Mermaid had no feet and could not dance. And a great desire came over him. (Wilde, *House* 70)

---

[6] In Andersen's "The Nightingale," "The emperor's castle, ... from top to bottom it was made of fine porcelain — so expensive, so fragile, that you really had to be careful if you touched it. You could see the most amazing flowers in the garden, and the prettiest were trimmed with silver bells" (140).

(Surely this moment would have held special appeal for Tanizaki, who is famed for his literary portrayals of foot fetishism.)

The Orient is a (feminized) locus of forbidden sexual desire for the Fisherman. But the "once upon a time" formula itself contains an exoticizing, distancing function that enables Wilde to eroticize *all* of the landscapes and characters he portrays. This extends to the safe cultural home of Britain, the (likely) venue for another erotic dance that represents the Fisherman's desires. The Fisherman's dance with the Witch, with the Devil looking on, takes place on a mountaintop near the Fisherman's own Catholic town. Although the Devil and the Witch dwell much closer to home, they are erotic, exotic figures. The wild Witch, who lives in the bay of the Fisherman's town, has "red hair streaming in the wind" and wears "a dress of gold tissue embroidered with peacocks' eyes" (Wilde, *House* 52). The Devil who watches on is described in the style of homosexual men of the period, with imagery of male-male desire (Duffy 343):

> A man dressed in a suit of black velvet, cut in the Spanish fashion. His face was strangely pale, but his lips were like a proud red flower. . . . A short cloak lined with sables hang from his shoulder, and his delicate white hands were gemmed with rings. Heavy eyelids drooped over his eyes.
>
> The young Fisherman watched him, as one snared in a spell. At last their eyes met, and wherever he danced it seemed to him that the eyes of the man were upon him. (Wilde, *House* 53)

During this period, the Orient itself becomes a locus of European sexual fantasy and is also associated with homosexuality (Duffy 344). But in Wilde's tale, this exotic Orient, and the homosexual desire it is associated with, exist not only in the faraway lands that the Soul visits but also close to the Fisherman's familiar home. That is, the distance created by the marvelous in the fairy tale enables the conception of desire and fantasy in geographical locales both central and peripheral to the British reader's imaginary.

"The Fisherman and His Soul" also employs the transformative magic of the fairy tale to meet the genre's demand for a perfect ending. Whereas Andersen's mermaid is left in a state of limbo, as a daughter of the air, Wilde's Fisherman is left complete, as the Fisherman is reunited with the (dead) Mermaid, and his Soul and the body are joined again. This wholeness transforms another character, the Priest, who had cursed mermaids and other magical creatures but feels changed by the flowers that have grown on the grave of the Fisherman and the Mermaid. Finally, the story's setting is marked by the events as the merpeople disappear: "Nor came the Sea-folk into the bay as they had been wont to do, for they went to another part of the sea" (Wilde, *House* 81–82).

Tanizaki's tale, on the other hand, ends on a more fragmented note, signaling a departure from the fairy tale form. Tanizaki's exoticizing use of the fairy tale—beginning with *mukashi mukashi*—is replicated in his exoticizing use of China as a setting. This is part of a greater trend for the "taste for China" (*Shina shumi*) in Tanizaki's early work; the Chinese location seems to function as a distant, fairy tale world for the Japanese author, one that is available for his erotic and gustatory consumption (see Nishihara 10; Sakaki, *Obsessions* 195; Aoyama, *Reading Food* 145). Like Wilde, though, Tanizaki complicates the binaries of his brand of Orientalism. "Ningyo no nageki" begins by exoticizing China and the Chinese nobleman protagonist for its Japanese readers, emulating the Orientalizing viewpoint of Wilde's Fisherman. However, Tanizaki's various "Orients" exist in more intricate power dynamics with transfigured notions of the "West" (see also Ito). This relationship manifests itself in the complex series of switches in perspective that occur in "Ningyo no nageki," as carefully outlined by Adrian Pinnington. First, Meng Shidao is presented as an exotic other; but then he encounters the Dutch merchant, and the tale focuses on the foreignness of the white merchant's body. This shifts the Japanese reader's perspective from outsider to sympathizer with the Chinese nobleman; the reader shares the nobleman's gaze on the merchant's foreign presence (Pinnington 84). The coinciding perspective of the Chinese nobleman protagonist and the Japanese writer/reader is then cemented by their shared enchantment with the Mediterranean mermaid. The mermaid's beauty, her animality, and her status as a precious possession are simultaneously encapsulated and surpassed by her whiteness: "Above all, what caught [the nobleman's] eye and enchanted his heart was the color of her skin, pure white, spotless, unblemished, without a hint of darkness" (trans. LaMarre 45–46).[7] Whereas Andersen's subject undergoes a torturous desire, Tanizaki's precious mermaid object becomes the representative and receptacle of racialized desire and fascination for the foreign other.

---

[7] In the mermaid's whiteness and Western origins, she is a literal representation of the archetype that Indra Levy describes in her book title *Sirens of the Western Shore: The Westernesque Femme Fatale* (2006). Whereas Tanizaki's mermaid is actually a European siren, Levy describes Japanese fictional (human) women characters who are "the alluring embodiments of Japan's cultural assimilation of the modern West" (5). Levy does not mention "Ningyo no nageki" but points to the famous character of Naomi in Tanizaki's *Chijin no ai* (A fool's love, 1924; translated as *Naomi*) as an example.

Despite the title, "The mermaid's lament" is not about the mermaid at all but about Meng Shidao's lament, his boredom, and his yearning for something new. His longing echoes in the final lines of the story: "In the direction of dear beloved Europe, toward the mermaid's Mediterranean home, the ship advanced along its ordained path, tracing its thread of desire through the depths of his heart" (Tanizaki, *Ningyo* 52). Andersen's "The Little Mermaid," Wilde's "The Fisherman and His Soul," and Tanizaki's "Ningyo no nageki" share an insistent plumbing of the bittersweet pain of yearning and wishing. They solidify this painful experience of unmet desire, respectively, into the mermaid's stabbing pain in her feet and severed tongue, into the Fisherman's fragmented body and Soul and his and the Mermaid's deaths, and into the nobleman's ennui, as well as his physical movement and separation from the enchanting mermaid.

Whereas Wilde's story provides the expected fairy tale closure, Tanizaki moves his narrative away from the fairy tale as the story progresses. His use of the *mukashi mukashi* fairy tale opening formula and the exotic setting suggests that the tale might end with the corresponding "happily every after," *medetashi medetashi*. Instead we leave the nobleman in this state of dissatisfaction, yearning, and transition. The ship sailing toward Europe—along the waters that are home to sirens—sails away from the "once upon a time" China, and the classic fairy tale arc of desire and wish-fulfillment is not completed. This departure from the fairy tale may be understood in itself as architextual, a relationship that Genette insists involves not only taking up genre conventions but also rejecting them, "the blending or scorning of genres" (*Architext* 83).

Wilde's and Tanizaki's admiration for art as artifice finds a suitable vehicle in the architext of the fairy tale form. Wilde articulates his "arts for art's sake" philosophy in the preface to *The Picture of Dorian Gray* (1890), published in between his two fairy tale collections:

> The artist is the creator of beautiful things.
> To reveal art and conceal the artist is art's aim. (3)

Influenced by Wilde's view, Tanizaki expressed similar sentiments in the earlier years of his career. In a famous 1927 exchange on the nature of literature, he debated the author Akutagawa Ryūnosuke's admiration for "truth" over "plot" in literature (Orbaugh, "Debate" 132). Tanizaki declared about both writing his own work and reading literature by others, "Unless it is a lie, I am not interested," explaining, "I have come to like stories that are twisted rather than straightforward, artful rather than artless, as crafted and complicated as possible" ("Jōzetsu" 72–73). This passion for artifice matches Jessica Tiffin's sense of the fairy tale's main effect in its "deliberate removal from the real" enacted by the "once upon a time" formula: "participation in the marvelous universe of the fairy tale—the enjoyment of the wonder fairy tale can evoke—depends entirely on recognition of the artificiality of that universe, the fact that it is a work of art" (13). Thus, the fairy tale's form as patently crafted object, its beautifying, pleasurable rendering of pain, and its unquestioned use of marvel can meet both Tanizaki's and Wilde's expectations of literary works.

Rereading the Prince's Enchantment

Abe Kōbō's short story / novella "Ningyo-den" (Legend of a mermaid, 1962) enjoys a deliberate misreading that is based on these types of images of mermaids as objet d'art for male aesthetic pleasure. Abe comically transforms the prince's objectifying enchantment with the mermaid, inviting laughter at this kind of absorption with the rules and roles of the fairy tale architext and the misapprehensions it causes. Probably best known as a novelist, Abe (1924–93) also worked as a poet, playwright, and photographer and on various film projects. Critical work on Abe has tended to circulate around an understanding of his texts as avant-garde, surrealist, science fiction, and fantasy and as international literature that transcends the Japanese context. The latter mainly concerns his experience growing up in Manchuria and his relative lack of ties to the Japanese mainland but perhaps also the appeal that translations of his works seem to have for overseas audiences. Unlike his better-known novels and plays, "Ningyo-den" has not been widely discussed or critiqued.

First published in the June 1962 issue of *Bungakukai* (World of literature) magazine, the publication venue and the story's events clearly indicate that "Ningyo-den" is targeted at adult readers. The tale is related by a narrator who, in a Poe-esque manner, is quickly established as mentally unstable, indicating that he has been institutionalized when he says, "The name of the condition that is written on my patient card is 'hypersensitivity to the color green'" (239–40). The remainder of the narrative gives the details of the events that brought about his phobia of the color green. Unlike Wilde's story, in which the prince figure visits the Witch and then moves from the land into the ocean, or Tanizaki's story, in which the mermaid safely returns to the ocean, Abe's story follows Andersen's plot slightly more closely: the mermaid and human prince meet in the water, and then the mermaid moves onto the land to live with the prince but eventually perishes as a result of his actions.

The narrator discovers a green-colored mermaid when ocean diving and is immediately besotted. He manages to take her home with him and keeps her in his bathtub for what he believes is an erotic relationship. But one morning, the narrator awakes to find an identical human copy of himself in the bathroom. He realizes that the green mermaid has special regenerative powers that support her carnivorous habits: she has been feeding on him at night while he sleeps and regrowing his body back from leftover body parts. In this sense, the strange creature is a traditional femme fatale who enthralls the narrator and uses him to satisfy her own appetites in a way that might destroy him. But eventually the narrator manages to defeat his antagonistic doppelganger and kill the mermaid. When finally destroyed, the mermaid desiccates and becomes a *miira* (mummy; 273), reminiscent of the *ningyo no miira* (mermaid mummies) popular in Edo-period (1603–1868) sideshows (see chapter 1). However, as the narrator himself comments, his story does not have a particularly happy ending. He develops his oversensitivity to the color green, and since his double has been arrested, he loses his job.

Although the narrator does not name any tale explicitly, he alludes to Andersen's story and mermaid mythologies a number of times. In one instance, he cites existing mythologies and discounts scientific explanations for eyewitness accounts of mermaids when he comments, "There was no room for any doubt, she was a living mermaid. Not a dugong or a dolphin or some sea beast of that ilk; the top half of her body identical to a human's, she was a genuine mermaid straight from the legends" (240). At another point, the narrator exhibits familiarity with Andersen's tale, identifying with the prince. If the mermaid is real, he worries, "then I will be the one to commit the terrible betrayal against her!" (248). As one critic, Hayashi Kōhei, points out, Abe's story also reflects the Japanese folktale known as "Ningyo no ongaeshi" (The mermaid repays a debt of gratitude), which is categorized as a tale of human-nonhuman marriage.[8] "Ningyo-den" is structured around the prohibition on looking found in such animal-wife tales: the human husband is forbidden to look on his wife while she is in a private space such as the bathroom, and when he breaks the taboo and peeks in, their life together is destroyed (Hayashi 322). Hayashi adds that Abe's story might be seen as a reversal of the "Yao bikuni" legend: instead

---

[8]Hayashi cites a version from Yanagita Kunio's collection of tales from Iwaki, Fukushima prefecture (321).

of a human (female) who eats mermaid meat, we find a mermaid who eats human (male) meat (327).[9]

The narrator demonstrates an awareness of mermaid stories and positions himself as the mermaid's prince, consciously commentating on his own role in the tale. Although the story is titled after the mermaid, the narrator establishes himself as its protagonist in the first paragraphs, complaining, "What I find very strange is no matter how many novels are written, and how many are read, not one single person seems to have noticed what a misfortune it is to have your life changed into a story with a plot," and "to become the protagonist of a story is to become imprisoned inside your self that you see reflected in the mirror" (239). This blindness imposed by the strictures of story is the main source of comic contrast.

Though the fairy tale may assert its own fictionality, "Ningyo-den" involves much more of Genette's "scorning" than "blending" of the fairy tale architext. Unlike Wilde's and Tanizaki's tales of wonder, Abe's cannot be described as "marvelous" in Tzvetan Todorov's influential definition, in which fantastical events are taken for granted and "supernatural elements provoke no particular reaction in either the characters or in the implicit reader" (54). In Abe's tale, the subjective first-person narrator is possibly insane; he doubts the existence of mermaids, and he constantly questions the mermaid's biology. This creates a different effect from the "marvelous" in the classic fairy tale, which readers are not expected to query. Abe's tale does not aim, as Tanizaki's does, to simply celebrate fabricated beauty, all that is complex and self-consciously artistic. Nor does Abe's tale invite wonder. Rather, it uses metafictional reflection to invite the reader to question the story and the narrator and to laugh at them.

The tale's humor is predicated on disrupting hierarchical pairs that are often highlighted by mermaid tales, such as self/other, human/animal, and masculine/feminine. Such destabilization is often associated with the figure of the double, a figure that is, interestingly, also found in Wilde's *The Picture of Dorian Gray*, in the shadow in "The Fisherman and His Soul," and in several of Tanizaki's works (see Posadas 68–108). In "Ningyo-den," the figure of the narrator's double is an exact replicate, challenging the permanency and immutability of the individual self as well as the binaries mentioned. This

---

[9] A more recent transformation of "The Little Mermaid" about mermaids who seduce and devour human men is Mizuno Junko's book-length manga *Ningyo-hime-den* (Princess mermaid, 2002; the title resembles Abe's but uses a different character for *den*). See Murai's discussion of the manga's use of the *guro-kawaii* (grotesque cute) aesthetic—Mizuno cites Aubrey Beardsley as an influence—as a feminist critique of the role of the sexually attractive female body ("Re-envisioning").

use of a "copy" can contest the notion of an authoritative "original" version of a tale, which recalls the replicating, transitory history of fairy tales and the practice of transformation that tales such as Andersen's undergo. Yet in Abe's tale, the non–fairy tale device of the first-person narrator involved in the narrative mitigates this effect: the first-person narrator complains about becoming "the protagonist of a story" (239), thereby authoritatively claiming a central role and defending himself against the challenge to his individuality that the copied selves pose.[10] The first-person voice gives the narrator of "Ningyo-den" more power than his doubles; he enjoys the privilege of retelling and reinterpreting events and ordering his confusing experiences into a coherent plot centered on himself. From a contemporary feminist fairy tale studies perspective, this privileged position of narration reflects the ways that agents for patriarchal societies have constructed cohesive categories of gender from confusing and multifaceted bodies and oral fairy tales.[11]

Abe's tale then exposes the way his protagonist works to build a cohesive narrative of gender: the narrator interprets the mermaid at his own convenience, but his misapprehension leads to his downfall. Much of the narrator's response to the mermaid concerns the way she blurs the boundaries between human and animal. The narrator wonders, "Was she actually a fish-like human, or was she only a human-like fish?" (241). He says,

> But how to explain that cool body temperature, like the wall of a moist basement? . . . On top of that, there was no getting around the fact that she showed no remains of an umbilical cord. It could only be seen as decisive evidence that she was not a mammal. You might say that she had something like breasts, although they were undeveloped. The unfortunate thing was they lacked nipples. And then, she had the screw-shaped tailfin of an osteichthye [bony fish], . . . and what's more, down her side she even had the lateral line that you only find on fish species. (242)

However, despite the narrator's unease about the mermaid's lack of humanity, he is driven by his sexual desire for her. According to his justification, "I

---

[10] The narrator of another of Abe's doppelganger stories, *Hako otoko* (Box man, 1973), is similarly shown by Baryon Tensor Posadas as "asserting his authorship over the narrative and declaring his interlocutors to be nothing more than figments of his imagination" (214).

[11] Ruth Bottigheimer in particular has illuminated the significance for gender of the editorial changes made by the Grimm brothers to their oral sources, in *Grimms' Bad Girls and Bold Boys: The Moral and Social Vision of the Tales* (1987).

don't have any special intention of claiming that I was a platonic person or anything" (263). In retrospect, he attributes his attraction to the mermaid to a chemical response. He recalls that when the adrenaline started pumping through his body, even her "nonhuman aspects, on the contrary, had a supernatural beauty" (242). Whereas Tanizaki's mermaid possesses what seems to be fleshly natural femininity but is in fact the beauty of objet, the narrator of Abe's tale retrospectively reduces the mermaid's attraction to his physical "adrenaline" reaction to her mostly animal body.

Perhaps in response to the narrator's unease about the mermaid's humanity, he focuses on her femaleness rather than her mermaidness, nearly always referring to her as *kanojo* (her) rather than *ningyo* (technically gender neutral). Through the narrator's mistaken determination to see the mermaid as a woman, Abe takes up a pop-culture question about mermaids that is often found in comedy: how can penetrative sex occur between a mermaid and a human man? Abe responds with rather more detail than most (though we shall see in chapter 4 that the "problem" is neatly solved by Kurahashi's inverted mermaid). Abe's narrator says bluntly of the mermaid, "The lower half of her body was fish. On her abdomen, she had some kind of hole for laying eggs, but we have holes like that in our ears and in our noses" (263). Since the narrator is attracted to the mermaid's eyes, his solution is licking the mermaid's eyes and drinking her tears, an act that he perceives as sex. Tears, traditional symbols of sadness, come to convey pleasure. This eye-sex also reverses and exaggerates mermaid fantasy traditions in which the mermaid's body is sexually enjoyed by men through the eyes—through looking. Abe's narrator treats the mermaid as the exotic, feminized China is treated in Tanizaki's work, as a fairy tale object of his own pleasurable consumption. However, the twist, Abe's narrator discovers, is that the mermaid is actually eating him: her tears make his body regenerate and allow her to continually feed on his flesh. This creates a truly carnivalesque cycle of consumption, emission, and reproduction, one that is rather more organic than the technology-based dystopias in some of Abe's other works (see Napier, *Fantastic* 73–77, 204–5).

The narrator's focus on the mermaid's femaleness affects the way he interacts with her, so that he constantly misinterprets her according to his own desire. His beliefs about gender roles lead to his view of himself as "consumer" rather than "consumed." As he relates, "I thought I had chosen her of my own volition and subjugated her. But the truth was the complete opposite, and in fact, I was captured by her as livestock to be farmed for meat and was only raised for that" (Abe 274). There is an ironic gap between the naïve narrator's and the perceptive reader's understanding of events, or perhaps between the narrator's contemporaneous and retrospective understandings of events. The reader is invited to laugh at the ridiculous juxtaposition of the animal mermaid against the human culture that the narrator assigns to her. When planning to trick the mermaid and eventually enjoy sexual contact with her, for example, the narrator offers her some raw meat, because "everyone knows that even two human partners will always go to a restaurant before they go to a hotel" (251). The mermaid accepts the meat, the narrator believes, "with the charming naiveté of a shy girl accepting a wedding ring" (252). When the narrator discovers the mermaid's true intentions, he experiences what the humor theorist John Morreall describes as a "cognitive shift" or "sudden change of mental state" (xii). The shift is shocking for the narrator but amusing for the reader, who has an "aesthetic interest" in enjoying the unexpected switch, rather than a "practical or cognitive interest" in its outcomes (Morreall 70).

Like Andersen's mermaid and her prince, Abe's mermaid and narrator are at cross-purposes. Unlike Andersen's, Wilde's, and Tanizaki's mermaids, however, Abe's mermaid never intends to communicate with the narrator, who has imagined himself as her "prince." In interpreting the mermaid as female, the narrator sees her as passive, innocent, in step with and interested in his own emotions, and available to satisfy his sexual desires. However, the mermaid's "othered" body, her disinterest in him, her carnivorous nature, her lack of language, and their sexual incompatibility show that she is none of these things. In this way, the story pokes fun at the narrator's inability to think outside the gender norms of his own society. The humor and the transformative twist in Abe's version lies in the male protagonist's ridiculous enthrallment with a deglamorized and defeminized mermaid.

Siren Songs and Silence

When the narrative viewpoint switches from the mermaid to the prince in these stories, and the yearning for the other becomes his domain rather than hers, the mermaid figure becomes successful in her quest. That is, whereas Andersen's mermaid fails to enchant the human prince, all of the mermaids here succeed. In each case—as for Andersen's mute mermaid—the ability for the mermaid to appeal to the prince is connected to her voice. Wilde's mermaid can sing (but not dance). Tanizaki's mermaid's tongue is loosened by a drink, and she talks him into taking her home. But Abe's mermaid is entirely alien, and it is her silence that allows the narrator to labor under his preferred (mis)understanding of the situation. Kawakami

Hiromi's (1958–) more recent short story "Hanasanai" (I won't let go, 1998) is another examination of the role of language and silence in the mermaid's bewitching of the prince and its relationship with the pleasurable magic of the fairy tale architext.

Kawakami's story is narrated in the first person by a character who never specifies a name or gender but gives the impression of being female. The narrator's male neighbor and acquaintance, Enomoto-san, comes to tell her that he has found a mermaid on the seashore, in a fish net (like Wilde's mermaid). Enomoto-san has brought the mermaid home and is keeping her in his bathtub (like Abe's narrator does). As in Wilde's and Tanizaki's tales, the mermaid's dazzling pale beauty is emphasized: "Its tail was long. The tail to the belly was covered with large, iridescent scales. From the belly upwards, there were no scales. The skin was white and smooth. The long hair was wrapped around the upper body, and a full breast was visible through the hair. . . . There were delicate, iridescent scales also on the ears. . . . The eyes and mouth looked as though they had been carved out of smooth white stone. . . . About one-third of the size of a human adult, it was a mermaid" (154–55). Enomoto-san, recognizing his dangerous obsession with his captive mermaid, asks the narrator to take the mermaid from him. The narrator takes the mermaid into her own bathtub and also becomes obsessed, finding it more and more difficult to leave the mermaid's side to eat or go to work. Finally, Enomoto-san and the narrator, realizing how the enthrallment is eroding their lives, force themselves to return the mermaid to the ocean.

In a sense, Kawakami's tale is a "prince's version," because it is narrated by a human protagonist and treats the mermaid as other. The mermaid is depicted as female, so the female narrator's obsession intimates a queer disruption of the classic fairy tale heterosexual romance. But it is the alien nature of this creature that is most marked: the mermaid is not referred to as "her" but as *ningyo* (technically gender neutral) or, out of politeness, *kono hito* (this person). Like many of Kawakami's short fantastical stories, "Hanasanai" captures the ambiguity of human communication, the self-protective and distancing dynamic of politeness, the importance of the unsaid in all relationships. The mermaid is implacably alien, but even the shared enchantment with her does not entirely bridge the distance between the narrator and the fellow human Enomoto-san.

Kawakami's depiction of the power of silence and speech, the unsaid and the unsayable, is one of the points where "Hanasanai" hooks onto the mermaid architext. Without a voice, Andersen's mermaid cannot communicate her love for the prince. Wilde's and Tanizaki's seductive mermaids are therefore accorded speech: Wilde's mermaid lures the Fisherman with her siren song, and in Tanizaki's tale, the mermaid's eloquent speech convinces the nobleman to return her to her ocean home. In Abe's and Kawakami's tales, though, silence is a kind of power. The mermaid's muteness in Abe's "Ningyo-den" leaves the male narrator free to assign meanings and motivations to her, which works to her advantage. In Kawakami's tale, the mermaid's silence also enhances her control and allure, which functions regardless of the gender of her victim. Only when Enomoto-san and the narrator return the mermaid to the waves does she speak, saying, "I won't let you go"—in Japanese, this is the single word *hanasanai*. A kanji character is used to specify the meaning of this word as "I won't let you go," as in 離さない. However, with a different kanji, written as 話さない, *hanasanai* would mean "I won't speak." The mermaid's moment of speech is terrifying because it disrupts her otherness and connects her to the human characters, but the single word also breaks her potent spell: paradoxically, the mermaid must let go when she says, "I won't let go," and she must speak to say, "I will not speak."

Having broken the spell, the only explanation that Enomoto-san and the narrator can find for their experience is simply, "We were bewitched" (Kawakami 171). Human enthrallment with the supernatural mermaid in all of these prince's versions of "The Little Mermaid" perhaps replicates the way readers themselves are captivated by wonder tales, immersing themselves in story. And if these pleasures in enchantment mirror some of the pleasures of reading fairy tales, the texts also give a sense that fairy tale pleasure may differ according to the gender of the character. In Wilde's and Tanizaki's stories, the male prince characters respond to the mermaids without question, throwing themselves into the joy of enthrallment. To be taken in by magic can be heartbreaking, but it is transformative—in Wilde's story, it causes the Fisherman's fragmentation and then wholeness and changes to surrounding characters in environments, and in Tanizaki's, it causes the movement of the nobleman across the water. These tales are dominated less by a sense of danger than by the pleasure of wonder and emotional abandon itself. Enchantment is almost worth the suffering it causes.

In Abe's and Kawakami's tales, enchantment is even more fraught with danger; it challenges the borders of the self and threatens the loss of individual identity. Abe's protagonist, conscious of the fairy tale architext that his own text is hooked onto, cannot take the same pleasure in art and artifice as Wilde's Fisherman and Tanizaki's nobleman take in their mermaids. Instead, Abe's narrator destroys the mermaid, attempting to expunge the marvelous from his life and restore order. Kawakami's female narrator seems the most suspicious of fairy tale wonder: she is uneasy with the mermaid's power to fascinate, but she is also uneasy when she is able to resist the magic and discard the mermaid. As a female reader, she might sense more risk in the pleasure of fairy tale enchantment, in which women are often displayed as objects of wonder rather than being empowered to enjoy the experience of wondering.

Through self-conscious interweaving with the fairy tale architext, these prince's tales seek out some of the pleasures of fairy tale transformation: Wilde and Tanizaki produce fetishistic pleasure in crafted, gleaming objects, which is taken in words and in female characters as beautiful manmade items, but importantly this is a pleasure in the marvelous fairy tale itself. Abe's tale invites readers' laughter at the narrator's misapprehension of the mermaid, inspired by grotesque bodily functions of devouring, destruction, and duplication. And Kawakami's short piece whittles down these more intricate tales to a vivid evocation of enchantment, the lure of silence, and the impossibility of human connection.

Carnivalesque inverted bodies and switches of power and gender roles are also seen in the woman-centered fairy tale revisions in chapter 4. But unlike the transformations that retell "The Little Mermaid" from the prince's perspective, the tales in chapter 4 remain firmly with the mermaid's point of view. They reverse or subvert the gendered bodies of Andersen's characters, but the reversals encourage some quite different reading pleasures and construct gender quite differently.

4

Mermaids Repeated, Inverted, and Reversed in Women's Fairy Tale Revisions

Fairy tales are controlled by poetic justice, reward for good and punishment for evil, or by the principle of "you reap what you sow." ... Learning from the older fairy tales, I thought in my own writing I would add to the skeletons of the tales the bare minimum of muscle needed to form their hyperreal, logical, and cruel world.
—Kurahashi Yumiko, *Otona no tame no zankoku dōwa*

This is a collection of stories that I parodied as I criticized them. They are parodies, but the cruel and the sexual aspects are just as they are in the originals.
—Matsumoto Yūko, *Tsumibukai hime no otogibanashi*

The fairy tales collected in this book, like candy, are sweet and hard and melt slowly, and will permeate the hearts of the people who read them.
—Higami Kumiko, in *Otogibanashi no wasuremono*

The appeal of the fairy tale, it seems, cannot be easily captured. From the quite divergent explanations in the epigraphs, we can only surmise that the fairy tale brings pleasure because it is something with a sharp edge, something with power. For Kurahashi, fairy tales offer the intellectual pleasure of close familiarity with the genre and with the satisfying forces that rule its narratives. For Matsumoto, an academic discovery of deeper "truth" drives our interest in a particular tale. And for Higami, fairy tales are appetizing, mysterious objects with the ability to affect their readers.

As these musings hint, all three literary transformations of "The Little Mermaid" examined in this chapter build on their authors' abiding interest in the fairy tale itself. Beyond the kind of enchantment with the fairy tale architext seen in the prince's transformations of the previous chapter, these transformations more explicitly signal their engagement with the fairy tale form and with Andersen's tale. Their story titles use the word *ningyo* (mermaid) or even *ningyo-hime* (princess mermaid, the little mermaid; see chapter 1), and their book titles use words for "fairy tales," *otogibanashi* and *dōwa* (see chapter 1). Matsumoto Yūko's "Otoko no kuni e itte shinda ningyo-hime" (The little mermaid who went to the man's country and died) is found in a 1996 collection of revisions of Andersen's, Perrault's, and the Grimms' fairy tales titled *Tsumibukai hime no otogibanashi* (Fairy tales of sinful princesses). Matsumoto's work saw the beginning of the "Grimm boom" of the late 1990s, but before this, in 1984, Kurahashi Yumiko had published *Otona no tame no zankoku dōwa* (Cruel fairy tales for adults), a collection of parodic tales that includes her transformation of "The Little Mermaid," "Ningyo no namida" (The mermaid's tears). Ogawa Yōko's more recent revision, "Ningyo hōseki shokunin no isshō" (The life of a mermaid's jeweler) is found in a book titled *Otogibanashi no wasuremono* (Lost property fairy tales, 2006), illustrated by Higami Kumiko.

The three short stories transform Andersen's "The Little Mermaid" by flipping bodies, gender roles, and relationships. They therefore fall under Linda Hutcheon's definition of parody as "imitation characterized by ironic inversion" and "extended repetition with critical difference" (*Theory of Parody* 6–7). Japanese literature has strong traditions of parody, as seen in practices of pastiche, and Edo-period (1603–1868) techniques such as *mitate* (doubling, juxtaposing, or likening an old and new work, often to comic effect) and *yatsushi* (casual/plain disguise) (Orbaugh and Mostow v). Both the traditions of allusion and "*mojiri* (twist, parody)" (Aoyama, "Love That Poisons" 37) have long been present on the Japanese literary scene, but Tomoko Aoyama also outlines a recent change in values, arguing that in writing since the 1970s, parody and pastiche have enjoyed new venues of expression.[1] Aoyama labels these fresh forms as the "new literacy," which she describes as "open-ended, decentred and dispersive" (35), as opposed to the established canon of *junbungaku* ("pure" or highbrow literature).

In the vocabulary of fairy tale studies, parodies such as Matsumoto's, Kurahashi's, and Ogawa's may be more narrowly described as fairy tale "revisions" due to their close, explicit relationship with "The Little Mermaid." The category of "revision" has tended to incorporate a drive for social

---

[1] See Aoyama's "Love That Poisons" (53). See also Howard Hibbett's similar claim in his work on Japanese humor, in a chapter titled "Parody Regained."

transformation, as in Adrienne Rich's notion of feminist "re-vision," which she describes as "the act of looking back, of seeing with fresh eyes, of entering an old text from a new critical direction" (35). Zipes, also, sets up "revision" as a subversive act, a category well fleshed out by his selection of feminist fairy tales in his edited collection *Don't Bet on the Prince* (1986). Zipes places "revision" in opposition to what he describes as the conservative, unoriginal process of "duplication" (*Fairy Tale as Myth* 8–9). But the latter category is somewhat contradictory and thus less helpful here; it cannot account for works such as Disney's animated adaptation, which is a highly creative yet gender-conservative transformation (see chapter 2). Similarly, the fairy tale revisions in this chapter share an interest in gender, and the revisions and their paratexts provide intellectual, critical pleasures that may be creative but do not necessarily challenge the gender status quo.

Setting aside "duplication," however, the concept of "revision" remains pertinent because it emphasizes transformations that focus on one specific tale (see also K. Smith 41), in this case "The Little Mermaid." Matsumoto's, Kurahashi's, and Ogawa's gender inversions and subversions respond directly to Andersen's tale. As such, they produce pleasures that are quite different from those generated by the architextual relationships with the fairy tale form that dominated the prince's tales of chapter 3. The revisions here especially invite intertextual pleasure, including laughter, at the differences between Andersen's text and their new versions.

In addition to the mermaid and fairy tale titles of these three transformations, they are linked to Andersen's story and the fairy tale genre through other paratexts—that is, textual material surrounding a narrative: titles, notes, prefaces, dedications, covers, and so on. Gérard Genette, describing paratextuality as one type of "transtextual relationship," highlights that paratexts are "characterized by an authorial intention and assumption of responsibility" (*Paratexts* 3). This chapter considers fairy tale pleasures and gender with attention to such authorial commentary and intervention. Matsumoto uses paratexts such as titles, morals, a postface,[2] and reference lists to clearly indicate her feminist position on the fairy tales she names and revises. Kurahashi uses a postface with a reference list, as well as morals to each story, to ripple out the effects of her bodily inversions and switching of gender norms. Finally, Higami Kumiko's illustrations to Ogawa's stories, as well as author and illustrator postfaces and a framing story for the

---

[2]In Japanese, these are called *atogaki* (lit. afterword). In English, *preface* and *postface* technically refer to commentary written by the author, whereas *foreword* and *afterword* refer to commentary written by others.

collection, work to question the reliability of fairy tale narrators and narratives. Examining these revisions in the context of such paratexts and viewing these paratexts as "thresholds of interpretation" (Genette, *Paratexts* 3) allow a consideration of the messages that authors deliberately transmit to their readers and particularly of the commentary the authors make on the pleasures of their fairy tale transformations.

Clearly, though the success of these revisions as feminist texts may be perceived differently, all three question gender norms. Whereas the transformations in chapter 3 switched to the prince's viewpoint, the fairy tale revisions discussed in this chapter adhere to the perspective of the mermaid protagonist. They deal in the species and gender contradictions and incongruities of the mermaid's body; their transformation hinges on the ways in which they reread or reverse the gendered body of Andersen's mermaid. As such, the revisions are presented in an order that highlights their increasingly complex reimaginings of gender through the repetitions and reversals they make to the mermaid's body and in an order of increasing focus on the pleasures of reading and transforming fairy tales.

Repeating and Rereading "The Little Mermaid"

Matsumoto's work provides a particularly clear example of the simultaneously conservative and radical forces that can operate within a text that is built on the critical, intellectual pleasures of revising a fairy tale. A writer, translator, and television personality, Matsumoto Yūko (1963–) debuted in 1988 with the Subaru Prize–winning novel on mother-child relationships and eating disorders *Kyoshokushō no akenai yoake* (For over eating girl dawn never comes).[3] Over the years of her prolific career, Matsumoto has taken up what the literary translation scholar Akiko Uchiyama describes as "intimate girl reading" of L. M. Montgomery's *Anne of Green Gables*, which is a hugely popular piece of classic girls' literature in Japan. Matsumoto has published around ten annotated translations, essays, travel guides, and companions to the work, demonstrating a sustained interest in intertextuality and the gender politics of translation (see Uchiyama, "Meeting"). This research-based, feminist approach is manifest in her work with the Western fairy tale canon. A sign of her interest in Andersen's story in particular is also found in one of Matsumoto's literary travel books, published the

---

[3] English title translations are taken from Matsumoto's homepage (Matsumoto, "Yūko Matsumoto Homepage").

year after her fairy tale revisions, which discusses Denmark and "The Little Mermaid" (*Romantikku na tabi e—Amerika hen*,[4] 1997).

Matsumoto's revision of "The Little Mermaid" cites Andersen's story as its fairy tale source in no uncertain terms. The protagonist's appellation and indeed a short summary of her tragedy is contained in the title, "Otoko no kuni e itte shinda ningyo-hime" (The little mermaid who went to the man's country and died). The tale was featured in a hardcover collection titled *Tsumibukai hime no otogibanashi* (Fairy tales of sinful princesses, 1996) and adorned with a cover illustration of the featured "princesses" gathered together: Snow White, Cinderella, and the heroine of "Bluebeard" on the front, and Sleeping Beauty, the little mermaid, Red Riding Hood, and the little match girl on the back. The 1999 paperback edition was renamed *Gurimu, Anderusen no tsumibukai hime no monogatari* (Grimms' and Andersen's tales of sinful princesses) and featured an illustration of Snow White in her glass coffin. The illustrator, Higami Kumiko, is also closely associated with fairy tales, as we shall see in her work for Ogawa Yōko's book. The princesses in Higami's work have unsmiling, distant expressions and closed rosebud lips, projecting a kind of sweet inscrutability. They seem to represent the mysterious surface of fairy tales, which conceal the machinations that Matsumoto undertakes to expose. Matsumoto's hardcover-edition *obi* (wraparound paper belt, used for marketing) promises the hidden depths and unconscious knowledge of Grimms' and Andersen's tales. It describes the book as a "sweetly frightening collection of cruel tales for adults" (*otona no tame no amakute kowai zankoku monogatarishū*); though Matsumoto's stories do not seem engaged with the mode of transformation we will observe in Kurahashi Yumiko's *Otona no tame no zankoku dōwa*, it may be that Matsumoto's publishers were mindful of Kurahashi's earlier success in their choice of advertising language.

"Otoko no kuni e itte shinda ningyo-hime" works to highlight the gender binaries that the author perceives in Andersen's tale.[5] The ocean is the world of women: it is a matriarchal, peaceful, polytheistic, primitive society with an oral culture (160). The men's world on land is literary, patriarchal, warlike, and Christian (159–60). That is, Matsumoto reads in Andersen's work the age-old equation of femininity with nature and masculinity with culture. Playing with homonyms, she equates women's menstruation, pregnancy (swelling), and childbirth with natural forces: "The bottom of the ocean was

---

[4]The title translates as "On romantic travels—American edition": the volume features the American Midwest as well as other literary travel destinations including Denmark, France, and Vietnam.
[5]Both Ulla Thomsen and Pil Dahlerup analyze "The Little Mermaid" in terms of such binaries (see chapter 1).

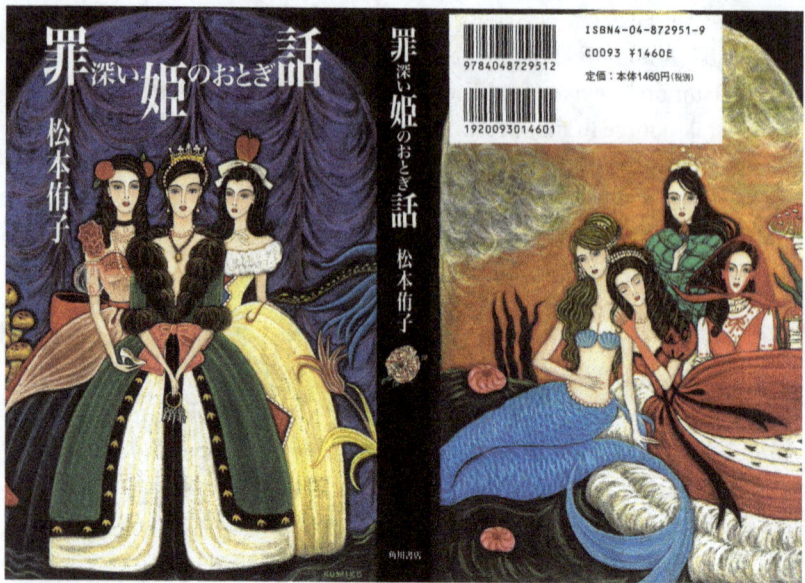

Figure 4.1. Cover for *Tsumibukai hime no otogibanashi*, with illustration by Higami Kumiko.

the country of women. The ocean [*umi*] was birth [*umi*], women's bodies flowed in tides, and that ebb and flow was the waxing and waning of women's bodies" (150). Matsumoto further uses the image of the peaceful ocean kingdom to criticize the patriarchal land. Because communication between the two cultures is impossible, the matriarchal state is inevitably oppressed, colonized, or obliterated by the aggressive patriarchy: "[The mermaid society had] epic poems that were not recorded in writing. The structure of their country was also primitive. These types of peoples are swallowed up by peoples who have writing and a nation, again and again" (170).

The story title, "The little mermaid who went to the man's country and died," paints a bleak picture of Andersen's tale, expressing Matsumoto's belief that the mermaid's particular "sin" is her attempt to leave the matriarchal realm and enter patriarchal society. The naïve mermaid is destroyed in the fray when she tries to cross from one side to the other. Although events of Andersen's tale remain the same, the mermaid's death is changed from a tragedy of unrequited love to the lamentable result of friction between these two diametrically opposite cultures. The tale's tragic ending is foreshadowed by the mermaid's realization: "The mermaid understood. Humans were completely different creatures from mermaids, and there was a great chasm between the two" (149).

This chasm is emphasized through the mermaid's loss of voice. First, in the moral Matsumoto affixes to her revision, she explicitly interprets the loss of voice as an injunction for women to be silent (185). Second, the story implies that simply having the ability to speak does not necessarily enable access to a public voice. On the individual level, the mermaid's loss of her voice in Matsumoto's story is nearly irrelevant, as the voice that she already had was constantly being ignored or misinterpreted. The revision expands on instances of miscommunication that are present in "The Little Mermaid": in Andersen's text, the mermaids sing to sailors on sinking ships, but their words cannot be understood and are taken as part of the storm (82). In Matsumoto's version, the mermaid is implicated in the disaster—she sings to please tired sailors; but instead she distracts them, and the ship hits an iceberg and sinks (149). Several such incidents drive home the impossibility of the mermaid's messages being heard.

In fact, humans and mermaids are so dissimilar in this story that even when the mermaid becomes human, she and the prince still cannot communicate—verbally or physically. Whether it be the mermaid's expressive eyes, her emotive dancing, or the sexual relationship between the two that Matsumoto infers from Andersen's story, the mermaid and the prince have completely different perspectives on the body. In this version, mermaids reproduce by laying eggs; they do not associate nakedness with sexuality as humans do (165). Physical closeness, then, does not aid communication any more than language does.

"The Little Mermaid" has not infrequently been a target of such feminist literary critique in Anglophone and European settings. One "cautionary tale" of a mermaid, contained within Joanna Russ's young-adult novel *Kittatinny: A Tale of Magic* (1978; see chapter 5), represents the 1970s and 1980s trend for rewriting fairy tales for children with a feminist twist (see Joosen 55–56). Published some decades later, Robin Morgan's earnest, socially inclusive sequel to Andersen's tale, *The Mer-Child: A Legend for Children and Other Adults* (1991), uses the little mermaid's half-human, half-mermaid son as a means to critique not only racism but prejudice against people with disabilities. Barbara G. Walker's "The Littlest Mermaid," included in a collection titled *Feminist Fairy Tales* (1996), offers a happier ending to the mermaid in the form of a more sensitive, respectful prince. This type of so-called politically correct transformation is the target of ridicule in James Finn Garner's "The Little Mer-persun," included in his second collection of fairy tale revisions, *Once upon a More Enchanted Time* (1995). Garner's parody of Andersen's tale succinctly grasps its seemingly old-fashioned notions of gender, as well as the history of feminist responses that followed. After rescuing the drowning human prince, Garner's politically enlightened mer-persun swims away before he wakes up, as she does not want "to endure any more emotional scenes, cultural imperialism, or Jungian archetypes" (36).

A line of feminist retellings of "The Little Mermaid" prior to these revisions is less prominent in Japan, where fairy tale transformations have focused more on uncovering or complicating psychological "truth." Matsumoto positions her own revisions less in relation to a history of feminist literary transformation and more within the field of scholarly fairy tale research. Her interest in fairy tales, she writes in the postface to her 1996 transformations, was stimulated when she was writing her second novel, *Shokubutsusei ren'ai* (Androgynous love, 1988). The novel is on the theme of sexual violence and includes a chapter titled "Sleeping Beauty" (63–72) that has characters critiquing Marie Bonaparte's developmental model of the sleeping beauty as representing "the masturbation taboo and repression of the clitoral orgasm" (Matsumoto, *Tsumibukai* 212) and who is awakened by the vaginal orgasm brought by a man. Bonaparte's (and Erich Fromm's) interpretations of fairy tales were quoted by Shibusawa Tatsuhiko in his essay collection titled *Erotishizumu* (Eroticism, 1967), which played a major role in the popularization of psychoanalytical readings of fairy tales in Japan from the 1990s onward (Murai, *From Dog Bridegroom* 18–20).

In such works forming the "Grimm boom" that Matsumoto's collection precipitated, popular collections supposedly uncovering the "true," adult content of Western fairy tales often support their claims through a list of references to their fairy tale source texts, as well as to Japanese and translated criticism and works of psychoanalysis. This is represented by the three volumes of the best-selling *Hontō wa osoroshii Gurimu dōwa* (The Grimms' tales that are actually terrifying, 1998–2005), published by two women authors under the pseudonym Kiryū Misao. The second volume (1999), which includes a revision of "The Little Mermaid," cites over one hundred primary and research texts in the list of references, including Kurahashi's and Matsumoto's books. However, Kiryū's seeming dedication to genuine scholarly practice is undermined by their insufficient information in their reference list entries, as well as by their admission of misconduct after Matsumoto took them to court for plagiarizing *Tsumibukai hime no otogibanashi* (see Murai, *From Dog Bridegroom* 31, 149n17). Kiryū's performance of scholarly practice, more than informing an analysis of their work, is an interesting indication of popular authors' awareness of the interaction between fairy tale criticism and revision. The abundant references also seem to be a show of authority to support the authors' claim that *dōwa* (children's/fairy tales; see chapter 1), which "we thought nothing more than things for children to read," actually contain "ideas and insights about humans, love, cruelty, nature, the gods, and more" (1). The degree of insight is debatable; in the main, Kiryū's books titillate with their infusion of sex and violence. Their mermaid revision, for instance, closes with the mermaid being burned to death in the town square and a devoted admirer of hers slitting his throat in despair ("Ningyo-hime: Uwaki na ōji to hitamuki na kinshi"; The little mermaid: The cheating prince and the single-minded knight).

Matsumoto, on the other hand, exploited the tale's existing elements of sex and violence to her feminist ends. She describes *Tsumibukai hime no otogibanashi* as "a collection of stories that I parodied as I criticized them. They are parodies, but the cruel and the sexual aspects are just as they are in the originals" (211); she adds, "I had the intention of clearly revealing the true meanings of the fairy tales, but I also wrote them anew as my own stories" (212). Following her aforementioned exploration of "Sleeping Beauty" in the novel *Shokubutsusei ren'ai*, Matsumoto says that her reading in the intervening years of feminist criticism of foreign films and literature and criticism of children's literature based on "political correctness" has also influenced her understanding of fairy tales (*Tsumibukai* 213). The list of references cites a few explicitly feminist works, such as Tajima Yōko's *Ai to iu na no shihai* (The control that is known as "love," 1992), as well as two different Japanese translations of "The Little Mermaid."[6] This bibliography also positions Matsumoto's book in relation to a number of analyses of fairy tales that claim to expose the "deep layers" of the genre, including Iring Fetscher's *Who Kissed Briar Rose Awake?* (1972; English title translation from Joosen 31; Japanese trans., *Dare ga Ibara-hime o okoshita ka*, by Okazawa Shizuya, 1984) and a string of similar titles by Kanari Yōichi: *Dare ga Akazukin o kaihō shita ka* (Who freed Red Riding Hood?, 1989), *Dare ga Shirayuki-hime o yūwaku shita ka* (Who tempted Snow White?, 1991), and *Dare ga Nemuri-hime o sukutta ka* (Who saved Sleeping Beauty?, 1993). Along these lines, we also find Maria Tatar's *The Hard Facts of the Grimms' Fairy Tales* (1987), translated by Suzuki Shō et al. in 1990 as *Gurimu dōwa: Sono kakusareta messēji* (The hidden messages of the Grimms' tales), and Mori Yoshinobu's *Meruhen no shinsō: Rekishi ga toku dōwa no nazo* (The deeper levels of märchen: The mysteries of fairy tales solved by history, 1995).

Despite or perhaps confined by this wealth of research, Matsumoto's parody dictates a particular reading of "The Little Mermaid" that brings up

---

[6]By the literary critic and scholar and translator of children's literature Yamamuro Shizuka (published 1976–77) and Aramata Hiroshi (published 2005).

some ideological contradictions and imposes certain limitations on interpretation. That is, Matsumoto's feminist messages for the reader are so clear that they could cut off other possible meanings for her stories. For instance, the moral appended to the end of the tale, over one page long, includes the following explanations:

> For the sake of love, the little mermaid lost her voice and so lost the ability to communicate her feelings; she experienced pain in her legs and so lost freedom of movement. In other words, women should be quiet and stay still. Women who actively try to communicate their feelings and try to love men will be punished. . . .
>
> The land (man's country, patriarchy, Christianity) is much mightier than the bottom of the ocean (woman's country, matriarchy, polytheistic goddess civilization). Just as the Amazons were killed by the Greek army in the Trojan War, just as the Heian-period matriarchy was broken by the Kamakura-period warriors, the little mermaid of the ocean country was left to die by the prince of the land. (185–86)

Robin Morgan's feminist "sequel" to Andersen's tale and James Finn Garner's mermaid parody of political correctness both reshape the endings to pursue their particular ends. Matsumoto, on the other hand, is determined to reveal a specific set of meanings for Andersen's story as it is.

The form of revision that Matsumoto employs—in which both the plot and the mood of the story are unchanged—leaves less room for new ways of understanding gender, perhaps even affirming the very images of women she wishes to criticize. Hutcheon identifies this risk as the "central paradox of parody": that is, "in imitating, even with critical difference, parody reinforces" (*Parody* 26). Angela Carter's renowned collection of fairy tale revisions, *The Bloody Chamber*, famously faced accusations of this sort, when Patricia Duncker asserted that the choice to engage with the fairy tale prevents Carter from subverting the gender categories that form its basic building blocks. Carter's stories, Duncker writes, cannot escape "the infernal trap inherent in the fairy tale, which carries its ideology in its own form" (6). Cristina Bacchilega effectively argues against this criticism by pointing to Carter's detailed knowledge of the fairy tales she transforms, given Carter's position as "an enthusiastic listener/reader of both folk and fairy tales, and as a writer who draws from many versions, oral and literary," and reimagines their meanings (*Postmodern Fairy Tales* 59).

Matsumoto's revision is certainly researched, referring to texts and cultures as diverse as Heinrich Heine's "Lorelei" (149), Friedrich de la Motte

Fouqué's *Undine* (185), ancient Greek figures such as the Amazons (150), the Kamakura period in Japan (150), ancient China (152), pre-Roman Etruria (171), and Japanese mythology (171). But rather than diversifying the tales' voices, this has more of an effect of universalizing a vast array of historical circumstances into a unified story of repression of women. Matsumoto aligns women with colonized peoples and men with their colonizers; heterosexual penetrative sex is a physical emblem of "invasion" of nations (160). She also posits her allegory of gender and colonialism as universal. This type of comparison of women's plight in developed countries with that of colonized peoples has been thoroughly criticized for generalizing and thus erasing the particular and unique problems of the groups it conflates (Loomba 163).

In crafting a critical revision that retells Andersen's tale to highlight its social injustices, Matsumoto enjoys dethroning Andersen's authority over the tale and providing a sneaky gasp at the gender prejudices she sees concealed within it. In other words, the author takes pleasure in revelation via repetition. However, this does prevent the story from questioning the underlying systems of classification that produce these prejudices, since the revision has no socially transformative intention of offering new understandings of gender. On the other hand, the postface to the *Tsumibukai hime no otogibanashi* collection paints a picture of an active reader who is not limited to Matsumoto's interpretation but can disseminate and choose her own meanings from a culturally different text. Matsumoto writes, "Women of color in the East may choose how they will read a story written and published by a white man from Western Christian civilization and whether they will pass it on or boycott it. The sieve we use for this sifting is our own consciousness" (220). That is, she envisions fairy tale transformation and reading as critical processes that take place between a text and its discerning female readers. She expects readers to "oscillate" between Andersen's tale and her own in the manner that Hutcheon describes (*Theory of Adaptation* xv; see chapter 1), inviting them to take part in the intertextual pleasures of repetition, revelation, and therefore transformation.

Whereas Matsumoto clearly articulates her feminist agenda, neither Angela Carter's work nor the texts analyzed in the remainder of this chapter prioritize politics in quite the same way. Instead, the following stories show a fascination with the genre of the fairy tale and its possibilities for change in itself. Rather than condemning the ways in which women may be stereotyped or oppressed, they take pleasure in rearranging the structures of gender.

Inverting "The Little Mermaid"

If Matsumoto's parody is revisionist in its attempt to look at "The Little Mermaid" with new eyes, to expose its damaging ideas of gender, Kurahashi Yumiko excavates quite a different history of the tale. From her acclaimed debut in 1960, Kurahashi Yumiko (1935–2005) produced a range of works, including experimental, metafictional, and dystopian fiction. In 1984, Kurahashi published *Otona no tame no zankoku dōwa* (Cruel fairy tales for adults), a collection of parodic tales that became a best-seller and her most popular work. The stories are based on not only Western and Eastern fairy tales (such as "Jack and the Beanstalk" and "Issunbōshi" [One-inch boy]) but also a diverse range of authors, including Tolstoy and Kafka, as well as two of the writers analyzed in chapter 3, Oscar Wilde ("The Nightingale and the Rose") and Tanizaki Jun'ichirō (*Shunkinshō* [A portrait of Shunkin]). Kurahashi's choice of the word *dōwa* for "fairy tale" (see chapter 1) serves to highlight the contradictions in her title, as it literally means "children's stories." Thus, the word "cruel" sits next to "children stories," and the idea of children's tales contrasts with the claim of adult audiences, announcing the dark, ironic humor that runs through the whole volume.

Interestingly, *Otona no tame no zankoku dōwa* places Kurahashi (born 1935) parallel to what Stephen Benson describes as the "fairy tale generation," five writers born between 1932 and 1947 and publishing in English from 1969 onward, "influential writers of fiction for whom the fairy tale served ... as a key point of reference, in terms both aesthetic and ideological" (2),[7] including Angela Carter, with whom Kurahashi has often been compared in Japan (Murai, "Translation and Reception"). Kurahashi's writing was often ignored or criticized by the conservative Japanese *bundan* (literary establishment; see Sakaki's "Kurahashi Yumiko's Negotiations"), though it has recently garnered both domestic and international interest as the established borders separating "high" and mass literature begin to disintegrate. Atsuko Sakaki writes that Kurahashi would have been hailed as a poster child for postmodern art and its corresponding poststructuralist criticism had she been writing in a Western language (Sakaki, "'Watashi'" 344). Tomoko Aoyama also names Kurahashi as part of the "open-ended, decentred and dispersive" flourishing of parody, the "new literacy," noting that she "continued to advocate the anti-Roman of anti-world or non-existent places and tear asunder ideological, religious, political and literary icons" (Aoyama, "Love That Poisons" 35, 39).

---

[7] Robert Coover, A. S. Byatt, Margaret Atwood, Angela Carter, and Salman Rushdie.

Figure 4.2. The 1998 edition of *Otona no tame no zankoku dōwa*.

Kurahashi's cruel story that revises "The Little Mermaid," titled "Ningyo no namida" (The mermaid's tears), is still recognizably Andersen's, and his tale is referenced as the source in the bibliography to Kurahashi's book. Andersen's main characters—the mermaid, the prince, the witch, and the prince's new wife—are all present in Kurahashi's tale. Her plot traces a similar arc: first, the mermaid sees the prince and desires him and then rescues him; she acts on her desire and leaves the ocean to be with him; the prince's marriage to another woman prompts her return to the ocean; then the story concludes with the mermaid's metamorphosis into yet another new form.

However, unlike Matsumoto's story published twelve years later, Kurahashi's "Ningyo no namida" diverts from Andersen's tale in both the narrative style and details of the plot. For the former, Kurahashi's point of reference seems to be the classic fairy tale as it is widely understood (see chapter 1); in her postface, she writes that fairy tales have "no unneeded portrayal of characters' psychology or descriptions of nature" (229). While this is a perceptive description of the Grimms' and other stories, it is less applicable to the highly descriptive and sentimental style of Andersen's literary fairy tale.[8] As a result, "Ningyo no namida" is a short, blunt transformation. Andersen's lively opening image of the sea palace, for example, is reduced by Kurahashi to simply "the bottom of the deep ocean" (11), distancing the tale even further from any real place or point in time.

Kurahashi also alters details of plot and characters in "The Little Mermaid," beginning with the body of the mermaid herself. In Andersen's first description, "They were six delightful children, and the youngest was the prettiest of all. Her skin was as delicate and clear as a rose petal, her eyes as blue as the deepest lake, but like her sisters she didn't have any feet. Her body ended in a fish tail" (79). Kurahashi's version mirrors Andersen's: "Of all the sisters, she was an especially beautiful mermaid, and her eyes were clear and the same blue as the deep ocean. From her torso to her head, each single scale was prettily formed and gave off an almost bewitching light. On top of that, the mermaid was different from her sister as, unusually, her navel was visible; the legs that grew from underneath it were long and attractive" (11). The protagonist is a bodily parody of mermaids: her bottom half (feet to navel) is human, and her top half is a fish's head. Amusingly, Kurahashi describes this mermaid as beautiful, though her body would seem ungraceful both in the water and on the land.[9]

While Matsumoto's project is to expose the tales' prejudices, Kurahashi's interest in *Otona no tame no zankoku dōwa* is closer to Wilde's and Tanizaki's love of the fairy tale as art form and crafted object (see chapter 3). Kurahashi

---

[8]The sentimental nature of Andersen's work seems less related to fairy tales and folklore than to other forms such as emotional Danish ballads and Romantic tales (see Easterlin).

[9]The awkward hybrid that Kurahashi describes is captured in René Magritte's painting *L'invention collective* (Collective invention), which pictures the same type of mermaid lying uselessly on the beach. Marc Sebastian-Jones and Tateya Koichi point out in their translator's introduction that this painting may have inspired Kurahashi (172), given that other of her stories have also responded to paintings (181n3).

revels in the cruelty of the fairy tale, citing G. K. Chesterton's comparison of fairy tales with modern novels to admire what she calls in her postface the "clear laws and logic of the fairy tale, which take the form of magic" (229). "Ningyo no namida" is built around a series of inversions to the traditional mermaid body, leading to a newly inverted hybrid mermaid-human, female-male body. The tale then follows these inversions through to their logical narrative endings, enabling a mischievous "troubling" of the physical, psychological, and emotional boundaries of established ideas of gender and even human identity.[10]

Kurahashi's inverted mermaid, with her fish's head and human lower body, does not maintain the same balance of animal and human as traditional mermaids but rather seems to be doubly animal. The mermaid's human half contains neither a head, the seat of reason, nor a heart, the symbolic receptacle of emotion. Rather, the human half is the lower portion, associated with instinct, sexual drives, and bodily emissions—in other words, animals. That is, in this body, the "animal" end of a human is attached to the actual animal's head. Then again, this animal/sexual mermaid, we learn, already has a soul, which would shift her to the "human" side of Andersen's scheme. Since she possesses a soul, however, the mermaid does not desire the prince for access to eternal spiritual life but purely for sexual attraction, shifting her back to the "animal" end of the spectrum.

When the mermaid rescues the prince from drowning, apparently her animal instincts take over. In Andersen's tale, the mermaid saves the prince and then kisses him. The Disney film had censored even this intimacy by having the mermaid wistfully sing to Prince Eric instead of kissing him. Kurahashi, on the other hand, logically builds on the powerful force of the mermaid's desire and has her mermaid engage in (her first experience of) sexual intercourse with the prince's unconscious body. This sex between the mermaid and the sleeping prince is described in seemingly neutral terms: "There was a hard, pointed tower of flesh standing up from below the prince's stomach. The mermaid, directed by a voice of instinct, tried putting that extraneous part into the insufficient part of her own body. It fitted perfectly" (14).

Because Kurahashi pares down the language to neutral shapes and configurations, she denies—perhaps reverses—customary imagery of feminine passivity and masculine invasion that Matsumoto had underlined. The scene also actively reverses another fairy tale tradition, that of the sleeping princess: in most versions of "Snow White" and "Sleeping Beauty," the

---

[10] For more on similar tendencies in Kurahashi's earlier work (1960–73), see Bullock.

prince falls in love with the beautiful sleeping woman and kisses her, and in Giambattista Basile's 1634 *Pentamerome*, in "Sun, Moon, and Talia," for example, the king even has sex with the sleeping princess and impregnates her. But this scene in Kurahashi's tale also recalls the Japanese foundation myth of the goddess Izanami and the god Izanagi, as it is narrated in the *Kojiki* (Records of ancient times, completed 712): "Izanagi asked Izanami, 'How is your body formed?' Izanami replied: 'My body is perfectly formed, except for one place where it does not come together.' Thereupon Izanagi said, 'My body is perfectly formed, except for one place where there is an excess. I would like to fill up the part of your body which does not come together with the part of my body which is excessive'" (*Kojiki*, bk. 1, trans. Borgen and Ury 66). Though power is seemingly shared evenly in this encounter, unequal expectations emerge in the *Kojiki*. In the next part of their encounter, the pair separate and circle a sacred pillar to be married; when they come together, Izanami speaks before her male counterpart, and for this wrong she is punished when she gives birth to defective children.

Another element of this myth that Kurahashi manipulates in her mermaid tale is the power of female ugliness. After giving birth to many islands and gods, the goddess Izanami dies delivering the fire deity. The grief-stricken husband, Izanagi, follows her to the land of the dead, but when he disobeys her injunction not to look at her, he sees her decomposing body and runs away in horror. In *Busu ron* (Theory of ugly women, 2005), Ōtsuka Hikari describes Izanami as Japan's first *busu* (a derogatory word for an ugly woman) and argues for a power of female ugliness stemming from "not only a disgust with the decomposing corpse but a fear of the absolute strength—the power of ugliness—of death" (32). Kurahashi's mermaid is aware that she possesses power in her ugliness: her grandmother has already warned her to avoid being seen by humans, as this will bring terrible misfortune (12). After the mermaid has sex with the prince, she imagines him waking up and seeing her "ugly upper body": crying, she runs back to the ocean (14).

Kurahashi's tale seems also to draw on other myths that feature deadly, ugly women, such as the ancient Greek stories of Medusa. But while the taboo is ostensibly on mermaids being gazed on by others, the destruction that occurs when the prince sees the mermaid is actually narrated as the consequence of the power of the mermaid's desiring gaze. The act of looking, rather than being seen, is emphasized: for example, when the mermaid first sees the prince, "forgetting her mermaid's body, she pushed her face at the window and peered into the rooms of the ship" (13). When she has sex with the comatose prince, the mermaid also forgets her mermaid's body (14).

Later the mermaid peeks into the ship again; her gaze is mentioned, but her being looked at is not. Female desire is represented as forgetting the gaze directed at one's own body and turning one's powerful gaze onto others. Hélène Cixous interprets the Medusa myth as a patriarchal fear of femininity: "She's not deadly. She's beautiful and she's laughing" (885). Kurahashi also moves the focus away from the patriarchal gaze and onto the desiring gaze of the female who has been feared and refuted as "ugly."

Kurahashi's more empowered mermaid is not required to exchange her voice or experience pain in order to become human. We might assume that she acquires a voice because she begins with a fish's head and gains a human one, but in the story, her only direct speech issues from her fish's head. She addresses a witch who, like Andersen's witch, immediately understands what the mermaid wants. Perhaps the closest communication in the story occurs between these two females, who barter to achieve mutually desirable outcomes. On the other hand, as in Matsumoto's revision, close communication between the prince and the mermaid does not seem possible. When Kurahashi's mermaid does have a human body, she cannot assimilate into human society; dresses make her uncomfortable, and she spends most of her time naked in bed (16).

Different from Andersen's tale, this mermaid's desire is not bound by the social and magical rules that are imposed on her: like Disney's Ariel and other disobedient mermaids, she swims up to the ocean's surface before she is permitted. Kurahashi's introduction of a rebellious mermaid who already has a soul sets a chain of revisions into motion. Like Wilde's Fisherman, the mermaid willingly discards her soul to gain the object of her desire. In this case, she exchanges it for a human upper body, with the opportunity to win her soul back if the prince will love her more than life itself (15). The revision, then, cannot conclude like Andersen's, with the mermaid gratefully becoming a "daughter of the air" closer to earning a soul. At the end of Kurahashi's story, the prince marries another woman, but the plot shifts once more when the mermaid again takes initiative to achieve her desire. She deliberately shows her ugly mermaid body to humans, which causes a storm: this time, instead of swimming the prince to shore, she takes him to the bottom of the ocean and bargains with the sea witch. The witch agrees to join the mermaid's human legs with the prince's human torso to form one new human body and happily takes the leftover body halves as payment. As one commentator points out, the new body created here is, in one way, a return to a binary system (as portrayed by Matsumoto) in which the male represents public "'head' of state" while the female embodies the physical and erotic lower half, but Kurahashi compels these two forces to combine and correspond within the bounds of one body (Kleeman 150). But what kind of communication is involved in this apparent spiritual closeness?

The Mermaid's Tears

The title "Ningyo no namida" (The mermaid's tears) resonates rhythmically and alliteratively with Tanizaki's "Ningyo no nageki" (The mermaid's lament); in meaning, both Tanizaki's and Kurahashi's titles also resemble a 1948 title to a translation of Andersen's story: "Ningyo no kanashimi" (The mermaid's sadness; trans. Katayama Shōzō, in Kawato and Sakakibara 69). However, contrary to Andersen's mermaid, who cannot cry, the tears of Kurahashi's mermaid flow freely. The tears become pearls, an idea borrowed from Chinese mythology,[11] also taken up in both Tanizaki's and Matsumoto's transformations. In Kurahashi's tale, the tears, which are already physical manifestations of intense emotion, become precious jewels, so that, as Max Lüthi puts it, "Feelings and relationships congeal into objects" (51). But the pearls are in such a surplus—the bed is covered with them (Kurahashi, *Otona* 18)—that they lose their value and perhaps their meaning.

While tears are emitted from the face and head and manifest emotion, the "tears" here are issued from the mermaid's lower half after the prince has pleasured their hybrid body, recalling the sexual arousal of Abe's protagonist licking the tears of the mermaid in "Ningyo-den" (see chapter 3). The tears/pearls seem to represent female bodily emissions that accompany sexual arousal and satisfaction. In one of Higami Kumiko's illustrations published with Ogawa Yōko's revision, "Dappi" (Shedding skin; 78), a mermaid draped in pearls is portrayed next to a seashell resembling a vulva with pearls inside it; another shell oozes a secretion. Higami's illustrations hint that pearls may also represent fish eggs: in "Sanran" (Spawning; 74), iridescent, pearl-like spheres spill from the mermaid in the same abundance as the pearls in Kurahashi's story. Finally, although these images deal with female emissions, tears as white pearls are also reminiscent of male ejaculation. This is turn may be reminiscent of the tragic fate of Andersen's mermaid to turn to foam.[12]

---

[11] For example, Tanabe Satoru cites a reference in the Chinese text *Shu(/ju)tsuiki*, written between 460 and 508, to a half-snake, half-person, related to mermaids, whose tears turn to pearls (33–34).

[12] Dahlerup has suggested that the mermaid turning to foam on the ocean "may be the symbol of unreproduced male sexuality" (162).

As with Abe's "Ningyo-den," the humor of Kurahashi's tale derives from its carnivalesque inversions and its focus on what Mikhail Bakhtin describes as "the prevailing logic of the ambivalent lower stratum [of the body]" (83). Each story in *Otona no tame no zankoku dōwa* has a moral affixed. Unlike Matsumoto's, it is more mystifying than explanatory; the moral of "Ningyo no namida" is, "People do not fall in love with the lower half of the body" (18). This seems to be another inversion that reflects Kurahashi's trademark dark irony. It reads like sexist advice recommending that young girls maintain their virginity in order to secure their man. It seems irrelevant to the story: the word it employs, *koi* (romantic love), is not used at all in the text, and another word for "love," *ai*, is used only once (15). And although Kurahashi's mermaid cannot enjoy the sexual activity with the prince that originally drove her to pursue him, her lower half does in fact achieve oneness with her object of desire. The author herself warns against paying too much attention to these morals, writing in the postface, "They are not there to confine the ways in which the stories may be read" (232). Just as Matsumoto wants to empower readers to choose whether to read or ignore the fairy tale canon and how to read it, Kurahashi encourages an unconfined reading of her own tales and their mocking morals.

Appending morals to each story is part of Kurahashi's sustained engagement with fairy tales, which extends from the *Otona no tame no zankoku dōwa* title to the postface about fairy tales and a bibliography of primary sources. This bibliography may be Kurahashi's pointed defense against the troubles she faced for her postmodern, parodic style. Earlier, the well-known critic Etō Jun had accused Kurahashi of imitating Michel Butor's *La modification* with her novel *Kurai tabi* (Dark journey, 1961), a claim Kurahashi rejected (see Sakaki, "Kurahashi Yumiko's Negotiations" 306–9). These accusations of plagiarism faced by Kurahashi—as well as Kiryū's aforementioned plagiarism of Matsumoto—provide another reason to identify the different types of fairy tale intertextuality, as this book does. Genette describes plagiarism as "undeclared but still literal borrowing," simply another form of relationship between texts, one that he includes in his narrowed category of intertextuality (*Palimpsests* 2). It is clear that further delineation would be useful, as in this context such a typology of the intertextual uses of fairy tales[13] could have a practical effect on authors' creative output as well as their livelihoods.

---

[13] This is the project of Kevin Paul Smith, who adapts Genette's types of transtextuality (*Palimpsests*) to describe different types of "intertextual uses of fairytales," in *The Postmodern Fairytale: Folkloric Intertexts in Contemporary Fiction* (2007). Smith does not discuss the issue of plagiarism.

Kurahashi's text is deeply engaged in an intertextual dialogue with mermaid traditions, fairy tales, and other mythologies. Action is privileged over descriptive writing in traditional oral/Grimms' fairy tale style; accordingly, connections between people are played out in new ways that are more concrete: that is, through the physical body, a unique hybrid (the mermaid + the prince) created from an unusual hybrid (the upside-down mermaid). Through inversions that reverse conservative figurings of gender and through "logical" diversions from Andersen's story, Kurahashi, like Angela Carter, "trace[s] violently contradictory genealogies" of Andersen's tale and other mythologies (Bacchilega, *Postmodern Fairy Tales* 59). The tale certainly undertakes a complex troubling of limiting notions of gendered roles and bodies. Yet it suggests no particular outcome for society; "Ningyo no namida" remains a cruelly playful and playfully cruel revision of Andersen's tale.

Reversing Roles in "The Little Mermaid"

Ogawa Yōko's collection *Otogibanashi no wasuremono* (Lost property fairy tales, 2006) neither purports to expose the adult, sexist themes of the tales nor follows their wondrous events to their logical ends but focuses, rather, on another aspect of the fairy tale genre: the repetition and renewal of fairy tales, their anonymity and cycles of loss and discovery. Andersen's "The Little Mermaid" would seem to hold a special appeal for Ogawa's fantastical and sometimes fairy tale literary sensibilities. Ogawa Yōko (1962–), of Matsumoto's generation, is a celebrated writer who is well established in the contemporary literary scene. Her work has been awarded numerous prizes, and she has been a member of the judging committee of the prestigious Akutagawa Prize from 2007 to the time of writing (2016). Special journal issues and books have been published about her work.[14] Many of her works deal with silence and muteness: a male character in *Hoteru Airisu* (Hotel Iris, 1996) has no tongue and cannot speak; another of her novels, which features a number of corpses, is titled *Chinmoku hakubutsukan* (Silence museum, 2000). Images of diving, swimming, and drowning appear in *Hoteru Airisu*, "Daibingu pūru" (Diving pool, 1989), and *Umi* (The sea, 2006). In another fairy tale connection, Mayako Murai (in *From Dog Bridegroom*) has identified "Bluebeard" narratives in "Domitorī" (Dormitory,

---

[14]Special journal issues on Ogawa were published by *Yurīka* (2004) and *Bungei* (2009) (see under "Ogawa Yōko" in the Works Cited). Books on Ogawa include Ayame Hiroharu's monograph *Ogawa Yōko: Mienai sekai o mitsumete* (Ogawa Yōko: Gazing at the world we cannot see, 2009) and a collection of criticism edited by Takanezawa Noriko, *Ogawa Yōko* (2005).

1990), "Kusuriyubi no hyōhon" (Specimen of a ring finger, 1992), and *Hoteru Airisu*.

Otogibanashi no wasuremono is immersed in the fairy tale world and does not explicitly cite research or even the sources of the (famous) fairy tales that are revised. The author's and illustrator's postfaces are neither self-reflective nor analytical; rather, both describe the work in a fairy tale manner, and both reference the setting of the framing narrative, a candy store. The book is a collaborative collection of four stories that Ogawa composed in response to illustrations by the artist Higami Kumiko, whose work centers on girls and fairy tales. Higami has provided cover art and illustrations for Matsumoto's book, as mentioned, as well as for girl studies works such as Takahara Eiri's *Shōjo ryōiki* (The territory of the girl; see chapters 2 and 5). Higami draws flat, expressionless, sometimes erotically posed pubescent girls and portrays sweet foods associated with girlhood such as cakes and desserts. Emblematic fairy tale animals such as butterflies, birds, and wolves frequently appear in her work. Her illustrations also depict elaborate costumes and shining jewels, evincing a version of the enchantment with artifice seen in Wilde's and Tanizaki's tales (see chapter 3). As with Wilde's and Tanizaki's publications, also, *Otogibanashi no wasuremono* presents the physical pleasure of a beautiful fairy tale object in the hands of the reader. All Higami's illustrations and stories seem to be loosely based on Western fairy tales. In addition to "The Little Mermaid," the other hypotexts seem to be the Grimms' "Little Red Riding Hood," Lewis Carroll's *Alice's Adventures in Wonderland*, and a combination of *Swan Lake* and Andersen's "The Wild Swans." The book's immersion in the fairy tale world, combined with a complicated presentation of gendered identities in its text and image, invites layered reading pleasures.

The Merman's Tale

Ogawa's revision of Andersen's tale is titled "Ningyo hōseki shokunin no isshō" (The life of a mermaid's jeweler). Unlike Matsumoto's and Kurahashi's tales, which are narrated in the third person, and unlike the distant, unconnected narrator of Andersen's story and many fairy tales, "Ningyo hōseki shokunin no isshō" is narrated in the first person by the eponymous jeweler. This narrator is a character not found in Andersen's story, a merman servant of the mermaid princess. His job is to create beautiful jewelry for her—an occupation perhaps inspired both by the jewelry in Higami's illustrations and by the episode in Andersen's story in which the mermaid's grandmother adorns the mermaid with flowers, pearls, and oysters.

Like Matsumoto's, Ogawa's mermaid tale essentially retains the events of Andersen's plot. Her method of revision is to tell it from a literal set of the "fresh eyes" Adrienne Rich had proposed (35): those of the new character of the merman. Ogawa's merman narrator retells the story of Andersen's little mermaid on two levels: first, he narrates the events of Andersen's story, watching as the little mermaid falls in love with a human prince, exchanges her beautiful voice for human legs and goes on to the land, and then sacrifices herself rather than kill the prince for the chance to become a mermaid again. The merman also retells Andersen's story, however, in that he reenacts a similar plot. Although he never explicitly confesses it, the merman jeweler seems to be in love with the mermaid; that is, he is in love with someone ultimately beyond his reach, just as the mermaid loves the unattainable prince. Also, like the little mermaid, the jeweler is mute and cannot speak his love. At the end of Ogawa's story, after the mermaid turns to foam, the merman avenges her death by killing the prince's human wife and dies in the process. In other words, like Andersen's little mermaid, Ogawa's jeweler makes an unacknowledged sacrifice for the sake of his love, which causes him to turn into foam on the ocean.

Ogawa seems to share Matsumoto's interpretation of the mermaids' realm as a matriarchal society; she inverts human gender roles and imagines a level of masochistic devotion on the part of the subservient mermen. The merman narrator begins his story by explaining that "in the merpeople's country, apart from the prince, every merman devotes his whole life to mermaids and dies without wanting anything in return" (82). He goes on to explain that mermen lose physical abilities according to their occupations: jewelers do not need voices, so they become mute; hairdressers do not need to hear, so they become deaf; and so on (84).[15] Males of the species are also physically limited in that any type of light turns them to foam and kills them. This means that only mermaids can swim to the ocean surface and be seen by humans, the narrator adds, so humans inevitably assume that no mermen exist.

In Ogawa's imagining, then, female mermaids move independently, can live in light, and have access to the human world. They live privileged lives and possess voices, power, material wealth, and the freedom to follow

---

[15] Ogawa's masochistic male figure has its precedents in Japanese literature, notably in the work of Tanizaki Jun'ichirō. Ogawa's mute merman servant is reminiscent of Tanizaki's figure of Sasuke in *Shunkinshō* (A portrait of Shunkin). The servant and student of the aristocratic musician Shunkin, Sasuke devotes himself to his cruel mistress and blinds himself for her sake. *Shunkinshō* is also one of the texts that Kurahashi parodies in her *Otona no tame no zankoku dōwa*, in "Kagami o mita ōjo" (The princess who looked in the mirror).

their own desires. The mermen, on the other hand, are confined to the darkness of the deep ocean. They live servile lives entirely for the sake of the mermaids, and they are mute or have otherwise lost the use of some physical faculty. The mermen's roles may be equated with traditional female ones (see also Ayame 225). On top of their limited access and submissive, self-sacrificing acts, the mermen perform domestic duties such as preparing meals, homemaking, grooming, telling stories, and singing lullabies (Ogawa, *Otogibanashi* 82).

Moreover, fairy tale gender roles also seem to be reversed when the merman protagonist avenges the mermaid after she has died for the sake of the human prince. Both the merman's method and his choice of victim suggest that he identifies with the mermaid rather than as her scorned lover. Instead of battling the prince who has rejected and caused the death of his beloved, the merman uses an item with feminine associations to take revenge on the human princess—the mermaid's competitor for the prince's affections. The merman crafts a beautiful necklace and swims to the surface to leave it on the beach, dying from exposure to starlight as he does so. The human princess cannot resist putting on the necklace; but then it grows gradually tighter until she cannot remove it, and it eventually chokes her to death. If the merman narrator is considered here as a stand-in for his beloved mermaid, this becomes a fairy tale conflict between two women involving feminine accouterments such as clothing or jewelry, in which the sexually experienced competitor is punished, as seen in the clash between the vain queen and the virginal princess in the Grimms' version of "Snow White."[16]

Higami Kumiko's illustrations feature beautiful feminine mermaids with breasts, long hair, and jewelry, but no mermen. This lack of a visual depiction of the merman might speak to another issue of gender in fairy tales. Mermaids are depicted as an egg-laying species, indicating that their physical interaction and procreation is not figured around the same heterosexual intercourse and genitalia as humans'. Ogawa's story, then, gives voice to a figure that is absent from the illustrations. The combination of Higami's illustrations and Ogawa's text might reveal the way fairy tales, in Bacchilega's words, perform the work of "showcasing 'women' and making them disappear at the same time," rendering them "man-made constructs of 'Woman'" (*Postmodern Fairy Tales* 9). In other words, Higami's flat images of girls

---

[16] As Sandra Gilbert and Susan Gubar point out, the queen's murder attempts "depend on a poisonous or parodic use of a distinctively female device as a murder weapon" (*Madwoman* 39): she tries to suffocate Snow White with corsets (*Madwoman* 253) and poison her with a comb. When defeated, the queen must dance herself to death in red-hot shoes.

Figure 4.3. Cover for *Otogibanashi no wasuremono*, with illustration by Higami Kumiko.

become portraits of an idea of Woman, whereas Ogawa's invisible mermen may be interpreted as "real" women behind the scenes, living with imperfect bodies, leading mundane lives in limited spaces, and performing housework for others.

However, the assumption that these mermen stand in for women because they are invisible and oppressed elides the more complex ways that Ogawa's tale reimagines gender. In creating the merman narrator, Ogawa inserts a powerless figure into the bottom of Andersen's already complicated hierarchy of matriarchal mermaid society, patriarchal human society, and sexless, disembodied air spirits close to God. At first glance, gender in Ogawa's mermaid society is defined according to physical difference: male and female are primarily distinguished by their inability and ability to be exposed to light, respectively. After this primary division, though, in Judith Butler's words, "gender reality is created through sustained social performances" (141). That is, gender is defined through the repeated enactments of femininity or masculinity and "corporeal styles" (140) of the (mer)men and (mer)women in their respective gendered spaces within their society. It is "inscribed on the surface of bodies" (136): in this case, the mermen work so much that they lose some physical faculty, the loss of which marks them as male, while the mermaids come to embody femininity through constant grooming and decoration. The incongruent juxtaposition of traditionally feminine roles with male bodies is a possible form of Butler's gender parody, since it highlights the naturalization of artificial gendered social roles. One critic, Ayame, believes that male readers, at least, would feel shocked at Ogawa's gender inversions (225).[17]

The Merman's Voice

In a statement that demonstrates Ogawa's sensitivity to the limitations and ideologies of gender, class, and hierarchy that language places on the speaker, she has commented that unlike the previous generation of writers such as Murakami Haruki, who felt that they had something they had to rebel against,

> When it comes to our generation, we could say that people writing novels aren't really conscious of the fact that they are using a language manipulated by the nation. Actually, they write novels with a sense

---

[17] Ayame Hiroharu focuses on men's reactions to a book that seems to be largely targeted at a female audience. Unlike Matsumoto, he apparently assumes that women are aware of and comfortable with the uneven social positions.

> of trust for language, feeling that it has every potential and that it is a tool with the strength to express what one cannot express. At the same time, every day they face the problem of language as a limited and restricted tool. All writers are struggling bitterly in the contradiction of trying to use words to express what cannot be expressed in words. (*Ogawa Yōko taiwashū* 97)

Words in Ogawa's works are not art and objects of aesthetic pleasure, as Wilde and Tanizaki treat them (see chapter 3). Rather, in response to Andersen's tongueless, helpless mermaid, Ogawa has created a mute, male narrator who, despite his very limited circumstances, seems to be what Gayatri Spivak would describe as a subaltern who finds the means to tell his story, who "can speak and know [his] conditions" (283).

However, the merman's claim to storytelling authority is difficult to assess, making him a possibly unreliable narrator. In narrative theory, the unreliable narrator is identified by discordance between the narrator's and the "implied author's" version of events (Wayne C. Booth, qtd. in Nünning 89) or by being evaluated as unreliable by the reader (Nünning 94). In the case of Ogawa's revision, readers might gauge the narrator's reliability from hints within the text, but this evaluation will be affected by their knowledge of Andersen's "The Little Mermaid." Actually, approaching Ogawa's text as a reader of Andersen's fairy tale both supports and contradicts a claim that this narrator is unreliable. First, the merman's account generally agrees with Andersen's text, making his version seem more trustworthy. On the other hand, the merman's account departs from Andersen's story on some small points. And the merman's love for the mermaid—more obvious to readers of Andersen who are familiar with the little mermaid's love for the prince—hints to the reader that the merman's judgment is clouded by his emotions.

The merman's reliability is called into question by the life that he describes. He is confined to darkness and obscurity at the bottom of the ocean. He does not have access to many of the events he narrates, so he can only construct the little mermaid's story from what he overhears and imagines. For instance, he does not witness her turning to foam but only sees what he believes is evidence of her death: clear drops drifting down into the ocean that he instinctively knows are the little mermaid's tears. "Mermaids cannot cry tears," he relates, "but I knew that these were tears. They were the tears of the mermaid who had stabbed herself and died, rather than kill the prince" (Ogawa, *Otogibanashi* 94–95). In Andersen's version, though, the mermaid does not stab herself. Later, the merman even describes his own death in the past tense, saying, "When I had melted in the light, I became foam on the ocean, and I was carried away by the waves" (96), before disappearing from the story. Having died, he gives no explanation as to how he is able to narrate events from beyond the grave.

Similar to Wilde's tale, "Ningyo hōseki shokunin no isshō" gives concluding information following the death of the protagonist, whose viewpoint we have shared up to that moment. After Ogawa's merman jeweler has described his own death, the story's closing paragraphs are narrated in the third person, describing the human princess being killed by the deadly necklace he had crafted. Whereas the third-person voice in Wilde's tale allows for a smoother transition from the Fisherman's point of view to an unidentified narrator, the switch from a first-person to a third-person perspective in Ogawa's tale is more difficult to assimilate. If the merman's plotline has continued to shadow Andersen's little mermaid's story, as it did across his unrequited love and his dissolution into foam, then it follows that the merman has now become an air spirit. Does the third-person, neutral narration then issue from his new body, positioned in the sky at a greater distance from the events? Since the merman's last act was one of vengeful murder rather than self-sacrifice, it seems unlikely that he has been allotted a chance at an eternal soul as Andersen's mermaid was. Readers might feel that the "implied author" has picked up where the "unreliable" first-person narrator left off, in order to satisfy us with the balanced, concrete ending that we demand of a fairy tale.

The merman's narrative and the third-person addendum are further differentiated by their different registers. The merman's low social status is cemented by his use of polite language: *desu/-masu* verb endings that are used in semiformal speech and simulate oral Japanese fairy tales (as in Tanizaki's tale discussed in chapter 3). The narrator uses honorific verb forms to address the reader (such as *gozonji deshō ka* for "were you aware?"; 82) and sometimes to refer to the little mermaid (*ossharu* for "speak"; 87) and, occasionally, humble verb forms to refer to himself (as in *wakatte orimashita* for "I knew"; 89). In contrast, the third-person narrative uses the plain dictionary-form verbs, which are more common in written communication and modern literature. The merman's subjective, first-person, oral narrative style is highlighted in contrast to the neutral, third-person yet literary style at the conclusion. The combination of styles disrupts what Bacchilega describes as the "powerful narrative strategy" of an "external or impersonal narrator" (*Postmodern Fairy Tales* 34), perhaps even exposing some of the effects of this strategy.

Further, the frame story to *Otogibanashi no wasuremono* fictionalizes the seemingly objective figure of the third-person narrator and the "implied author" and suggests that this voice is also unreliable. The frame story takes place in a candy store. The opening part is a monologue spoken by the candy store owner directly to a customer. No detail is given about the customer, allowing the reader to entirely inhabit this position within the story and become the "you" that the candy store owner addresses. The candy store owner is similarly anonymous, using the uniformly polite, gender-neutral language of customer service—albeit perhaps with slightly condescending overtones—and giving no indication of gender or age. Upon being asked about a room at the back of the shop, the candy store owner tells the customer/reader about a grandfather who accidentally discovered some anonymous fairy tales in a lost property room in a train station in Italy. The grandfather was inspired to embark on a search for lost fairy tales around the world; he collected the stories, transcribed them, and then had them translated by experts. The grandfather himself eventually disappeared in his quest for more stories. According to the candy store owner, the stories that the grandfather collected are now held in the "reading room" (5) at the back of the candy store. The candy store owner invites the customer/reader to go into the room and read some of the stories while waiting for a purchase to be gift-wrapped. The candy store owner recommends that the customer take a piece of candy upon choosing a book and "turn the page as leisurely and slowly as the candy melts in your mouth" (13).

This part of the frame story precedes the contents page that lists the four fairy tale revisions. The frame story therefore fictionalizes the authors of these four stories—including the author of "Ningyo hōseki shokunin no isshō"—as anonymous writers whose work has been discovered on a fantastical international quest. The candy store owner has already warned that these fictional authors are unreliable, saying that the stories have "no historical value" and that "all of them are written by mere would-be writers, fantasist and delusionist types" (9). The frame story's emphasis on anonymity and the candy store owner's disparagement of these authors undoes the traditional figures of reliable "implied author" behind the "unreliable narrator." But while disparaging the writers of the stories themselves, the candy store owner takes more time explaining the grandfather's process of selecting translators: "He called on specialists in each language and asked them for translations. He was not distracted by their degrees and titles; he searched for people who were brilliant and had a sense for the work" (12). In this way, the narrator also challenges the traditional privileging of the "original" story over its "derivative" translation.

Thus, traditional hierarchies of authorship, translation, illustration, and narration are mixed up, rendering the reliability of different storytelling figures ambiguous. In another reversal outside the frame narrative, *Otogibanashi no wasuremono* itself was created in an unusual order: Ogawa composed text to match Higami's pictures, whereas it is more common for illustrators to respond to a writer's text. As a contrast, in Matsumoto's book *Tsumibukai hime no otogibanashi*, Higami's pretty illustrations of girls decorate the text and intensify the fairy tale atmosphere of the work. As in Matsumoto's book, in "Lost property fairy tales" (*Otogibanashi no wasuremono*), the girls' pink lips are closed; they gaze out but do not speak to their viewers. But whereas Matsumoto promises to reveal deeper truths about the fairy tales and these princess protagonists, Ogawa's stories seem to delight in deepening their sense of mystery and anonymity. Ogawa writes of the mermen outside the picture and focuses on lost characters and what characters might lose as much as on what readers can discover about them. The illustrations and text seem to develop a deeper relationship when they divert from their usual hierarchies, which in turn attributes the creation of this fairy tale to even more authors and thereby complicates the idea of any authoritative "voice" of the story.

Finding Pleasure in Loss

The dissolving merman jeweler is a transfiguration of the little mermaid who dissolves into sea foam, and this theme of vanishing is one of the implied pleasures of this tale. In Roland Barthes's terms, readers may find "pleasure" in the "*comfortable* practice" of reading Ogawa's familiarly tragic story of unrequited love. But more than that, the effects of Ogawa's play with gender roles, her focus on muteness, and her misgivings about language, voice, and authority also evoke Barthes's "text of bliss": "the text that imposes a state of loss, the text that discomforts (perhaps to the point of certain boredom), unsettles the reader's historical, cultural, psychological assumptions, the consistency of his [*sic*] tastes, values, memories, brings to a crisis his relation with language" (14). Most importantly, Barthes's vision of "bliss" involves forgetting the self, "the *dissolve* which seizes the subject in the midst of bliss" (7). Whereas Andersen's mermaid experiences joy when she becomes an ethereal air spirit one step closer to heaven, in Ogawa's transformation, the merman narrator's story climaxes in the moment he describes his own body's disintegration and his disappearance.

Paratexts underline the recurring imagery of loss and disappearance in *Otogibanashi no wasuremono*. The brief closing part of the frame story consists of the candy store owner asking readers how they are and inviting them to revisit the "lost property reading room" at any time. On the following pages are the author's and the illustrator's single-page postfaces. Both women reference the frame story's candy store and "reading room" setting by comparing the process of reading to the act of eating candy. Ogawa, still mistrustful of the expressive possibilities of language, figures reading not as intellectual decoding but as a mysterious physical communion with Higami's expressionless girls: "Each girl that Ms. Higami Kumiko portrays has suppressed the emotion from her face, but in her mouth, she is tasting a single, one-of-a-kind piece of candy. I expect that if readers stare at these girls for long enough, the flavor will reach your mouth too" (116). Higami, in her afterword on the opposite page, then compares the process of reading with absorbing candy into one's body: "The fairy tales included in this book are like candy: they are hard and sweet, and they will melt slowly, and they will filter into the hearts of the people who read them" (117).

The girls' pleasure pictured here differs from other gendered understandings. Andersen's and Ogawa's images of a mermaid and a merman turning to foam and Barthes's descriptions of reading pleasure are somewhat reminiscent of male orgasm and ejaculation: achievement of ecstasy is marked by bodily emission, a kind of loss and dissolution. The ecstatic loss of self was also seen in the enthusiasm with which Wilde's and Tanizaki's princes threw themselves into enchantment with their alluring, unreal mermaids and in Ogawa's merman's unquestioning, masochistic devotion to the mermaids he serves. Thus, Wilde's, Tanizaki's, and Ogawa's male protagonists share with Andersen's mermaid a dedication to their own extreme pain and suffering and the inevitable release it builds to. Their pain is a physical expression of a kind of immersive, vicarious pleasure in intense emotional experience that they offer up to the reader.

Ogawa's and Higami's postfaces, though, introduce a different type of reading pleasure, a girlish delight in tasting, assimilating, and sharing the flavor of candy. As we shall see in chapter 5 on girls' mermaid stories, candy is a recurring item of girlishness and is used to imagine the way girls might share and absorb stories. Girls can absorb the stories into themselves, individually—just as they eat candy—but part of their pleasure is found in sharing this experience with other girls, through eating the same candy and reading the same stories together. Whereas Kurahashi and Matsumoto present reading as open-ended and reader-centered, for Ogawa and Higami, reading is an ambiguous process that involves a certain loss through disintegration, as well as a certain gain through absorption.

The word *wasuremono* in the collection's title, *Otogibanashi no wasuremono*, means "lost property" but more literally "forgotten things." The title could also be rendered as "Forgotten fairy tales" or as "Lost and found fairy tales" (Murai, *From Dog Bridegroom* 64). "Forgotten" or "lost" could refer to any number of things, including the publication itself, which has largely been neglected in the critical work on Ogawa to date. Ayame argues that the *wasuremono* that Ogawa has uncovered in her stories is the cruel nature of fairy tales, something he believes has been forgotten in recent incarnations of the genre (225), although Kurahashi had certainly already highlighted this element, and it was also a major tenet of the late 1990s "Grimm boom."

Ogawa's work rejects ideas of the "true" nature of a particular tale. Her revision is narrated in repressed, humble language by an unnamed, mute, dead merman, and it is concluded with an unmarked third-person addendum. In the frame story, an unidentified speaker describes the tale as a translation of a transcription of a story—the place of origin and the original language of which is unknown—collected by a man who has since disappeared. As such, the volume enacts a more profound imagining of literary fairy tales that takes into account their oral history, bringing the authority of any narrative, any narrator, and any author sharply into question. *Wasuremono* describes the merman's gendered self as it is forgotten in his blissful moment of disintegration, but it also stretches to cover the pleasure of consuming and digesting such images of loss and the pleasurable confusion of experiencing fairy tales as forgotten, anonymous, and uncertain.

Such a pleasurable loss of self is another magical metamorphosis enabled by the fairy tale form, reminding us of the fairy tale's potential for transformation. Andersen's mermaid finds another shape when she becomes a "daughter of the air" on her way to gaining an eternal soul. Wilde's Fisherman and his Mermaid leave a grave with strange flowers that deeply affect the prejudiced local Priest. In Kurahashi's story, of course, two characters transform into a new hybrid, formed of the legs of an upside-down mermaid fused to the torso of a human man, with new, obscure means of communication between the unbridgeable gap that Matsumoto perceives between the sexes.

Ogawa's merman may disappear before the end of "Ningyo hōseki shokunin no isshō," leaving a violent legacy, but the framing story to *Otogibanashi no wasuremono* closes the book on a different note. The reader of the lost tales, we learn from the candy store owner, has finally decided on a ribbon for his or her gift-wrapped purchase: it will be "the color of tears." This returns us again to the reader's enthrallment with the mermaid's yearning and suffering, that important element of Andersen's story that Ogawa revisits. Ogawa's portrait of an anonymous reader moved to sadness by the forgotten fairy tales reminds us that these tales offer their readers an opportunity to vicariously experience the often painful metamorphoses of the characters and in doing so to indulge in the pleasure of the self, transfigured by reading.

5

Girls Reading and Retelling "The Little Mermaid"

> If the role of the critic is to discriminate selectively and express dissent, then it is only my ability to think as a girl that qualifies me as such. As well as informing critical ability, thinking like a girl also permits the discovery of all sorts of things: "fantastic" things—things that give us a sense of pure joy, things we yearn for, and, of course, creative works of art.
>
> —Takahara Eiri, "The Consciousness of the Girl: Freedom and Arrogance"

Though the mermaid might appear to be nothing more than a lonely sailor's sex dream, she has in fact become a popular figure in children's stories, a free and magical creature who fascinates young girls in particular. Andersen's "The Little Mermaid," which hinges on birthdays and painful physical changes, cemented the tale as one of coming of age, and we have seen in chapter 2 how this tradition continues in recent analogues such the Disney film adaptation. In fact, growing-up plots feature in many more mermaid stories for preadolescent and teenage girls. As revisions such as Matsumoto's show (see chapter 4), from a feminist perspective, mermaids are not always ideal role models for young readers. However, while it is important to address these kinds of problematic fictional representations of women, concerns over what girls read can also tend to reflect histories of anxiety about women's reading habits and ignore other possibilities for girls' fairy tale transformations. Certainly, the transformations of "The Little Mermaid" discussed in this chapter, written for and about girls, evoke a myriad of pleasures and possibilities for girls' reading, transforming, and writing of fairy tales.

Here I turn to growing fields of girl studies, predominantly the Japanese field of *shōjo* (girl) studies, to gain a fresh perspective on girls' mermaid stories and in particular their intertextual pleasures. Both vulnerable and informed girl readers of fairy tales are depicted in Jane Gardam's short story "The Pangs of Love" (1983) and Joanna Russ's novel *Kittatinny: A Tale of Magic* (1978). A vivid example of the usefulness of Japanese girl theory is then seen in the responses to Yoshimoto Banana's novella *Utakata* (Bubbles, 1988). Whereas Banana's[1] work was often dismissed as shallow mass culture by members of the literary elite, scholars of the *shōjo* have produced more perceptive analyses. Their work directs me to identify the more dispersive mode of transformation of fairy tales that takes place in the novella. This in turn serves as a model for analyzing another girls' text that has been derided for its associations with mass culture: the film *Aquamarine* (dir. Elizabeth Allen, 2006), adapted from Alice Hoffman's novel of the same title (2001), which depicts girls actively enjoying a critical reading style. Finally, girl characters' cocreation of fantastic worlds is shown to be a means of expressing agency in the face of adult-male violence in Sakuraba Kazuki's novel *Satōgashi no dangan wa uchinukenai (A Lollypop or a Bullet)* (2004).

Western and Japanese girl studies provide sympathetic and imaginative tools for understanding girls' pleasures in fairy tale retellings. Anglophone studies of girlhood blossomed in the 1970s with Angela McRobbie and Jenny Garber's essay "Girls and Subcultures" (1976); the topic has since continued to gain attention from disciplines such as sociology, education, history, and media studies, though it only "coalesced" into the field of girl studies in the late twentieth century (Kearney, "Coalescing" 1). Dedicated girls' studies journals and research associations emerged from late in the first decade of the twenty-first century onward; it seems that the field will continue to grow and can certainly inform work on fairy tale retellings. However, Japanese theories of the *shōjo* (girl) are especially helpful for this analysis because of their accessibility, due in part to their cross-cultural origins and their emphasis on girls' reading communities. The *shōjo* is an imaginary figure and an idea built from texts, offering an entry point to girls' stories for nongirl, non-Japanese critics. The term is distinct from the standard word for "girl," *onna no ko* (lit. female child): *shōjo* is "a cultural construct, symbolizing a state of being that is socially unanchored, free of responsibility and self-absorbed—the opposite of the ideal Japanese adult" (Orbaugh, "Shōjo" 458). That is, the *shōjo* is an idea or a perspective rather than an actual young female. This is underlined in Takahara Eiri's concept of "girl consciousness" cited in the epigraph (and outlined in chapter 2),

---

[1] I follow the common practice and refer to the writer with her pen name (Banana was born Yoshimoto Mahoko).

which he defines by the attitudes of "freedom" and "arrogance," asserting that "being a girl has nothing to do with age or sex" (186).

In Japan, *shōjo* culture was set into motion by the widespread implementation of secondary education for girls from 1899, as a part of education reform in the Meiji period (1868–1912) of modernization and rapid social change (Honda, "Genealogy"; Honda, "Invalidation"). This established a set period of recognized girlhood and cultivated girls who could read and write. Publishers took advantage of this new market, and during the first half of the twentieth century, following successful ventures for boys, popular magazines aimed specifically at girl readers began to appear. These magazines featured illustrations, serialized *shōjo shōsetsu* (girls' novels), and readers' columns to which girl audiences contributed letters. The serialized fiction was often then published as stand-alone book volumes.

Recent *shōjo* studies works prove applicable to fairy tale works from outside Japan because of the strongly cross-cultural traditions of the Japanese girls' culture that developed from this point. Foreign girls' stories arrived in Japan as part of the influx of translated children's literature that also included classic fairy tales such as Andersen's and the Grimms'. What were to become the classic girls' novels included European, British, and North American favorites such as Frances Hodgson Burnett's *Little Lord Fauntleroy* (1886, trans. 1890–92), *The Secret Garden* (1911, trans. 1917), and *A Little Princess* (1905, trans. 1927), as well as Johanna Spyri's *Heidi* (1881, trans. 1920). The popularity of particular works in Japan was often due to the efforts of women translators, who themselves had become devoted readers after benefiting from new education opportunities for girls. This is seen in two of the most famous girls' works, Louisa May Alcott's *Little Women* (1868–69, trans. 1906) and L. M. Montgomery's *Anne of Green Gables* (1908, trans. 1952): *shōjo* studies research has demonstrated that early women translators of these novels managed to convey affection for the heroines and their stories while containing them within socially acceptable behaviors, thereby strengthening their appeal for girl readers (see Dollase, "Shōfujin"; Uchiyama, "*Akage no An*"). Such translated classics were loved alongside Japanese-authored texts, most notably the woman author Yoshiya Nobuko's wistful, girl-centered episodes collectively known as *Hanamonogatari* (Flower tales, 1920–21).

From the classic novels, girls' genres developed into various forms. There was a boom in highly literary and groundbreaking *shōjo manga* (girls' comics) in the 1970s. Famous examples continue the cross-cultural tradition through their imaginary European settings: Ikeda Riyoko's *Berusaiyu no bara* (The rose of Versailles, 1972–73) takes place around the French Revolution, and child vampires wander through eighteenth- to twentieth-century Europe in

Figure 5.1. The 2009 Kawade shobō edition of Yoshiya Nobuko's *Hanamonogatari* (Flower tales) (*left*) and one of Matsumoto Yūko's companion books to *Anne of Green Gables* (see chapter 4): *Akage no An no kyō ga shiawase in naru kotoba* (Words to make today happy from *Anne of Green Gables*) (*right*).

Hagio Moto's *Pō no ichizoku* (The Poe family, 1972–76). From the following decades, *otome-chikku* (maidenesque) and other shōjo manga of the 1980s and 1990s are known for their girlish fairy tale aesthetic, with Takase Ryō, for example, retelling Andersen's "The Little Mermaid" in "Otogibanashi no gogatsu" (Fairy tales of May, 1989) and "The Snow Queen" in *Orenji poketto* (Orange pocket, 1990). These associations of girls with fairy tales and the widespread appropriation of foreign cultures and texts remain strong traditions in contemporary Japanese *shōjo* culture. The 1980s and 1990s also saw the proliferation of novels published under imprint labels such as Cobalt (Kan and Fujimoto 22). As we shall see, it was during the economic bubble of these latter two decades that the *shōjo* was accorded a more prominent role in mainstream culture, albeit often as an emblem of the ills of consumerism. Nevertheless, in the twenty-first century, the *shōjo* form continues to expand into genres such as science fiction, fantasy, and "light novels"— entertaining short novels for young adults (Kan and Fujimoto 22).

The breadth of cultural sources for Japanese girl culture is reflected in Japanese girl studies, especially in the work of the pioneering scholar Honda Masuko. Honda traces a genealogy of *shōjo* imagery from classic to contemporary texts. She describes the visual "signs of the girl" through the fluttering movement of ribbons and frills denoted by the onomatopoeic term *hirahira* and its audible and language equivalent as "lyrical word chains" of poetic, fragmentary expression ("Genealogy" 20). Honda also defines *shōjo*-hood as liminal and suspended, a period outside adult responsibilities and physical demands, which she pictures through Eastern and Western fairy tale heroines: "Sleeping Beauty slept for a hundred years, while the girl protagonists of 'Ubakawa' (The Old Woman's Skin) and 'Hachikatsugi' (The Bowl-Bearer) covered themselves and, as pupa in their own small rooms, waited for their maturity" ("Genealogy" 36). In another work that is particularly pertinent to the theme of mermaids, *Ofiria no keifu: Aruiwa, shi to otome no tawamure* (The genealogy of Ophelia; or, Playing on death and the maiden, 1989; see chapter 1), Honda discusses texts ranging from Japanese folklore and *shōjo* manga to Australian film. Drawing on Gaston Bachelard's essays on the philosophy of water, among other diverse sources, she pursues the meanings of cultural associations between girls, water, and death.

Another important element of *shōjo* identity that Honda defines is the private, protected girls' sphere that is created by shared reading and writing practices. Honda describes, using Benedict Anderson's terms, the "imagined (or fictive) community" of girls that developed through readers' columns in 1920s and 1930s girls' magazines ("Invalidation" 14); in these columns, readers and writers of girl texts interacted through letters (see also Dollase, "Early Twentieth Century"; Dollase, "Ribbons Undone"). This tradition has continued through to manga periodicals, and the centrality of girls' textual friendships is also explored in recent critical work.[2] The treasured space created by these textual connections among girl readers extends, of course, beyond consumption practices. As seen in the mermaid transformations addressed here, girls' stories themselves place a high value on friendships between girl characters.

For fairy tale transformations, approaches that highlight girls' complex textual interactions prove especially informative. Tomoko Aoyama analyzes intertextuality in girls' fiction, identifying and defining "girls' intertextuality" as "absorption and transformation" rather than "simple imitation" or "repetition of preceding texts" ("Transgendering" 56). She shows that "parody, allusion, quotation, adaptation and travesty play significant roles" in *shōjo* genres and that "the choice of these embedded texts and particularly their transformation strongly indicate the difference from, and often the

---

[2]The theme of girls' friendship is conveyed in titles such as *Passionate Friendship: The Aesthetics of Girls' Culture in Japan* (Deborah Shamoon, 2011) and *Straight from the Heart: Gender, Intimacy, and the Cultural Production of Shojo Manga* (Jennifer Prough, 2011).

antagonism towards, the non-*shōjo*, particularly adult male culture. Thus these texts within texts help to construct and define the exclusive *shōjo* world, within which the writer, the protagonist, and the reader share the same texts woven into the primary texts" ("Transgendering" 57). Aoyama and her co-editor of *Girl Reading Girl in Japan* (2010), Barbara Hartley, compare the contemporary literary *shōjo* with the premodern dutiful *musume*, "daughter of the patriarchal family in the early and mid-Meiji Period" (2). They argue that their book shows the ways different girls, "through their layered readings of print text, visual images, and three-dimensional practice, engage in highly sophisticated and complex borrowing and interweaving of themes and ideas across texts" (5). Aoyama and Hartley further identify reading as an important strategy employed by the *shōjo* to "subvert and resist the structural marginalization attempted by both the adult male and the woman who acted on his behalf" (2). Aoyama and Hartley's approach, then, endows the *shōjo*'s liminal, girlish perspective with even more critical potential.

The critical possibilities for Japanese girl studies are reflected in the writing style of particular works. At the beginning of Honda's seminal chapter, she announces her use of two languages, one to narrate her remembered girl self and another academic voice; she hopes that "like a toccata and fugue, . . . the different keys of these two language registers resonate in mutual harmony as they express the various aspects of 'girlhood'" ("Genealogy" 20). Similarly, Kawasaki Kenko's erudite analysis of Yoshimoto Banana's writing begins with an account of her "falling in love" with the work and giggling on the phone about it with a girlfriend (50). This criticism interwoven with girl subjectivity challenges the authoritative voice of male-dominated spheres such as the *bundan* (literary establishment). This critical code, like the stories and readers' columns it explores, also addresses the reader as a fellow girl, inviting her to enjoy being a part of a girls' reading community. The reverse side of this coin, however, is the risk of an overly idiosyncratic and perhaps privileged or exclusionary understanding of girlhood. This is what makes the imaginary nature of the *shōjo* concept so important: it is a way of seeing and reading, or what Takahara calls a "girl consciousness," that different readers can adopt. The *shōjo* cannot and should not claim to be a universal representation of Japanese girls or girlhood. Both the strength and the weakness of these frameworks lie in their personalized visions. It is my argument here that embracing these liminal, uneven perspectives can open our eyes to new readings of girl-centered texts. In the mermaid stories discussed in this chapter, girl characters within the stories are shown to actively read and reimagine fairy tales, so that the author's conscious act of transformation is performed again by the characters she has created. *Shōjo* studies concepts such as girls' intertextuality provide an eloquent account of the pleasures of girls' transformative fairy tale texts.

Vulnerable and Critical Girl Readers

As discussed with regard to animated adaptations of "The Little Mermaid" (see chapter 2), the influence of fairy tales on children has proven a major concern for adult gatekeepers of the genre. In the same vein, the stories in this chapter evince a near obsession with girls' reading that reflects broader cultural preoccupations about what girls (and women) read and how these preoccupations affect them. Mermaid tales by Jane Gardam and Joanna Russ explore these concerns over children's fairy tale consumption and girls' reading habits. Russ's tale, included as a stand-alone story in Jack Zipes's collection of fairy tale revisions, *Don't Bet on the Prince*, is found within her young-adult novel *Kittatinny: A Tale of Magic* (1978). The novel's eponymous protagonist, Kit, is a reader of fairy tales and other stories. Kit leaves the everyday reality of her family home and embarks on a journey through a kind of wonderland; during her adventures, she discovers a story about a mermaid whose love of fairy tales brings her to an unhappy end. Gardam's short story "The Pangs of Love" (1983) also operates on several metafictional levels: it endows Andersen's little mermaid with a new younger sister, a voracious reader who uses Andersen's story to explain to the human prince how he hurt her sister but who nevertheless reenacts a similar story arc herself.

These images of girls who love stories form part of broader, continuing debates on the effects of reading on girls and women. Concern over female readers is expressed in both Japanese- and English-speaking contexts; one example for the latter is seen in the founding debates of the modern field of fairy tale studies. In 1970, Alison Lurie argued that some lesser-known fairy tales provide powerful female role models for readers ("Fairy Tale Liberation," reprinted in *Don't Tell the Grown-Ups*). In 1972, Marcia R. Lieberman responded that "an analysis of fairy tales that children actually read indicates instead that they serve to acculturate women to traditional social roles" (383). While Lurie and Lieberman disagree on which stories girls are reading and therefore on the effects of reading fairy tales, both seem to assume that girls are quite passively influenced by what they read.[3] Despite being tackled

---

[3] Donald Haase takes up this topic in a chapter section titled "Gender and the Passive Reception of Fairy Tales" (25–27), highlighting a gap in the research on how fairy tale reading actually affects women.

by both critical and fictional texts, this assumption has maintained a strong influence on children's literature (see Joosen 52–53). Its power may well lie in its place within broader collective anxieties about women's reading.

Fears around women's reading have been well documented in both Japanese- and English-language cultural contexts over the past two centuries. In Japan, several Meiji-period print articles attacked fiction and newspapers as putting girls at risk by exposing them to new future possibilities (Patessio 192); one such piece outlines a condition dubbed "shōsetsu-byō" (novel disease), in which novels could disturb students' emotions, leading them to forget themselves (Yamada Toshiko, ctd. in Patessio 198–99). In an overlapping period in Victorian and early Edwardian England, frequent public discussion of women's reading, though varied, included negative stereotypes about women's defenselessness against the ideas in the texts that they consumed (see Kate Flint's *The Woman Reader, 1837–1914*). Women's reading of novels and fiction was often met with especially fierce disapproval. Later, in English and European modernism, Andreas Huyssen finds that "real, authentic culture" remains a male domain (191), whereas woman are associated with mass culture and viewed as "subjective, emotional and passive" readers of poorer-quality literature (189). In the context of Japanese modernity, complex public negotiations of womanhood occurred around women's production and consumption of print culture, as has been traced in interwar women's magazines (see Sarah Frederick's close study). Debates and discussions on this topic continue, particularly around the influence on girl audiences of mass-culture novels and films such as *Twilight* (novel by Stephanie Meyer, 2005; film adaptation dir. Catherine Hardwicke, 2008).[4] In fact, I return in the next section to the way debates about girls' reading and viewing habits intensify when they concern commercial culture.

Commentary on women's reading habits extends to fictional portrayals of girl and women characters who love to read books. In *Girl Reading Girl in Japan*, Aoyama and Hartley discuss this figure of the "reading girl" in detail. Aoyama had elaborated earlier that "from the age of *The Tale of Genji* (eleventh century), the figure of the girl preoccupied with tales, stories, romance, and fantasies—all of which have been regarded as belonging to 'women and children' rather than to mature and respectable men—has appeared again and again in fiction" ("Transgendering" 56). Though these recurring reader characters are often well loved, they can also embody cultural fears over the negative effects of reading on girls and women. Aoyama notes that the

---

[4]See Lisa Bode's article on twenty-first-century depictions of "impressionable" female teen viewers and readers of *Twilight* (712).

female narrator of the eleventh-century *Sarashina nikki* (Sarashina diary) is obsessed with stories but later feels remorse over her preoccupation (57), and in Jane Austen's *Northanger Abbey*, the girl protagonist, Catherine, must learn to repudiate the gothic novels that had so captured her (56). Comparably, in Gustave Flaubert's *Madame Bovary*, romance reading leads Emma to her eventual suicide (also discussed by Huyssen). Working against this cultural backdrop of women depicted as victims and vulnerable readers, later research has highlighted such figures as that of the "pathologized woman reader" in twentieth-century Western cinema, whose reading is presented "either as a sign of her illness or a potential cause of it" (Badia 240). This history of anxious representation of female reading practices in Japanese and English is both reflected and challenged by girls' intertextual practices and pleasures in the girls' mermaid stories collected here.

The British writer Jane Gardam's (1928–) tale "The Pangs of Love" (1983), though it is seemingly targeted at adult women,[5] features a striking example of "girls' intertextuality." The short, tongue-in-cheek piece stars a younger sister of Andersen's mermaid who is "a difficult child of a very different temper" (35), cynical and tough. She breaks the rules and swims to the ocean surface before she is even fourteen (36). Gardam's youngest mermaid sister is a voracious reader, and this habit is linked with her criticism of her sister's emotion-driven actions in Andersen's story. The seventh mermaid reads Descartes (38) and says, "I've always tried to be good. . . . I've just tried to be rationally good and not romantically good, that's all" (40). This younger mermaid also meets the prince and quotes Andersen's story to him, revealing that it was not the prince's wife but actually the little mermaid who saved him from drowning. The mermaid changes "the prince" to the second person and adds her own commentary, so that she and the prince engage in a metafictional discussion of Andersen's story:

> "'Then she ducked beneath the water, and rising again on the billows managed at last to reach you who by now' (being fairly feeble in the muscles I'd guess, with all the stately living) 'was scarcely able to swim any longer in the raging sea. Your arms, your legs' (ha!) 'began to fail you and your beautiful eyes were closed. . . .'"
>
> "What antique phraseology."
>
> "It's a translation from the Danish." (39)

---

[5] It was published in a collection that included tales originally published in *Vogue* and *Women's Journal*.

The seventh sister accusingly informs the prince of the little mermaid's fate:

> "She died for love of you and you never gave her one serious thought. You even took her along on your honeymoon like a pet toy...."
> "I always loved her," said the prince. "But I didn't realise it until too late."
> "That's what they all say," said Numera Septima. "Are you a poet? They're the worst. Hardy, Tennyson, Shakespeare, Homer. Homer was the worst of all. And he hadn't a good word to say for mermaids." (37)

Gardam's mermaid seems well armed against the dangers of romance. In a literary exchange with the sea witch, the mermaid says she does not believe in falling in love, criticizing poetic accounts of romance by Shakespeare, Petrarch, and the Brownings (42). The mermaid herself is also evaluated by the third-person narrator in literary terms, described as "the kind of girl well-heeled men do run after because she never ran after them, very like Elizabeth Bennet" (42).

Despite the younger sister's wit, she is not immune to romantic love. She falls in love with the same prince as her sister and has a bathtub affair with him on the land, in her mermaid form. Later, the mermaid has nearly convinced the prince to give up his "earthly speech, clothes and possessions and power" to come and live in the sea with her, but ultimately he cannot risk "los[ing] soul and body and self-respect" if the mermaid were to leave him for someone else (44). So the prince gives up and goes home, leaving the mermaid clenching her fists but denying that she is disappointed or angry. At the end of Gardam's story, the seventh mermaid is adamant that she is a rational being who, through her experience of being rejected by the prince, is "free now—free of the terrible pangs of love which put women in bondage" (45). The story portrays women in a bind. It depicts a new generation of girls who are educated and conscious of feminist ideas and the possibility of independence. They are critical readers of romantic love in literature, but there is no new model of relationships available to them. The mermaid continues to pit herself against the romantic, restrictive love espoused in poetry, but her critical reading pleasure is curtailed by her circumstances.

Joanna Russ's more didactic young-adult fiction treats girls' reading more positively. Russ (1937–2011) came to prominence as a science-fiction writer in the late 1960s and early 1970s and was also a feminist literary critic famous for her ironic work *How to Suppress Women's Writing* (1983). *Kittatinny*, her only work for children, depicts girls' reading of fairy tales as both dangerous and empowering. The protagonist, Kit, on her mystical journey stumbles across a book with a story titled "Russalka or The Seacoast of Bohemia." It tells of a mermaid named Russalka[6] who is already a little snobbish but brought to ruin by a love of books, particularly of the book of fairy tales that has drifted into her ocean home. That is, Russalka is a vulnerable female reader of fairy tales. She is also a yearning adolescent girl like Andersen's mermaid: she becomes enamored of humans and seeks out the human prince in his castle. But on land, she cannot communicate with her voice, and her reading and writing skills are useless as no one in the prince's castle can read (47), except for a wizard, who cannot interpret her handwriting (49–50). When she keeps attempting to explain herself through notes, "eventually all her writing materials were taken away from her on the grounds [of] 'compulsive graphomania' (scribbling all the time)" (49–50).

Words such as "graphomania" that may be difficult for young-adult readers appear frequently in the fairy tale of Russalka. The sea witch's magic is "all titration, distillation, radiation, hydration, and oxidation, for the person you and I call an old witch was really a distinguished scientist" (46), and a human wizard uses magic described as "necromancy, cheiromancy, geomancy, aeluromancy, and megalopolismancy" (49). As seen in the parenthetical definition of "graphomania," explanations for the difficult vocabulary are added through asterisks, parentheses, footnotes, and asides. We learn, for example, that "'glacous' means iridescent, like mother-of-pearl" (43). The types of wizard magic just given are listed with the following footnotes, which become increasingly obscure:

1. "Necromancy" means performing magic by means of the dead.
2. "Cheiromancy" means performing magic by means of birds.
3. "Geomancy" is magic by means of the earth.
4. "Aeluromancy" is magic by means of cats (I don't know whether you use the cats or the cats do it themselves.)
5. "Megalopolisomancy" is magic by means of very large cities. (49)

The narrator of *Kittatinny* (omniscient, occasionally narrating in the first person) gives asterisked explanations elsewhere in the novel, so that it is unclear whether these explanations are provided in the "Russalka" story for Kit or by the *Kittatinny* narrator for its young-adult readers. In any case, the amusing instructive tone of the narrative opens a channel for communication between narrator and reader.

---

[6]Rusalki (sing. Rusalka) are seductive female water spirits in Slavic mythology ("Rusalka"); Russ may have chosen a spelling that has an interesting resonance with her own surname.

This connection between narrator(s) and reader(s) highlights the role that reading plays in both "Russalka" and *Kittatinny*: it has major effects on girls who do it. "Russalka" functions as a cautionary tale for Kit: it portrays reading fairy tales as dangerous for bored, bright girls, implicitly because they may absorb the damaging ideologies of romance that the tales embody. And since no one can read Russalka's writing or understand her, the story suggests that female education and knowledge, or in fact any knowledge possessed by a female, is treated as illegitimate and indecipherable by patriarchal society. Because Russalka's amphibious body is so different from the human prince's, he assumes that she is cursed. This prevents him from ever understanding her and even causes her death. When, under the prince's orders, the wizards reverse the metamorphosis spell, she reverts to her original frog-like state and dies out of water. She manages to say one word on her dying breath, directed at both herself and the prince: "Fool!" (51). Through the story of Russalka, Russ criticizes men's ignorance of female knowledge, but, as Zipes summarizes, she is also "angry at women who sell themselves for a 'romantic' vision of love" (Introduction 18).

On the other hand, in the novel as a whole, reading is essential to Kit's growth. She puts herself into the story she reads and imagines herself as the sea-maid, the prince, the sea-witch, and other characters (53). Kit's fantastical journey in her adolescence, including her encounter with Russalka's story, is the kind of fairy tale–esque girl's retreat from the world that Honda describes. It forces Kit to accept different sides of herself, so that upon her return to reality she is able to express and act on her lesbian desires and to escape a limiting domestic role. So Russ's novel describes an active reading girl, who reads a tale about a vulnerable girl who dies from reading fairy tales. *Kittatinny* clearly engages with ideas of girls as passive, malleable readers, then after that seems to provide an encouraging, supportive message that through being critical readers who engage with multiple perspectives, girls can avoid these pitfalls.

Rereading the Girl in Commercial Culture

Gardam's and Russ's stories reflect ideas about the way reading influences girls and women, but these widespread and ongoing debates become especially fraught when they concern commercial culture.[7] In Japan, from early on, women were used to symbolize intellectual concern with the structures

---

[7]In fairy tale studies, Zipes has pursued the effects of the child's (though not always the girl's particularly) changing patterns of consumption of the culture industry; see *Relentless Progress*.

of mass capitalism (see, for example, Frederick 20, on interwar magazines). With the heightened affluence and consumption of the economic bubble of the 1980s and 1990s, the figure of the *shōjo* was co-opted to represent these concerns, which negatively affected commentary on girl cultures. The case of Yoshimoto Banana's novella *Utakata* provides a strong example of a "girl" fairy tale transformation by an author whose work has been derided and ignored as shallow and commercial but has been reread in more interesting ways by *shōjo* studies scholars. This example of Banana in turn provides a useful model for the analysis of girls' reading practices in the film *Aquamarine* and for understanding the use of the girl perspective in Sakuraba Kazuki's novel *A Lollypop or a Bullet*.

In the 1980s and 1990s economic boom in Japan, the *shōjo*, as Sharalyn Orbaugh observes, "became an object of intense interest" and an image of "relentless consumerism and free play" ("Shōjo" 459), viewed in opposition to model adulthood. One of the most well-known and frequently cited pieces of research to link the *shōjo* to commercialism is the anthropologist and folklorist Ōtsuka Eiji's *Shōjo minzokugaku* (Ethnography of the shōjo, 1989). Ōtsuka studies artifacts and practices including school uniforms, girls' cute handwriting styles, and Rika-chan Barbie-style dolls to assemble an account of *shōjo* culture. The close association he draws between the figure of the girl and "cute" and "sweet" commercial products has materialized in a number of academic and mass-media discussions, often theorized under the notion of *kawaii* (cute).[8] However, Ōtsuka's and subsequent approaches transpose adult-male—often patriarchal—distress over mass popular culture onto a universalized figure of the girl. They are motivated by a perception that the girl—and by implication society—needs to grow out of this self-absorbed, unproductive existence (Robertson 158–59; Shamoon 4; Treat 375). This view is not limited to Japan; girls in the West have been similarly viewed as "exemplarily deluded consumers of culture industries" (Driscoll 267), often in need of intervention.[9]

---

[8] For more on the notion of *kawaii*, see Kinsella.
[9] In a valuable work on girls and cultural theory, Catherine Driscoll addresses the problems of this model by delineating the "girl market" and "girl culture": "An idea of the girl market is employed to sell participation in girlhood. . . . But rather than being equivalent to the girl market, girl culture names the circulation of ways to articulate identities as girls. Girl culture does not denote advertising, sales, or commercial discourse on who buys what popular cultural products, because these do not delimit circulating representations of girls or necessarily identify any social group as girls" (268). Driscoll proposes analyzing the way girlhood is constructed by those who identify with girl culture, rather than understanding girls as a stable "demographic, a group defined by shared socioeconomic characteristics" (268).

This conflation of the *shōjo* with commercial "cute" culture makes it risky to use *shōjo* scholarship in fairy tale studies. The problem has led Mayako Murai to avoid the *shōjo* paradigm in her English-language work on Japanese fairy tale transformations (*From Dog Bridegroom*). Some cross-cultural similarities in girl cultures notwithstanding,[10] Murai also argues that a *shōjo* approach risks "perpetuating the marginalization of women and the fairy tale, both of which are often connected with childishness in Japan" and in the cross-cultural arena may also work to "reinforce the Western infantilization and feminization of Japanese culture" (36). Here I address these difficulties first by proposing Japanese *shōjo* studies as simply one means for thinking about fairy tales and that these particular *shōjo* studies frameworks be applied to what are identifiably *girls'* fairy tale texts—not to all Japanese texts. Second, I engage with *shōjo* studies that do not conflate the girl with consumerism and *kawaii* but rather focus on other notions of girl identity such as reading and friendships. Mobilized in this way, a *shōjo* studies perspective looks beyond images of the girl as the quintessential consumer and enables us to see the way the selected transformations of "The Little Mermaid" interact with and are shaped by girl culture.

The case of Yoshimoto Banana offers a prominent example of certain practices of criticism of Japanese girl culture. A literary star of recent decades whose work is widely translated into English and other languages, Yoshimoto Banana (1964–) broke into the spotlight in 1989 with her novella *Kitchin* (Kitchen), launching what the *Mainichi shinbun* (Mainichi daily news) dubbed the "Banana phenomenon": "any book she published immediately became a huge best-seller; journals and magazines published special issues; interviews and dialogues were published; and celebrity idols named Banana as their favorite author" (Kondō 335). Banana's work often portrays characters recovering from painful experiences; her fans at the peak of her popularity reportedly included many young people, especially girls and women, who wanted to feel "rejuvenated or healed" (Kondō 335). Banana's young female protagonists are routinely read as *shōjo*, and her engagement with fairy tales—such as "The Little Mermaid" in *Utakata*—can only strengthen this association.

---

[10]In Driscoll's work on Western girl culture, she examines Japanese girl culture in the context of the "globalized girl market" (285). Though she notes some possibly Japan-specific elements, Driscoll also identifies similarities in the histories of Western and Japanese ideas of the girl, as well as a degree of shared participation in contemporary globalized girl markets. These commonalities point to the feasibility of careful cross-cultural deployment of culturally specific girl theory such as Japanese *shōjo* studies.

A number of *shōjo* studies scholars have shown that Banana's "girl" writing has been consistently interpreted in terms of consumer culture. Yoshimoto Banana became the face of contemporary commercial culture, and for some critics, the difference between Banana and her father, the literary and cultural critic Yoshimoto Taka'aki, exemplified a highbrow/lowbrow intellectual gap between generations (see Treat). Anxious responses to Banana's work include that of the literary scholar Masao Miyoshi, who complains that in Banana's writing, "girl baby talk drones on about the cool and abundant delights of gourmet commercial life" (qtd. in Treat 365n33). Miyoshi's patently inaccurate recollection of Banana's writing certainly indicates the strength of popular conflations of the *shōjo* with consumer culture in Japan (Treat 365n33). However, Aoyama uses the example of Banana's work to show how "girl critics" such as Saitō Minako and Kawasaki Kenko have used varied approaches to "write against the grain of male-dominated literary criticism and journalism" ("Genealogy" 45). As with other stories in this chapter, the *shōjo* studies approach of certain critics encourages a more sympathetic and careful reading of Banana's transformation of "The Little Mermaid."

Banana transforms "The Little Mermaid" in her novella *Utakata* (1988). The title itself is evocative of Andersen's tale: the word *utakata* means "bubbles," "in elegant poetic diction ... with strong connotations of ... evanescence" (Aoyama and Hartley, in Kawasaki 62n4). The girl narrator is named 鳥海人魚 Toriumi Ningyo: the name is made up of the characters for bird, sea, person, and fish, with of course the latter two—the given name—forming the word for "mermaid." Ningyo's mother tells her, "Your father and I put bird and sea and person and fish into your name so that you would be loved by everything on the earth. And as your mother, I liked 'ningyo' because I wanted you to become a woman like the little mermaid, who will discard even her life for the sake of love" (11). Andersen's tragic heroine is not everyone's idea of an inspirational namesake. In fact, Ningyo's tale is about learning to accept her parents and distinguish herself from them. Primarily she must face her discomfort with her parents' unconventional relationship: her mother is her father's long-term unmarried "mistress"; the father supports Ningyo and her mother financially but has never lived with them.

The kind of "girl" fairy tale transformation used in *Utakata* does not produce a recognizably feminist revision; it does not especially challenge the limitations of gender roles. In line with the recurring theme of father-daughter clashes in these girls' mermaid tales, Ningyo does reach the explicit realization that she is living in a "patriarchy" because of her financial dependence on her father (56). However, the drive for personal "healing" in this and other of Banana's works (see Sherif) overrides the kind of feminist reversals found, for instance, in Matsumoto's critique of Andersen's tale (see chapter 4) or in Russ's offering of an alternative female coming-of-age journey. Banana's mermaid narrates her lived experiences of a moratorium similar to what Honda describes, which ends with what Ningyo imagines as a kind of Sleeping Beauty awakening: "So this is my little story of how my mother's short travels made me feel as though I suddenly woke from a long sleep" (20). However, as Kawasaki notes, Banana's work does not conceal the girl's body during her "sleep"; it focuses on the "time of the girl" itself, rather than the girl's move to adulthood (60). Ningyo is a university student and mentions that she is not a virgin (Yoshimoto Banana 44), which might separate her from certain visions of girlhood. But all of Banana's works seem to enjoy what Takahara describes as a "girl consciousness," a perspective that is not limited to actual young females but rather a writing style that enfolds readers into the girl identity. This pervasive *shōjo* presence in Banana's writing shapes her transformation of fairy tales.

Banana's means of engaging with fairy tales in *Utakata* is debated. Ōtsuka Eiji argues that *Utakata* shares similarities with *mukashibanashi* (folk tales; see chapter 1) because Banana's girl narrators distance their narratives from the present reality through a lack of proper nouns and techniques that resemble the *mukashi mukashi* (once upon a time) opening formula ("Yoshimoto Banana ron" 205–6). However, Kawasaki is critical of Ōtsuka's structural analysis. Certainly, Kawasaki's insightful, *shōjo*-centric interpretation helps to identify the novella's more complex transformation of "The Little Mermaid." Kawasaki focuses on Banana's "blurred border" between the body and the world. In Banana's work, this blurred border, "rather than filtering this world or imposing some system of semioticization, accepts the meteorological system of the world without mediation" (61–62). As such, characters intermingle with their surrounds, seen, as Kawasaki also points out (58), in the opening passage of *Utakata*:

> After I got to like Storm, I stopped thinking of love as something like cherry blossoms or fireworks. It seemed to me more like the bottom of the sea.
>
> On a white expanse of sand with the tide's ebb and flow, I sit, fascinated, watching the blue of the far away sky melt into clear water. Here, everything is equal to the point of sadness. (Yoshimoto Banana 9; trans. Aoyama and Hartley, in Kawasaki 56)

Ningyo describes herself as at one with the ocean, the dwelling place of mermaids. In this vein, Kawasaki writes about Banana's use of climate in her writing—for example, single descriptions of "blue sky" to express emotion (61)—and advises, "We must take note of the weather conditions in Banana's world" (62).

Kawasaki's advice directs us to the character Arashi, whose name is the word for "storm." When Ningyo meets Arashi for the first time, she is attracted to him and feels close to him, so that he is a kind of prince figure in her mermaid tale. Arashi may in fact be her half brother: he was abandoned as a child on the doorstep of Ningyo's father, who denies that Arashi is his son but has raised him anyway. Significantly, Arashi is named for a violent weather system that is vital to Andersen's tale and its hypertexts. In "The Little Mermaid," a great storm arises when the mermaid first gazes on the prince. The storm might signify the prince's destructive role and the mermaid's tempestuous passion, as well as foreshadowing the mermaid's fate to metamorphose into the elements of water and air. In Kurahashi's "Ningyo no namida," when the mermaid gazes desirously at the prince, she breaks taboo and allows her monstrous body to be seen by humans, actually calling up the storm (see chapter 4). In Miyazaki's *Ponyo on the Cliff by the Sea*, the mermaid drives the storm, running on the crashing waves toward her prince (see chapter 2). Banana's text, however, removes the distance between the mermaid, the prince, and the symbolic weather—in *Utakata*, both the force and object of desire become synonymous with the storm itself in Arashi.

Just as Banana blurs characters with their surrounds, she also renders the borders between different characters permeable, so that they all "absorb" and "transform" elements of Andersen's mermaid. Though the narrator of *Utakata* is named "Mermaid," it is her mother who enacts themes of pain from Andersen's tale. Ningyo's mother contemplates suicide with a knife, recalling the stabbing pain that the little mermaid suffers with each step and the sword her sisters proffer to use to kill the prince. The characters' experience of pain in *Utakata* is, like the little mermaid's, linked closely to desire. Powerful desire is distributed to all the characters, as Ningyo realizes: "My mother and my father, and also probably Arashi and I, are the type of people who cannot close our eyes no matter what: terribly selfish and given to deep desires" (Yoshimoto Banana 90).

This desire makes the almost lovers and possible siblings Arashi and Ningyo seem to melt into each other. When they first meet, the two are aware that they are family of a sort, but each is romantically interested in the other and independently tries to confirm that they are not blood relatives. However, part of Ningyo's attraction to Arashi seems to be founded on her sense that they are related. She remarks glowingly when they first meet that he seems so familiar (22); she feels that she knows his true self and that there is no sense of strangeness (23); he seems like an old friend (25); he feels like a member of her inner, intimate circle (27); and he hugs her with "the warmth of a real brother" (48). Ningyo's attraction to Arashi is characteristic of Banana's work, which often introduces the possibility of incestuous ties and erodes traditional nuclear-family structures in various ways. Ningyo's mermaid-like yearning for her pseudobrother perhaps also reflects the narcissism that has been associated with the *shōjo* (see Treat 364); what Ningyo and Arashi's interest in each other indicates here, though, is the way desire and pain ebb and flow between these characters without impediment.

Narrative and writing also connect Ningyo and Arashi. In one scene, Ningyo begins to compose a letter to Arashi, and the writing flows and then "escalated until it read like a diary" (Yoshimoto Banana 76): Ningyo's writing to Arashi becomes writing to herself. In fact, although Ningyo is the narrator of *Utakata*, it is Arashi who plays the role of "writing boy." Arashi aspires to be an author and recounts a fairy tale–like story he wrote as a child about Mr. and Mrs. Crocodile (40–41), who are saved from debt by contributions from the local animals. Finally, Mr. and Mrs. Crocodile discover the money left for them, and as thanks, Mrs. Crocodile distributes flowers to all the creatures in the forest. Arashi says he wants to become an author who writes this kind of "boring," "happy thing" (39). His humble approach to reading and writing is noticeably different from that of the ignorant wizards who diagnose Russalka with "graphomania" in Russ's story or the anxious prince figure Ray whom we will encounter in Hoffman's *Aquamarine*, who grasps at knowledge and confidence through books. Arashi's *shōjo*-like interest in fairy tales is another example of the way the figure of the girl is diffused throughout different characters in *Utakata*.

Banana's approach to "The Little Mermaid" is transformation through dissemination. This transformative style is reflected in miniature in Arashi's fairy tale, in which the news of Mr. Crocodile's debt spreads across the forest to all the animals, and Mrs. Crocodile distributes flowers to them. Rather than parodying Andersen's tale or producing new versions of the same characters, Banana diffuses and disperses its significant elements. The mermaid's pain and desire are experienced by all the characters, and the storm that is connected with these desires emanates from the character Arashi. The *shōjo* consciousness infuses the whole novella, flowing between the boy writer, the girl narrator, and the storytelling parents who named her Mermaid. The *shōjo* perspective of critics such as Kawasaki Kenko allows us to grasp this transformative style with more clarity than do perspectives of girls as receptacles and representatives of artificial mass culture.

Girls' Communal Reading

Other works that are even more heavily invested in commercial production and privileged visions of female adolescence can nevertheless also be understood as articulations of girl-centered culture. Whereas Russ's Russalka and Gardam's seventh mermaid sister have reading habits that set them apart from their sisters and communities, the girl characters in Alice Hoffman's U.S. novel *Aquamarine* (2001) and the film adaptation of the same title (dir. Elizabeth Allen, 2006) are defined by their friendships, a central tenet of Japanese *shōjo* studies. The novel and film of *Aquamarine* present clear examples of girls' friendships and girls' intertextuality. Allen's film in particular transforms not only Andersen's "The Little Mermaid" but also other popular mermaid film traditions and portrays girls reading texts both pleasurably and critically.

Though many responses to Allen's live-action film adaptation of *Aquamarine* highlight the positive example it presents to its young viewers, others are deeply critical of its shallow, commercial leanings. Much like in certain critiques of Banana's writing, reviewers frequently denigrated *Aquamarine* in terms of commercial girls' products such as sweet, artificial foods and plastic toys (see Fraser, "Reading and Retelling"). Positive commentary on the film, on the other hand, tended to point out that—in the words of one review title—"tweens will learn a few good lessons in *Aquamarine*" (Long). While responses to *Aquamarine* depend on the reviewer's feelings about its "tween" girl audience,[11] it is striking that both negative and positive write-ups tend to return to an image of uninformed girls influenced by what they read. However, this common view ignores the way the film itself portrays girls' shared enjoyment of texts.

The novel *Aquamarine* was written by Alice Hoffman (1952–), a popular author of fiction for both children and adults, and released by the mass publisher for schoolchildren Scholastic, pitched at preteen girls. Hoffman uses fluid, simple language in this gentle story, which in some editions is accompanied by watercolor illustrations. *Aquamarine* is about two twelve-year-old lifelong best friends, Hailey and Claire, who, in the vein of Andersen's story of growing up, are on the brink two major changes: first, they are approaching the onset of their teenage years, and second, they are on the verge of being separated, as Hailey's family is moving away. The tale has the girls discover a

---

[11] As Bode finds in her work on adult responses to the teen hit *Twilight*, "it is often difficult to separate the evaluation of [the film] from the reviewer's disposition towards the teen girl audience" (709).

mermaid—the eponymous Aquamarine—and help her to go on a date with a human boy. Hoffman's novel draws quite strongly on Andersen's text: the teenage mermaid is the youngest of many sisters (32), who call for her from the ocean (52); she falls in love with the first human she sees (34) and in one moment appears to have disappeared into bubbles (56). When her love interest, Raymond, sees her, "he looked as though he was drowning" (68); like Andersen's prince, then, he narrowly escapes a sort of ocean death.

Elizabeth Allen's film adapts Hoffman's use of Andersen's story but also incorporates some contemporary mermaid tales. From Andersen's text, it retains a few symbolic elements such as tears, fireworks, and dancing. It develops the theme of adolescence, presenting Hailey and Claire as giggly, clumsy preteens who ride childish bicycles. Hailey is a tomboy, and Claire is shy: their clothed bodies are contrasted with those of the teenagers around them: their confident, blond mermaid friend and bikini-clad, tanned, popular girls. Firmly grounded in a shared girls' culture, *Aquamarine* privileges girls' friendships over heterosexual romance. As such, it can be interpreted as a girl-centered transformation of Andersen's text but also of two famous mermaid films in English: *Splash* (dir. Ron Howard, 1984), and Disney's *The Little Mermaid* (dir. Clements and Musker, 1989).[12] To begin with, all three films use fish-out-of-water comedy during the mermaid's time on land, presenting a charmingly naïve heroine. The mermaid's lack of understanding of the human world causes her, in *Splash*, to name herself after a street; in the Disney film, to comb her hair with a fork; and in *Aquamarine*, to rub fairy floss (cotton candy) against her face instead of eating it.

Much in the style of Disney's *The Little Mermaid*, *Aquamarine* inserts a father-daughter conflict into Andersen's and Hoffman's texts. Whereas the mermaid in Hoffman's story is simply fading away because she is out of the ocean, Allen's teenage Aquamarine has escaped an arranged wedding. Like Disney's mermaid Ariel, Aquamarine is given a three-day time limit on the land; she must win the prince's love to prove to her angry, sea-king father that "love exists," or he will force her to come home and marry the merman of his choosing. However, unlike the imposing King Triton in Disney's adaptation, in this girl-centered film, Aquamarine's father does not physically loom over the story but stays off-screen, making his presence known only through a storm and an angry phone call. And instead of Disney's male animal sidekicks, Aquamarine is aided by her human girlfriends in her struggles. Apart from the fearsome father, they face the problem that,

---

[12] These films are also compared by the literature and fairy tale critic Christy Williams in "Mermaid Tales on Screen: *Splash*, *The Little Mermaid*, and *Aquamarine*."

like *Splash*'s heroine, Aquamarine turns back into a mermaid when she is in contact with water (a common comic and dramatic device in mermaid stories on-screen) and also when the sun goes down.

Though the films all essentially remove physical pain from the mermaid's experience of desire and love, *Aquamarine* imagines romance differently from Andersen's and these other tales. Aquamarine does not come onto land for the sake of the "prince." Rather, she is focused on proving to her father that "love exists" to gain independence and selects Ray almost arbitrarily when she admires him kite-surfing. Hailey and Claire are also infatuated with Ray but instantly agree to help Aquamarine gain his love, because she can grant the girls' wish to stop Hailey from moving away. When Aquamarine's three days are up, she asks Ray if he loves her. He replies quite reasonably, "We've had one date.... I like you, I really really like you.... Why do I have to be in love with you today?" Audiences might compare Aquamarine's more realistic experience with that of Disney's sixteen-year-old Ariel, who has a magical white wedding with Prince Eric after they have known each other for three days of Ariel nodding and smiling without the use of her voice.

Like the girls themselves, the film's ending prioritizes girls' friendships without shunning heterosexual romance. Having failed to prove the existence of love, Aquamarine is summoned by her father back into the ocean for her arranged marriage. However, Hailey and Claire bravely jump into the roiling water to help their mermaid friend because, they explain, they love her. At this moment, the father's sea storm subsides because Aquamarine has, after all, proved that "love exists." This functions as a twist on the fairy tale romance but feels quite natural after the girls' period of intense bonding. From this supportive friendship, the mermaid gains independence and a potential boyfriend, and the human girls gain confidence and vicariously learn about dating boys. This kind of emphasis on girls' friendships has long been a pillar of literary girls' culture but has only been established in North American film more recently in the 1990s (Kearney, "Girlfriends" 130). The trend looks set to continue, with Disney fairy tale films recently acknowledging the importance of female friendships. As opposed to the 1989 animation about a little mermaid who is focused on her romance with a human prince, in Disney's 2013 adaptation of Andersen's "The Snow Queen," *Frozen* (dir. Chris Buck and Jennifer Lee), the plot is driven by the relationship between two sisters.

An important part of the girls' friendship in *Aquamarine* is the time the girls spend reading together. The film proposes an image of girls' reading that seems to address the dilemma faced by Gardam's seventh sister, who has a critical reading ability but no way to enjoy or benefit from it. In an addition to Hoffman's novel, in the film, Hailey and Claire are devoted readers of magazines for girls. They cement their friendship with Aquamarine when she joins them in a happy montage of magazine reading. Moreover, in this scene and throughout the film, the girls' reading is not associated with risk or illness but rather appears pleasurable as well as critical. When the girls finish their reading session, Aquamarine perceptively comments on the magazines' ultimately unhelpful advice on romance: "You have to be flirty but demure, devoted but not desperate, available but elusive. . . . It's so annoying! But strangely addictive." Later, Hailey also demonstrates a critical view of her own knowledge when she tells Aquamarine, "When you find love, it's really beautiful. Or at least that's what I've read in magazines." Likewise, earlier in the film, when the gob-smacked girls first see Aquamarine, she explains to them impatiently that she is a mermaid: "fabled marine creature, half woman and half fish, best known for sitting on rocks, staring in mirrors, and obsessively combing our long, beautiful hair, blah blah blah." This mermaid is self-consciously aware of how she is stereotyped within mythology. She layers this critical analysis with pleasure when she reads magazines together with her human friends. It is the girls' pleasure and willingness to engage with the magazines and other texts that enable them to enact what Aoyama describes as "the critical power of the *shōjo*" ("Transgendering" 61). This girls' critical reading pleasure might be understood as a fictional representation of the "resistance" that the cultural studies theorist John Fiske, for example, argues is enacted by real fans and consumers of popular culture. However, the girl studies scholar Catherine Driscoll points out that nonconformity has always been employed as a marketing strategy for commercial products for girls and that it is therefore not useful to assess girls' consumption of cultural products in terms of conformity or subversion (269). Regardless of how much this critical approach to texts manages to support or subvert systems of capitalist consumption, it should be understood as a part of rather than an exception to girl cultures.

In contrast to the girls, the prince figure in *Aquamarine*—more developed than Andersen's or Disney's prince—is painted in Hoffman's novel as a "reading boy" with very different motivations from the community-minded and subversive "reading girl." Hoffman's prince has read a great number of books but worries that it is still not enough for college (47); he has also "read so many books he thought he knew how every story ended" (74). In other words, different from the girls and unlike the "writing boy" Arashi in *Utakata*, Hoffman's prince seeks authority and validation from his reading. This model of masculinity, however, is apparently not compatible with

Figure. 5.2. Girls reading magazines in *Aquamarine*.

"tween" visual culture; in the film, Ray is not a reading boy at all but an outdoorsy adventurer who wants to defy his father by deferring his first year of college to go traveling. These changes across mermaid stories indicate that images of masculinity and reading would also do well to be explored from a girl studies point of view.

A *shōjo* studies approach allows a more sympathetic interpretation of the film's girl-centered transformation of Andersen's tale and other recent mermaid stories. *Aquamarine* reshapes Andersen's themes of adolescence and sexual maturity, as well as decentering the heterosexual-marriage plot that has risen from the erasure of Andersen's Christian moralizing. It instead tells a tale of girls' friendships and portrays girls' critical, pleasurable reading styles. These were mostly overlooked by reviewers, who continue to rely on images of female reading as passive and indiscriminating.

Girls' Communal Retellings

In *Aquamarine*'s sweet portrait, girls cement their friendships through pleasurable and critical *reading*. However, in Sakuraba Kazuki's novel, we find girls actively *retelling* the dark, painful elements of mermaid stories. Pleasure in reading and retelling in Sakuraba's novel is a bonding process but also a temporary refuge for girls who inhabit a much more difficult universe. The violent world of these adolescent characters brings out the tragic, destructive elements of Andersen's tale. This darkness is reflected in the title, *Satōgashi no dangan wa uchinukenai*, which literally translates as "candy bullets don't penetrate"; the alternative English title printed on the book's cover is *A Lollypop or a Bullet*. In this story, girl characters cocreate imaginary worlds through "absorbing" and "transforming" Andersen's "The Little Mermaid" and other mermaid texts. Sakuraba has stated that in her writing, she has come to use the *shōjo* perspective as a "tool to reflect the realities of many different people's lives" ("Intabyū" 81–82); in *A Lollypop or a Bullet*, she uses the perspective of a marginalized, powerless girl character to reflect on male violence.

A Lollypop or a Bullet marked Sakuraba Kazuki's leap from the realm of "light" fiction to more mainstream labels. First published in 2004 in the Fujimi mystery series imprint for young adults, it was so popular that it was republished for more general audiences under Kadokawa bunko. Sakuraba (1971–) had achieved popularity with her *Gosick* young-adult novels (2003–11) (the title is an invented Romanized word that resonates with the loanword for "gothic"). After the reportedly unexpected success of *A Lollypop or a Bullet*, she went on to be nominated for the Naoki Prize for popular literature with *Akakuchibake no densetsu* (Legend of the Akakuchiba family, 2006) and then to win with *Watashi no otoko* (My man, 2007), which was made into a film in 2014. While Sakuraba moves quite flexibly between several literary echelons—which is somewhat unusual—many of her works share certain features. Sakuraba is a girl reader and woman writer who favors girl protagonists. A self-confessed *bungaku shōjo* (literature girl; Sakuraba, "Sakka"), the literature and literary girls she creates reflect her lifelong obsession with reading and books. *Gosick* is a mystery series in which an eccentric girl detective solves puzzles from the vast library she inhabits. Two girls bond over books in *Shōjo ni wa mukanai shokugyō* (An unsuitable job for a girl, 2005; see Fraser, "Unsuitable Job"), and *Seinen no tame no dokusho kurabu* (Reading club for young people, 2007) comprises a series of episodes set at different points in history in the book club at a girls' school.

A Lollypop or a Bullet is an angst-ridden story that opens with "a newspaper article extract" reporting the discovery of the dismembered body of thirteen-year-old girl, Umino Mokuzu. The remainder of the novel is narrated in the first person by Mokuzu's friend, fellow middle-school student Yamada Nagisa. The girls first meet when Mokuzu transfers into Nagisa's class. Other students comment on Mokuzu's foreboding name: it resembles the expression *umi no mokuzu to naru*, which literally translates as "become seaweed of the ocean" and refers to death by drowning in the ocean. This name makes a dark twist on girls' culture; as the "girl critic" Saitō Minako points out in relation to Yoshimoto's choice of the penname Banana and the character name Ningyo, such absurd or overtly symbolic names are a tradition in Cobalt series girls' novels in particular (177). Here, Mokuzu's name induces her death to haunt the story. Nagisa's narrative details the events leading up to Mokuzu's gory end: we learn that Mokuzu is being physically abused by her father, and it becomes clear that he will be her murderer.

In contrast to Mokuzu's disturbing name, Nagisa's evocative given name means "beach" or "shore," while her common family name, Yamada, means "mountain rice field." Nagisa describes herself as a pragmatist who is determined "not to worry about or get involved in anything trivial that isn't related to staying alive" but only think about money and other such "real bullets" (Sakuraba, *Satōgashi* 9). She plans to finish junior high school and then leave to join the local defense forces to earn a living shooting actual bullets. Despite these differences, the girls share a marginal position and a lack of support from the adults around them and the systems these adults are supposed to uphold. They live in a small, shabby fishing town in Tottori prefecture that has, as Nagisa cynically puts it, "every single thing that city people prefer to put in the country. A nuclear power plant. A prison. A juvenile detention center. And a Self Defense Forces garrison" (18). As for their families, Mozuku's father is abusive and her mother absent; Nagisa's father is dead, her mother is busy working to make ends meet, and her elder brother is a *hikikomori*—a young recluse who does not leave his room.

Contrary to Nagisa's practical purpose of "real bullets," Mokuzu constructs her identity through fantasy. She introduces herself to her increasingly bewildered new classmates as a mermaid princess visiting the human land. In addition to her tragic name, one source of this fantasy seems to be a hit song released by her once-famous father many years ago. The lyrics tell the story of a man who falls in love with a mermaid but then—evoking Japanese folk beliefs in the miraculous properties of mermaid meat (see chapter 1)—makes her into sashimi and eats her (9). In this patriarchal script for femininity, a male narrator-subject positions the female mermaid as an object of desire and consumption. Listeners are complicit in ignoring or even aestheticizing the male singer's violence toward the mermaid. Nagisa remembers the final verse of Mokuzu's father's popular mermaid song in which the mermaid is killed, and she therefore finds it frightening. But the song is "romantic" and "elegant," still sometimes used in commercials for cars, as well as for feminine products such as makeup and pantyhose (8–9).

However, apart from Mokuzu's father's song, additional elements are woven into her *shōjo*-style invocation of mermaids, so that she and Nagisa "absorb" and "transform" the pain that is so central to Andersen's tale and other mythologies. Due to an old injury from her father's abuse, Mokuzu cannot open her legs widely apart, so that they resemble a mermaid's fused tail. This disability renders walking difficult for Mokuzu, which Nagisa explicitly compares with the stabbing pain that Andersen's mermaid experiences with each step on land (22).[13] In what seems to be Mokuzu's own added flourish, she explains bruises inflicted by her father as the effects of marine pollution on her sensitive mermaid skin. Finally, just as Andersen's mermaid turns to foam at the end of his fairy tale, Mokuzu brags that she possesses the ability to turn to foam at will and "disappear."

Mokuzu's horrible demise that opens and closes the novel is simultaneously aligned with and yet removed from delicate visions of Andersen's mermaid dissipating into the ocean. In an early episode, Mokuzu performs a magic trick for Nagisa in which she seems to vanish from her house. The next time Mokuzu disappears from her house, it is because her father has dismembered her body into small pieces and carried it out, a grotesque twist on the little mermaid dissolving into bubbles. Mokuzu's experiences of violence and her death are mermaid-like yet disgustingly visceral and real. She moves more freely in the water and fantasizes about a mermaid existence, but she is denied the death by water that Honda Masuko finds associated with the beautiful eternal *shōjo*; instead, Mokuzu's dismembered body is scattered on a mountaintop, closer to the fertile earth that Honda relates to culturally defined adult femininity (*Ofiria* 16).

A *shōjo* in desperate need of the protective cocoon that Honda describes, Mokuzu attempts to create a kind of wonderland from her suffering. This draws on a long tradition of preadolescent and adolescent girls discovering different worlds, from *Alice's Adventures in Wonderland* (Lewis Carroll, 1865) to *Spirited Away* (dir. Miyazaki Hayao, 2001) and of course Russ's *Kittatinny*. More than Carroll's Alice and her happy contemporary counterparts, though, Mokuzu's experience is comparable to that of Ofelia, the girl protagonist of Guillermo del Toro's film *Pan's Labyrinth* (2006). The violence that Ofelia experiences in real life—Spanish civil unrest under Franco—is paralleled by the grotesque, dangerous, and fantastical labyrinth that she visits, where she is assigned difficult tasks. Neither Mokuzu's nor Ofelia's world, that is, provides her with an escape from her

---

[13] Although it is beyond the scope of this book to pursue, a number of transformations connect mermaid characters with disability, including the physically abused daughter in Munro Sickafoose's short story "Knives" (1995), wheelchair-bound elderly ladies in *Ponyo on the Cliff by the Sea*, a drug-addicted, wheelchair-bound mermaid in Timothy Schaffert's short story "The Mermaid in the Tree" (2010), a disabled human girl in Robin Morgan's *The Mer-child* (1991), and a deaf girl in Jane Yolen's *The Mermaid's Three Wisdoms* (1978).

difficult life but rather warps its violence into more imaginative and magical forms. Nor does either "wonderland" provide a safe space for psychological growth, as it did, for example, for Russ's heroine, Kit. Ofelia and Mokuzu drag their traumas with them into their fantasies and indeed to their deaths. At the end of *Pan's Labyrinth*, Ofelia is shot and seems to escape to her magical "wonderland" permanently. The visual medium presents the viewer with a compelling experience of the wonderland, and its existence remains ambiguous because the story ends in this fantastical realm. On the other hand, Mokuzu's imaginary world is entirely invented and does not hold the power of vivid third-person descriptions or on-screen depictions. When Mokuzu is killed and deprived of language, her fantasy remains only with Nagisa.

Another major function of Mokuzu's mermaid identity seems to be her attempted rejection of her femininity as others perceive it. Mokuzu introduces herself to her new class using *boku*, a boyish word for "I" (Sakuraba, *Satōgashi* 12). She tells her classmates that she is a mermaid and that mermaids do not have sex distinctions: they all have feminine-looking bodies but no genitalia (13). Her attempts, of course, only draw more attention to her female body. The slender, pale, beautiful Mokuzu (12) attracts a male classmate—Kanajima—whom Nagisa later admits she was interested in. Yet any "prince" plot or its resulting rivalries are aborted. The development of friendship and understanding between Mokuzu and Nagisa is prioritized, eluding intervention by male characters. Indeed, the girls are uncomfortable with heterosexual romance. The father's control over his daughter's body explains Mokuzu's discomfort, and this dynamic is reproduced in scenes of violence between Mokuzu and her classmate and former admirer, Kanajima. Kanajima attacks Mokuzu in anger (118–19) and then blames her for provoking him (125). When he later apologizes, she refuses to forgive him because only her father has ever hit her (154). She then rips off Kanajima's shirt and beats him before they both collapse into tears (153). Nagisa looks on in bewilderment, her romantic interest in Kanajima shattered by these scenes.

Mokuzu's conspicuous discomfort with her body could imply sexual dimensions to her father's abuse, but it also fits Honda's notion of girlhood. Honda uses the *hirahira* onomatopoeic fluttering of ribbons and sleeves to capture the ephemerality and paradoxes of the *shōjo*. This transient and elusive *hirahira* movement, Honda writes, signals the girl's liminality and her "alogical and unworldly" private sphere ("Genealogy" 35–36). It is an expression of the girl's desire to withdraw from view and "slumber in the cocoon" (35), but it is nevertheless this "eye-catching movement" that "provokes" and "inevitably draws the attention of others" (34). Mokuzu's use of the mermaid to construct her identity and body is a kind of storytelling equivalent of this fluttering of ribbons and frills. It is deeply connected with ideas of the girl, and it is an attempt to retreat to a private, girl-centered world; but it nevertheless draws the attention of others. In this way, also, Sakuraba overlays a realistic narrative of violence with a *shōjo* aesthetic.

The link between Mokuzu's mermaid fantasy and her disturbing family dynamic also finds some precedence in other mermaid tales. Despite Andersen's lack of attention to the little mermaid's father, many transformations explore father-daughter relationships.[14] While mermaid tales of fathers abusing their daughters are not abundant,[15] mermaids are certainly frequently held captive by powerful and authoritative men. Disney's Ariel and Ghibli's Ponyo (see chapter 2), Kurahashi's mermaid (see chapter 4), and Gardam's seventh sister all rebel against the control of their fathers. Powerful, kindly father figures in these stories can reflect a desire to restore a patriarchy that perceives itself as threatened; in the Disney film, for instance, the rebellion of the mermaid daughter is contained into heterosexual romance. In other cases, women writers align themselves with their rebellious mermaid-daughter protagonists in their attempts to gain access to the male-dominated literary land, where their voices cannot be heard—and where, in Russalka's case, their writing is illegible. Notably, Kurahashi's mermaid rejects fatherly control of her body in the way Kurahashi herself challenged the authority of "literary fathers" in her parodic, radical writing throughout her career (see Sakaki, "Kurahashi Yumiko's Negotiations").

In *A Lollypop or a Bullet*, Sakuraba challenges the narrative perspective on male violence through a storytelling structure that emphasizes girls' agency through their friendships based on imaginary worlds. Contrasting the novel to its commercial predecessor, the *Gosick* series, Sakuraba states that she intended *A Lollypop or a Bullet* as a "small" act of "terrorism": "I created the kind of *shōjo* that appear in light novels, and I use light novel narrative voice; but what I've written is a realistic story. In a standard light novel, the *shōjo* fall into crisis and they're saved, but in this work, they're not saved. I wrote it to penetrate a real problem" ("Intabyū" 80). Sakuraba's use of the girls' story contains seeds of the *shōjo*'s subversive ability. This critical capacity is enacted through the novel's structure, in which the climactic event of violence—Mokuzu's murder—is revealed at the opening of the novel. The structure strips the traditional shocking climax or "twist" of

---

[14] This pairing is interrogated in *The Father-Daughter Plot: Japanese Literary Women and the Law of the Father* (2001) and is described by Esperanza Ramirez-Christensen in the introduction as "at once the most superfluous and the most revealing" (1).

[15] An abusive father cripples his daughter in Munro Sickafoose's short story "Knives" (1995).

its power. That is, rather than permitting hope for a happy ending or eliciting sentimental tears for a helpless victim of abuse and murder or inviting a thrilling exploration of the murderer's mental landscape, the novel portrays a complex situation in which the most important factor is not the father's psychology or Mokuzu's violent fate at his hands but rather Mokuzu's own construction of her identity and the way she develops it through her friendship with another girl.

To an extent, the novel enjoys the kind of pleasure in pain and suffering seen in other transformations of Andersen's heartrending mermaid story. The adolescent yearning of Andersen's mermaid and the bittersweet self-destruction sketched in Tanizaki's, Wilde's, and Ogawa's transformations are echoed in the angst of Sakuraba's novel. *A Lollypop or a Bullet* offers the reader dramatic immersion in the teenager's powerless railing against a violent world. Yet despite a sense of fateful, beautiful tragedy, the structure and focus of the work enables an aestheticizing of pain and darkness that remains girl centered rather than objectifying its girl protagonists.

The narrative is built around the development of the unlikely friendship between Nagisa and Mokuzu. Nagisa seems to be well liked, and Mokuzu is strange, violent, and rude. At first, Nagisa is irritated by Mokuzu's fantasizing and by her tendency to inflict emotional injuries with her words, which Nagisa labels as "candy bullets." But the girls grow close, spending time together and, for instance, meeting to swim in the ocean at night. Instead of rejecting Mokuzu's imaginings of the mermaid realm, Nagisa begins to accept them. Nagisa changes her view of Mokuzu's "candy bullets," coming to see them as just another weapon to use in the battle to survive childhood and become an adult: "I don't think I will forget that right now, when I was thirteen years old, there were other soldiers around too, fighting with their hack weapons and shooting out strange bullets here and there, and that some survived and others died" (188). Through this violent imagery, Nagisa insists that every child makes her own attempt to fight to survive. Through this focus on the girls, the powerful father is—like Aquamarine's off-screen sea-king patriarch—denied the role of protagonist of Sakuraba's story.

If father-daughter relationships have been one common thread among these girls' mermaid tales, then another is the girl's association with candy—as in Sakuraba's title. The abundance of candy in "girl" literature might move us to add it to Honda's "signs of the girl." *Aquamarine* features girls eating candy several times: the mermaid first meets the human girls when she eats their gummy worms, and she later tries fairy floss and discovers ice cream. Candy is also frequently seen in Higami Kumiko's girlish artwork, probably inspiring Ogawa Yōko's use of the "swan candy" as the central image of her candy store frame story for the *Otogibanashi no wasuremono* collection discussed in chapter 4. As noted, Ogawa in her postface likens the consumption of her fairy tales with eating candy with unexpected flavors; in fact, we will see a similar image of reading as eating sweet food in Nonaka Hiiragi's commentary on fairy tales in chapter 6.[16] In the title of Sakuraba's novel, *A Lollypop or a Bullet* (or the literal translation of the Japanese title, "Candy bullets don't penetrate"), Sakuraba juxtaposes this association of girls and candy with the hard, real violence of bullets. This suggests a more serious intent and greater danger to girls' culture than commercial *kawaii* market images of "candy" would generally invoke. Sakuraba's "candy bullets" indicate that the girl character's transformation of the mermaid tale is her act of self-defense and her assertion of her own "girl" agency.

A Lollypop or a Bullet is therefore another text that features girl characters actively reading and retelling mermaid mythologies together. Sakuraba finds the ambiguous figure of the mermaid the perfect fit for girls who are uneasy with cultural constructions of heterosexuality and femininity. The mermaid allows her girl characters to discover an intense bond that momentarily eclipses patriarchal power. However, while fairy tales here are a powerful tool in girls' bonding and their construction of their identities, they remain "sweet," feeble weapons against the physical violence of an adult man.

Sakuraba's unhappy protagonist, Mokuzu, is not the only girl figure to feel the mermaid's appeal. Andersen's tale of painful physical transformation and leaving the family home has been transformed into a range of girls' stories of growing up. The constructions of gender in these girls' transformations of "The Little Mermaid" take on greater significance in relation to broader discourses about girls' consumption of texts. Whether girls' texts—including fairy tales—are judged to provide positive or negative role models for girls (whatever that means for the individual critic), they are frequently framed in terms of "influence." Debate about the influence of reading on girls is tied up in social anxieties over women's reading and in the overuse of the "girl" as a convenient icon for mindless consumption of mass culture. A study such as this that does not observe the way girls actually read and respond to texts cannot make any claims about real girls' reading styles. What I can argue here is that there are numerous ways to imagine

---

[16]Since fairy tales and folklore often depict girls and women eating, research using work on the relationships of food, orality, and literacy in Western fairy tales (for example, Louis Marin's *Food for Thought*, 1986) and on food and gender in literature (for example, Tomoko Aoyama's *Reading Food in Modern Japanese Literature*, 2008) could further enlighten studies of the construction of gender and reading in Japanese and English fairy tale transformations.

and interpret girls' reading beyond the reductive understandings that continue to be rehearsed. We might add that, paradoxically, if girls really do absorb their reading material in passive, unquestioning ways, they would also absorb active and critical modes of reading that are presented to them in works such as these transformations of "The Little Mermaid." The images of girls reading and retelling in these tales themselves contradict many of the critics' dismissals of them.

Pleasurable, active approaches to texts are vital to girl cultures. These transformations of "The Little Mermaid" and its images of desire and pain demonstrate that examining depictions of reading and retelling, and especially of intertextual and critical pleasures, can aid our understanding of why and how fairy tales are transformed. They also show that for stories for and about girls, the Japanese figure of the *shōjo* provides an apparatus through which to better identify and analyze these pleasures.

6

Beyond Happily Ever After in Women's Post–Fairy Tale Transformations

> I won't turn to sea foam. That story, that kind of thing, well that's an old story, and it's fantasy, and the medicine I took is a new medicine, and I'm a child of today.
>
> —Watanabe Peco, "A Mermaid of Today"

A recent collection of short manga episodes by the contemporary woman artist Watanabe Peco, titled *Henshin monogatari* (Tales of metamorphosis, 2008), opens and closes with a two-part story that transforms "The Little Mermaid." In Watanabe's opening episode, titled "A Mermaid of Today" ("Heisei ningyo"; lit. Heisei-period mermaid), a girl mermaid named Rin acts on her desire for her prince. Rin has just left *shōjo*-hood and come of age. She explains that her ancestor was the model for Andersen's mermaid but that Rin's own metamorphosis to human was not equally painful because—as quoted in the epigraph—the fairy tale world has modernized. The gentle, bright episode closes with the sense that Rin will soon win the affections of her chosen human prince. Then, following six other stories, Watanabe's collection finishes on a second installment about Rin, "Henshin fuzen" (Metamorphosis malfunction). Rin and her prince are living beyond their "happily ever after": they are now married with a daughter. Rin is dealing with life as an ex-mermaid; Rin's husband, due to stress and guilt over his father's death, is experiencing erection problems, the "metamorphosis malfunction" of the title. Together, these two parts neatly capture the transition from the girls' texts of chapter 5 to the women's post–fairy tales of this chapter. Just as Watanabe's mermaid tale moves from a girl fairy tale reader in the first installment to the anxieties of modern adulthood in the second, so we move now from the girls' intertextuality of chapter 5 to women's transformations about adult relationships and gender performances.

The first transformation discussed, "Gill Girl," is an episode of the U.S. television series *Dark Angel* (prod. James Cameron, aired 2000–2002), created by both men and women. The two novels were both written by Japanese women: Nonaka Hiiragi's *Ningyo-hime no kutsu* (The little mermaid's shoes, 1994), and D[di:]'s *Sentō no ningyo-hime to majo no mori* (The little mermaid of the public bath and the witch's forest, 2008). All three have women protagonists. And as "post–fairy tales," these transformations all position their plots as occurring *after* the publication of Andersen's "The Little Mermaid." That is, similar to Jane Gardam's "The Pangs of Love" (see chapter 5), characters in these texts explicitly name "The Little Mermaid" as a work of literature and use it with specific meanings in their own texts. So the events of these narratives are set against Andersen's story positioned as an existing—and past—literary text. Though the stories are not sequels to Andersen's tale, they also consider what may occur in adult women's lives beyond the "happily ever after" of union with a prince. This emphasis on women's lives after the ending of a fairy tale is one of the several meanings of the "post-" appellation; these transformations are not only post–happy ending, but post-Andersen, postmodern, and postfeminist.

These texts also share an interest in women's bodily and creative agency, which is articulated through their portrayal of the protagonist as a storyteller, performer, or artist. Andersen's story may encourage these themes: some thinkers interpret "The Little Mermaid" as an allegory of the difficult experiences of authorship. Jack Zipes, for instance, writes that the tale of the mute mermaid captures the predicament of an artist whose patron or audience—the prince—does not recognize or value her performance (*Hans Christian Andersen* 112). Barbara Fass, also, discusses the way the artist protagonist of Thomas Mann's *Doctor Faustus* identifies with the little mermaid, situating this allusion within the theme of "the artist's painful endeavor to locate his place within a society hostile or at best indifferent to the creative imagination" in nineteenth- and twentieth-century Anglo-European literature (291). And in an essay linking the mermaid's muteness with the pain in her legs, the critic and avant-garde writer Kanai Mieko refers to both "The Little Mermaid" and other tales such as "Aunty Toothache" and "The Wild Swans" to argue that Andersen's depiction of pain and of taboos against speaking encapsulates the difficult experience of storytelling itself ("Anderusen no Shitsū" 50–51). Elsewhere, Kanai writes that it is possible to interpret the mermaid's pain and voicelessness as "the pain of an unrequited love that is not allowed to be confessed" ("Anderusen no ashi" 281). But Kanai goes on to suggest another dimension: "In these tales, the passion of love is met with the doubled severity of pain in almost self-inflicted punishment. For example, if we compare the mermaid's experience with the nightmarish punishment the young poet inflicts on himself in 'Aunty Toothache' . . . (and this is a punishment for the act of writing poetry, which might be another experience of being controlled by one's passions), we become able to read from Andersen's work the fate of the poet itself" ("Anderusen no ashi" 281). In Kanai's interpretation, artistic creation is allowing passion to control one's body, and Andersen's protagonists must punish themselves for this taboo act by inviting pain on their bodies. Likewise, transforming "The Little Mermaid" enables the authors of post–fairy tales to draw a link between the woman protagonist's pain with her anxieties about her agency and her role as an artist.

This interest in the function of pain also forms part of a greater preoccupation in these texts with gendered bodies. Unease and ambivalence about gendered bodies, the changes they undergo, and the characters' control over them underpin their engagements with the hybrid, half-woman body of Andersen's mermaid and her shift from home to the alien human land. Moreover, in these texts, unlike the girls' stories of chapter 5, female bodies share the spotlight with male bodies. But whereas stories featuring male bodies such as Wilde's, Tanizaki's, and Abe's (see chapter 3) questioned "humanity" (= masculinity) through prince characters against othered mermaids-as-objects, these women's texts problematize the gender inscribed on all sorts of physical bodies. Female but also adult-male bodies are "troubled," as with the erection problems experienced by the "prince" in Watanabe's manga. Men characters in these transformations evince allergies and rashes, superpowers and disability, and undergo scientific experiment.

Given this disruptive approach to bodies, any pleasure that characters are depicted as experiencing in these stories seems ambivalent at best. The transformations, though, invite readers and consumers to take pleasure in the dystopian or difficult conditions their characters face. The texts further appeal to the reader through engaging with fairy tales: all these transformations undertake extended and postmodern intertextual play with multiple fairy tale texts and traditions. This is mostly enacted by their female protagonists, who negotiate the different versions of fairy tales available to them, often using the tales to explore their experiences of sexual objectification, sexual autonomy, storytelling, artistic agency, and performing gender. The images of gender here cannot be described as entirely feminist, revisionist, or parodic but are rather more woven with ambiguity and uncertainty. This is tied to the postmodern, postfeminist, "post–fairy tale" form.

The creation of a post–fairy tale in itself rejects the finality of the "happy ever after" and even any kind of clear-cut resolution typical of the fairy tale.

These tales and their female protagonists are in-between and uncertain, as we will first see manifested physically in the hybrid, science-fiction body of the protagonist in the *Dark Angel* series. The very human protagonist of Nonaka's novel, on the other hand, uses Andersen's tale to understand her roles as wife and mother, only to find herself left in a suspended state of "waiting." Finally, the third novel's protagonist, named Fū, also refers to fairy tales such as Andersen's to structure her perceptions and experiences of contemporary city life, and we leave her more lost and confused than when the story began. The relationship that these transformations have with "The Little Mermaid" is as open as their endings. Despite explicitly naming Andersen's story as a central source text, these works tend to spiral away from it, using Andersen's tale as a springboard to a wider engagement with the fairy tale form. This could well be a general characteristic of recent postmodern fairy tale transformation.

Hybridity and Happy Endings in Post–Fairy Tales

In an episode titled "Gill Girl" (season 2, episode 8, dir. Bryan Spicer, writ. Marjorie David), the postdisaster science-fiction series *Dark Angel* (prod. James Cameron, aired 2000–2002)[1] finds in the mermaid the perfect vehicle for its sustained interest in separated families, hybrid bodies, and women's agency, objectification, and sexual control. *Dark Angel* is set in Seattle in 2019, in an economic depression caused by an "electromagnetic pulse" that globally disrupted electrical power, destroying all computer records and changing the nature of society. This is therefore a "post-tale" of a dystopian near future beyond the current comfort of the developed world. The eponymous action heroine[2] is a young woman with the masculine-sounding name Max, who has selected the surname Guevara in what may be a reference to the legendary Cuban revolutionary (Jowett 33; McConnell 188n34). Max is a genetically modified human who was created and trained as a "secret weapon," with enhanced physical powers and analytical abilities. At nine years old, she and a group of children escaped their training facility, Manticore (named for a legendary hybrid creature usually depicted with a lion's body and a human head). Now around nineteen years old, she has teamed up with her computer hacker and cyber-journalist love interest,

---

[1] The series is listed under Cameron's name in the Works Cited. Quotations and mentions from specific episodes are cited in the text with the season number and episode number.
[2] James Cameron (1954–), one of the series's creators, also directed films with some of the most famous female action figures of Hollywood film in recent decades, including Ellen Ripley in *Aliens* (1986) and Sarah Connor in *The Terminator* (1984).

Logan, to battle corrupt powers and criminal gangs, while constantly evading recapture by Manticore. Max also seeks to uncover her origins—her mother—and works to reunite her "family," the other "transgenic" children who escaped with her and were soon parted.

This story of hybrid bodies is a blend of genres and traditions. The urban dystopian landscape and the theme of technological modification of human bodies have led to the series being categorized as part of the "cyberpunk" science-fiction genre. Cyberpunk is one of the genres favored by postmodernist fiction (Nicol 164), but it also links *Dark Angel* to a contemporary Japanese imaginary. There is a complex history of cyberpunk textual interactions between Japan and the West (see Takayuki Tatsumi's *Full Metal Apache: Transactions between Cyberpunk Japan and Avant-Pop America*), but relevant here is the fact that many Japanese popular-culture products express a cyberpunk aesthetic that has been adopted by Western texts. Douglas McGray, in his influential article on Japan's "gross national cool," names *Dark Angel* as one of the U.S. cultural products to "draw heavily" on Japanese manga and anime (46). I would add that the imagery of Max—sensuously feminine and vulnerable yet tough—seems to be especially drawn from the *sentō bishōjo* (beautiful fighting girls) of Japanese anime and manga (not necessarily cyberpunk) traditions, who are "beloved precisely for the purity, frailty, and sweetness they evince at the height of battle" (Saitō Tamaki 93).[3] Thus, though *Dark Angel* has very little direct connection with individual Japanese texts, the series and the portrayal of Max in particular reflects a contemporary fantasy fiction environment that is informed by Japanese popular-culture forms.

The episode of *Dark Angel* that forms a post–fairy tale transformation of "The Little Mermaid" is titled "Gill Girl." In it, Andersen's tale as well as the more recent Disney animated adaptation provide a means for Max to frame her experiences of otherness and her search for a happy ending. The mermaid's hybrid body and the shadow of ambiguity it casts over her gender and sexual identity finds a good fit with the series's postfeminist construction of women's pleasure. Postfeminism here is a conceptual framework

---

[3]Saitō Tamaki defines beautiful fighting girls as adolescent. Max is slightly older and tougher; she wears leather and rides a motorbike. But she is young looking, not muscular or "butch," as Saitō describes traditional European and North American action heroines (7). Also, like the beautiful fighting girl, Max is sexualized and vulnerable: for instance, she is periodically rendered physically helpless by seizures (season 1, episodes 4 and 16). A similar figure, which has been identified in "culturally hybrid" texts that are part of international visual popular culture, is Sharalyn Orbaugh's "busty battlin' babe" ("Busty Battlin' Babes" 226). Max's government-manufactured body fits with Orbaugh's description of powerful female bodies that have been artificially manufactured to work for male creators or state organizations (226).

that describes the attitude that rejects or ignores the ideals of earlier feminist movements. The postfeminism framework is defined as one that exposes the "undoing" and "undermining" of 1970s and 1980s feminism that occurs in many recent popular texts (in English) that nevertheless position themselves as entering into an informed dialogue with these feminist ideas of the past (McRobbie 27). Projecting an image of this kind of engagement with female empowerment, *Dark Angel* offers its viewers pleasures that are structured around ideas about gender that can be confining and "troubling" at the same time. This contradictory ability gives the series some flexibility to amuse a diverse audience.

"Gill Girl" establishes itself as post–fairy tale when it introduces Andersen's fairy tale as an existing published work in the opening scenes. Max helps Logan babysit his niece, and in order to calm the excited girl, Max reads "The Little Mermaid" to her from an illustrated book. When they run out of time before they reach the ending, the girl asks, "Did the mermaid ever get to see her family again?" and Max simply revises the story, replying, "Yeah, and they all lived happily ever after." Following this introductory interlude, the episode plays out an encounter with the science-fiction version of a mermaid: a human woman whose body is genetically modified to live in water and breathe with gills. Throughout the whole episode, Max and other characters continue to demonstrate awareness of the different hypertexts of "The Little Mermaid" and its transformative possibilities, expressing their preferences for particular versions. In this sense, the episode is a postmodern text that, as Linda Hutcheon puts it, "takes the form of self-conscious, self-contradictory, self-undermining statement" (*Politics* 1).

The story of "Gill Girl" progresses through a number of events frequently found in mermaid tales and traditions. The genetically modified mermaid is first discovered when she is caught in a fishermen's net as in Wilde's tale (see chapter 3); the fishermen then sell the mermaid to a strip club, where she is put on display in a large water tank, shown to the public just as mermaid mummies and other curiosities were shown in the Edo-period (1603–1868) exhibitions and nineteenth-century Western freak shows (see chapter 1). The mermaid's male counterpart—her mate—then comes to find her. Max and her associates encounter the merman and collude to rescue the mermaid before she is captured by Manticore agents; at Manticore, she would be observed or dissected by scientists, another fate that frequently threatens mermaids.[4]

---

[4] See, for example, Ron Howard's film *Splash* (1984) and Jonathan Shiff's Australian girls' television series *H20 Just Add Water* (2006–10).

In response to these events, Max and Logan use Disney's animated adaptation of "The Little Mermaid" as shorthand to describe the happy ending they aim for, also indicating their own need to overcome the impediments that prevent them from becoming romantically involved. Max is especially insistent about the place of her own story within different fairy tale forms. Early on, Max and Logan debate the way Max changed Andersen's ending for the little girl listener:

MAX: Why do writers always have to go for the tragic endings anyway? What's wrong with a happy ending once in a while?
LOGAN: I prefer the Disney version myself.

Later, Max again asserts her wish for a happy ending by holding the picture book in her hands as she tries to convince Logan to undertake the high-risk mermaid-rescue operation. Then at the climax, she rashly dodges bullets to save the mermaid, explaining, "I'm going for the Disney version." In this way, Max sets the Andersen and Disney architexts at odds, both "blending" and "scorning" the aggregate fairy tale architext, as her bleak, "broken world" demands her to (Genette, *Architext* 83).

Despite Max and Logan's confidence that they are able to play out their preferred version of the mermaid tale, the meaning of the "mermaid" label itself is repeatedly contested. That is, Max insists on naming the fish-hybrid transgenic a mermaid, making a sentimental allusion to both Andersen's story and to Disney fairy tale films. On the other hand, the antagonist, a ruthless Manticore agent, denies the "gill girl" her fairy tale labeling when he contemptuously dismisses the fishermen who caught her as "idiots" for believing her to be a mermaid. Interestingly, apart from Max, the other parties to name the transgenic a mermaid are these fishermen who sell her and the touts at the strip club that buys her. These male characters utilize the sexualized mermaid figure as a marketing strategy in their commercial transactions. Thus, the "Gill Girl" episode generates conflict through introducing contesting meanings and possibilities for the "mermaid" label (romantic female agent versus marketable commodity versus ignorant folklore) and through alluding to different endings of famous mermaid architexts (literary tragedies versus Disney romances). Furthermore, the events of the episode often clash with both the elements of the classic fairy tale and the conventions of Disney fairy tale films. That is, while Max and Logan express a preference for one hypertext of "The Little Mermaid" and frame their struggle as a fairy tale, in this particular episode that transforms fairy tales, the genre itself is put into competition with the gothic, action, and cyberpunk texts that combine in the series.[5]

The Hybrid's Postfeminist Pleasures

For Max, there is a great deal at stake in determining which label is affixed to the mermaid's body and in determining which version of the fairy tale Max and the mermaid are enacting. As the eponymous "dark angel" of the series, Max's contradictions and ambiguity as a "beautiful fighting girl" and a genetic hybrid are reflected and magnified in the body of the mermaid. Max's and the mermaid's contradictory bodies and identities seem to limit the pleasures available to them, but their limited circumstances form a vital part of the pleasures—visual and otherwise—that are offered to consumers of their stories.

In "Gill Girl," the mermaid-like contradictions of Max's femininity coexist through the series's postfeminist usage of the visual medium. Like the captured mermaid put on display in the strip club, Max is the object of a powerful and dehumanizing male gaze, but like the mermaid's siren ancestor, she utilizes her sexual attractiveness as a weapon against the same male powers. This is played out most obviously in the scene that shows Max enter the male space of the strip club in order to rescue the captive mermaid. Laura Mulvey's famous analysis of this kind of strip-club scene commonly found in Hollywood film helps to untangle the dynamics of the gaze at play here. In "Visual Pleasure and Narrative Cinema," Mulvey explains,

> Traditionally, the woman displayed has functioned on two levels: as erotic object for the characters within the screen story, and as erotic object for the spectator within the auditorium, with a shifting tension between the looks on either side of the screen. For instance, the device of the showgirl allows the two looks to be unified technically without any apparent break in the diegesis. A woman performs within the narrative, the gaze of the spectator and that of the male characters in the film are neatly combined without breaking narrative verisimilitude. (33)

The strip-club scene in "Gill Girl" begins as Mulvey describes it, as camera techniques invite an objectifying gaze on the female body from television

---

[5]For a reading of Max as a gothic heroine, see McConnell. Jowett describes the series's combination of science-fiction, gothic, and action genres in "To the Max."

viewers who align with strip-club patrons and male staff. Max, not allowed access to this male-only venue through the front door, is instead forced to pose as a stripper to gain entry, creating an opportunity to showcase her body.[6]

At this point, though Max only ever cites the happy ending of the Disney film, she could easily be taking advice from Disney's outrageous sea witch Ursula to use her "body language" to achieve her purpose: we watch as she deliberately switches into a sexy persona and walks with an exaggerated sway. The camera zooms in on her backside in tight jeans and then shifts to slow motion as she removes her outer shirt; the moment is replayed several times, capped off with a shot of an expression of calculated seduction on her face. Cinematic techniques encourage the viewer to enjoy Max's body and sex appeal, but the scene also implies—as Ursula's song and dance had in the Disney film—that sexuality and female sexual attractiveness are matters of performance. Here, Max performs performance, so to speak: she poses as a stripper. When Max has gained entry to the club, the first shot shows the female performers onstage from below, encouraging continuity of the gaze of television audiences and strip-club customers. However, in Mulvey's terms, there is an apparent "break in the diegesis" when we see Max looking worriedly at the captured mermaid and then marching purposefully toward her, minus the suggestive strut. Having proved her ability to play the stripper role, Max then demonstrates her disdain for it, interacting with her male friends in the club in a decidedly unsexy manner.

The scene therefore showcases Max's sexual attractiveness for the audience's "visual pleasure" while simultaneously inviting them to identify and empathize with her as the fully realized protagonist of this series. She is endowed with a postfeminist version of agency that has been described as the figure of "the do-me feminist," who deliberately utilizes her attractiveness and sexuality to her own ends (Genz and Brabon 92). This postfeminist stance, in which "raunch culture and do-me feminism blend the sometimes conflicting ideologies of women's liberation and the sexual revolution" (Genz and Brabon 91), allows for the simultaneous objectification and empowerment of a protagonist such as Max.

The series's intense interest in sexual objectification and agency is underlined in other episodes that complicate the protagonist's own experiences of desire. We know that Max—who begins the series as a cat burglar—owes

---

[6]This cheap device is common in the series. Max poses as a prostitute or stripper in several other episodes (season 1, episodes 1 and 4) and at one point exposes her breasts to distract an opponent (season 2, episode 16).

her agility to the feline DNA used in her creation. One side effect is a breeding cycle that periodically sends her into heat. Portrayals of this event shift between humor and intensity as Max experiences a clamoring instinct to mate but attempts to repress encounters that do not meet her everyday emotional needs or reflect her usual attractions (season 1, episodes 3 and 21). In the "Gill Girl" episode, we learn that the mermaids lay eggs, a process that Max may view as more desirable than her own troubling breeding cycles, which cause her body to rage beyond the kind of control she demonstrates with it at the strip club.

Unlike the girls' texts of chapter 5, these women's post–fairy tales do not focus their interest only on female bodies. In *Dark Angel*, different postfeminist visions of femininity are refracted through Max herself and then doubled in the mermaid figure, but competing models of masculinity are split into separate male characters: namely, the love interest Logan, Max's fellow transgenic escapee Alec, and the merman. The first model is found in Logan, an intelligent and articulate dissenter against the oppressive regime. The prince counterpart to Max's mermaid, he has refined tastes in art and food but rebels against the patrician values of his wealthy, privileged family. Nevertheless, Logan struggles with his masculine identity, for most of the series frustrated at being confined to a wheelchair by an old injury. He repeatedly attempts to overcome his disability, for example, creating mechanized leg braces that allow him to jump and run.[7] In this respect, Logan somewhat matches Genz and Brabon's typology of the "postfeminist man," who is "slightly bitter about the 'wounded' status of his masculinity" (143) and "frequently relies upon a prosthetic appendage to his masculinity . . . in order to disguise the fact that he is no longer whole and hegemonic" (133–34).

Logan's literally damaged masculinity is contrasted with that of another prominent male character, Alec. Max's fellow genetically modified transgenic, Alec is an irreverent alpha male and the one to irritatingly convince Max that she must pose as a stripper to rescue the mermaid. As a hybrid, Alec's manufactured body might also be considered, like Logan's, "no longer whole and hegemonic," but it is, on the other hand, extremely powerful and capable. Alec's attractive body is, like Max's, displayed for the viewing pleasure of the television audience, but he is not subjected to the same objectification by other characters from within the plot. Finally, the merman character, who appears only in the "Gill Girl" episode, represents a third type of masculinity. He shares some features with Ogawa

---

[7] Like Andersen's little mermaid, he feels pain in his legs. Other transformations also use mermaid figures to depict disability and desire for free movement—see chapter 5, note 13.

Yōko's merman (see chapter 4): he does not speak, and his body—with gills—disables him on human land; but he is still determined to rescue his loved one. Lacking aggressive, macho masculinity, he is pale and not as muscled as Alec or Logan. Since these mermaids are revealed to be an egg-laying species, the merman does not seem to play a human-male role in reproductive sexuality. Although he does not have a fish tail and therefore presumably has human male genitals, he seems to be emasculated—lacking a voice and an active sexual role—in the way that other mermen such as Ogawa's are. That is, in this episode, each of these models of masculinity is found to be somehow problematic. Further, they cannot easily coexist. Unlike Max and the mermaid, the merman and these two other characters do not bother to communicate, and though Logan and Alec may be allies, they never become friends. As such, the series is interested in a range of gendered physical forms as part of its characteristic cyberpunk insistence on artificial interference that renders the human body out of its inhabitant's control.

Whereas male characters are disconnected and disparate, Max and the mermaid connect with each other through shared bodily experiences. Posing as a performer in the strip club, Max gains backstage access to the mermaid's tank. Though this mermaid, like Andersen's, cannot speak, the two are able to communicate through the military hand signals they both learned at Manticore. Max's understanding of the mermaid firstly serves to highlight the evil nature of the Manticore agent antagonist, who refuses to call the girl a mermaid and refers to her as a "thing" and "it." He ignores the mermaid's dolphin-like chatter and obnoxiously shouts "English!" at her. Yet Max and the mermaid's ability to communicate seems to be facilitated by something more than their shared manufactured hybridity. Significantly, Alec, a male transgenic who also knows the hand signals and has access to the tank, does not seem to communicate with the mermaid. Perhaps Max's romantic fairy tale notions make her more willing to listen. Or perhaps Max and the mermaid occupy the same role: in the strip club, their positioning as reluctant female performers on display to the male gaze deepens their bond.[8] Beyond their animal origins and in-betweenness, Max and the mermaid are connected by their need to deal with both the fetishizing male gaze and the destructive figures of "science" that threaten to appropriate and dissect their feminine, othered bodies.

---

[8]Unusually, the series portrays sex work such as stripping and prostitution sympathetically but without sentimentalizing it. Elsewhere, Max expresses solidarity with sex workers, defending them against extortion and calling them "my sisters" (season 1, episode 10).

Figure 6.1. Max next to the captured "gill girl" in *Dark Angel*.

In *Dark Angel*, the visual medium and the postfeminist approach enable the creation of a sympathetic and sometimes pleasurably empowered protagonist, who inhabits an attractive body that is displayed for the "visual pleasure" of the audience. The tensions of this hybridized body are articulated through the figure of the mermaid, who is literally put on display in the male space of the strip club. However, the mermaid is able to escape, and her story is neatly concluded at the end of the "Gill Girl" episode: she and the merman happily return to the ocean together, with Max and Logan farewelling them from the shore. In contrast, just as Logan's young cousin departs before Max can finish reading "The Little Mermaid" to her, in this episode, the audience leaves Max and Logan halfway through their story, their problems still looming. The *Dark Angel* series itself ends on an unresolved note: the existence of hybrids is exposed, and they must prepare to go into battle with a human world that treats them as "freaks." The "Gill Girl" episode, then, features a postmodern, multivoiced, self-conscious reading and retelling of Andersen's story, in which the tragedy of Andersen's self-sacrificial, othered heroine competes with Disney's ordered romance, but neither script reaches its conclusion.

The Mermaid's Legs

Despite differences in medium, genre, and cultural context, like "Gill Girl," Nonaka Hiiragi's realistic novel *Ningyo-hime no kutsu* (The little mermaid's shoes, 1994) presents another example of a female protagonist who uses fairy tales to understand her own life. More specifically, the protagonist, Mariko, uses the imagery of the mermaid's legs and fairy tale shoes—as seen in the title—as well as a motif of food, often with fairy tale undercurrents. Mariko is not as confident as Max about her power over the fairy tale; any pleasures she takes in this process of fairy tale framing are ambivalent at best. Yet as we shall see, in a postface to the novel, Nonaka as the author then invokes fairy tale structures in a different way, encouraging a rereading of Mariko's text and a new perspective on the pleasures of this particular fairy tale transformation.

Nonaka (1964–) is a reasonably popular writer who has not been widely discussed in the critical arena. Her debut prize-winning work, *Yomogi aisu* (Mugwort ice cream, 1991), was based on her experience as a Japanese woman married to an American man and living in the United States, perhaps reminiscent of the little mermaid's experience in a foreign land when she has lost language. Nonaka's subsequent move back to Japan saw works set in her native country, and her transformation of Andersen's story forms part of this latter category. The protagonist of *Ningyo-hime no kutsu* is a young woman named Mariko who begins as a circus performer famed for her beautiful legs. Then she becomes pregnant and happily gives up her starring role in order to marry and have the child. The third-person narration skips between flashbacks to Mariko's childhood and her married life from her wedding up until the time when her daughter is three years old. It is therefore a post–fairy tale plot that explores events after the typical "happy ending" of the wedding.

Ningyo-hime no kutsu opens by zooming the narrative camera in on Mariko's legs, which are to inform the titular "shoe" motif used throughout the novel. Mariko, like Max, is positioned as a literal performer for an objectifying male gaze who exerts some control over her own sexuality. In the circus, she performs the "rolling globe," in which she lies on her back and spins a large globe on the soles of her feet. Mariko is a spectacle in "shocking pink," "gold lamé," and "spangles" (7), her popularity due more to her beautiful legs than her skill: men line up and comment that she is more arousing to watch than a talented stripper is (8), and the audience carry themselves into the circus tent on their legs, "made for practical use," to look at Mariko's decorative legs (9). Initially, Mariko seems to benefit from this gaze, enjoying a sex life in which she can pick and choose her partners. At this stage, she is involved with three men, whom she nicknames A Lunch, B Lunch, and C Lunch, as if they were three options on a set menu.

When Mariko becomes pregnant by one of these lovers, though, she herself tries to adjust the significance of her legs after she quits her starring role to marry and have the child. She "lowers the hem of her skirt" and works to change her legs from beautiful decorative objects to functioning tools (45). Mariko's reliance on ideas from "The Little Mermaid" begins here: her pregnancy makes her aware of her own body, weighing her down from the buoyant feeling of love, and her legs hurt with each step. However, she tells herself that the little mermaid endured the same pain for the sake of the prince's love. This theme of pain is extended to the pain of childbirth that Mariko endures for the sake of her family. After the couple's daughter is born, the family lives a quiet life, in which Mariko attributes a similar mermaid-like sacrifice to her husband. He develops an allergy to the family dog but tolerates his constant rashes for the sake of the daughter, who loves the dog. Mariko, through perceiving her husband's symptoms as a sacrifice, is able to feel affection for his red, puffed-up flesh, another post–fairy tale example of a disobedient or difficult male body.

Despite Mariko's affection for her husband and their supposed domestic bliss, she remains somehow unsatisfied, and her unease about her new role is expressed through food imagery and fairy tale framing. Images of food metamorphosis capture Mariko's anxiety about aging. In *shōjo* stories, protagonists experience food in relation to their girlhood: mermaid meat in "Yao bikuni" makes the protagonist an eternal girl (see chapter 1), and in Lewis Carroll's *Alice's Adventures in Wonderland* (1865), Alice eats food that temporarily changes her into many different forms, simulating adolescent development. Mariko recalls that as a child she was amazed by foods that change form, such as fairy floss (cotton candy; 19) and popcorn (20). But she views such food metamorphoses with a growing unease after a fan compares her beautiful legs stuffed into her stockings to a novelty candy that explodes out of its plastic packaging when pricked with a toothpick. In the face of this unease, Mariko initiates a love affair. She visits an ex-lover who is a pâtissier, eating his cakes and listening to his "sweet words" (136) before they begin the affair. Mariko starts using makeup again (115) and wears the high-heeled shoes that are associated with the youthful sexualized beauty of her circus-performer life (125).

Mariko's initial use of "The Little Mermaid" thus expands to encompass multiple fairy tale texts and images. The fairy tale intertext in *Ningyo-hime no kutsu* that brings together food (the poisoned apple) and shoes (as a punishment for the witch) is "Snow White." Mariko often refers to this tale, which Nonaka then rereads in her author's postface. Sandra Gilbert and Susan Gubar, in their famous analysis of "Snow White," see the roles of angelic daughter and wicked stepmother as an inevitable cycle in which the passive princess grows up to be the aggressive queen, who is doomed to compete with a younger girl. Mariko seems to instinctively grasp this interpretation when, in the novel, she reads fairy tales aloud to her daughter. Thinking about "Snow White," she wonders if as a mother she has now left the role of princess and become the wicked queen. Perhaps acknowledging her new wicked role, when she prepares to meet her lover, Mariko seeks admiration from both her daughter and the mirror, asking her mirror, in the traditional lines from the fairy tale, who is the fairest (115). Gilbert and Gubar suggest that the mirror's voice in "Snow White" that tells the queen that she is no longer the most beautiful woman is "the patriarchal voice of judgment that rules the Queen's—and every woman's—self-evaluation" (*Madwoman* 38). Mariko never gets an answer from her mirror, but she certainly seems to have internalized "patriarchal judgment" of her female body. She continues to value "princess" youth and beauty over wicked queenhood, as if these are her only options.

At the end of the story, Mariko does not outwardly acknowledge that she is listening to any voice of the patriarchy, but she does become disillusioned with the men in her life. Her appetite for candy is replaced with the meaningless childhood habit of putting beads in her mouth, an act that cannot provide sustenance or flavor, only nostalgic comfort. On the way home from a disappointing meeting with her lover and then a visit to her father, she trips on her high heels—those symbols of her feminine desirability—and falls down the stairs. The novel closes with Mariko lying on the concrete waiting for help, with the implication that the fall has caused her to miscarry her second pregnancy, and the comment, "Now, she had come to the realization that all she could do was endlessly, endlessly wait" (Nonaka, *Ningyo-hime* 174).

Mariko's fate reflects that of the "*matsu onna* (the woman who waits)" (Sarra 30), frequently appearing in Heian-period (794–1185) *waka* poetry and classical Japanese works by women, such as *Kagerō nikki* (Kagerō diary; Sarra 30), *Genji monogatari* (The tale of Genji), and *Makura no sōshi* (The pillow book; Sarra 246–47) and maintaining a presence in subsequent literary traditions. This traditional position of "woman who waits" cuts Mariko's mermaid plot short: unlike Andersen's mermaid, Mariko cannot continue her journey into free movement on a higher plane. Rather, she is frozen in a kind of limbo phase of painful legs that, for her, symbolize sacrifice for the sake of others.

Mariko is literally trapped as well as emotionally restricted to the role of the wicked queen. Her situation is explicated by Ikoma Natsumi in one of the few pieces of criticism on this novel, in Ikoma's book on gender in Japanese and English fairy tale retellings. Ikoma quite accurately describes Mariko as "a heroine untouched by feminism" who, "to the end, never clearly comprehends the unequal treatment she has been given by a male-centered society" (276). In this sense, Mariko cannot be described as a postfeminist protagonist; she neither acknowledges nor rejects feminist ideologies. Ikoma believes that the novel's realist narrative is closer to nineteenth-century English literature: when Mariko has three lovers, she unknowingly steps outside the bounds of appropriate behavior for women, so like fallen women in Victorian literature, she must be punished—hence her fall at the end of the story. Ikoma argues that the novel's confinement to Mariko's perspective in its third-person narration demonstrates the limits of this traditional realism, which "cannot offer affirmative, alternative choices of action to oppressed characters" (290). Thus, according to Ikoma, due to the realist narrative, neither Mariko nor the novel itself can avoid the sexist social norms that *Ningyo-hime no kutsu* depicts.

Although the fairy tale form differs from the nineteenth-century English realist novel, it can function in a parallel manner: as Cristina Bacchilega has shown, the traditional third-person narration works to "silently assume" and "naturalize" culturally constructed gender roles (*Postmodern Fairy Tales* 35, 34). However, where the work as a whole might be positioned in relation to feminism is another question. Nonaka herself articulates a more transformative perspective on her novel in her postface following the story.

The Author's Afterword to Post–Happily Ever After

Nonaka makes an interesting use of the postface to provide commentary on Mariko's use of fairy tale imagery. While such sections are rarer in English, Japanese novels almost routinely include *kaisetsu* (commentary), and *atogaki* (postfaces) are not uncommon. Gérard Genette believes that unlike the preface, which can direct the reader's interpretation, a postface following the text "can hope to fulfill only a curative, or corrective function" (*Paratexts* 238–39). His somewhat dismissive evaluation seems unhelpful in this context: in fact, it is the "curative, or corrective function" that makes the postface to *Ningyo-hime no kutsu* so dynamic, because Nonaka uses her postface to reread her own fairy tale transformation. That is, the commentary in itself becomes a type of revisionist post–fairy tale in which Nonaka questions the tempting sweetness of the life women are offered, hinting that it conceals a more mermaid-like painful suffering.

Nonaka writes that her novel is interested in unhappy endings like the little mermaid's, as well as in supposedly happy endings for princesses like Snow White, Cinderella, and Sleeping Beauty. Querying the "beyond happily ever after," she asks what happens *after* these princesses achieve the romantic love they dream for:

Made with baking powder, plenty of egg white, and risen soft and fluffy, girls' sweet dreams are actually very bitter when you try to taste them—probably.

This novel is like a poisoned apple. I wrote it, with love, for all those princesses. (177)

Here, Nonaka revisits "Snow White," as well as invoking the other food images from her novel: changing, expanding foods (popcorn and fairy floss), the association of sweet foods with romantic and sexual relationships, and disillusionment and loss of appetite.

Nonaka is not the only woman author to have employed food imagery to visualize her interaction with fairy tales. Angela Carter famously used the imagery of cooking recipes to reject the notion of a single, "godlike" author of a fairy tale, instead imagining generations of (women) cooks/creators: "Who first invented meatballs? In what country? Is there a definitive recipe for potato soup? Think in terms of the domestic arts. 'This is how I make potato soup'" (Carter, introduction x). So far, we have seen an association between girls and candy in chapter 5 and employed by Higami and Ogawa in their postfaces to *Otogibanashi no wasuremono* in chapter 4: Higami and Ogawa position themselves as candy store owners or fellow girls to their girl readers, suggesting that reading their book is like consuming candy with unexpected flavors. Nonaka's bitter cake and poisoned apple for her girl reader is more sinister, but not without parallel. In line with her production of "cruel" fairy tales in 1984, Kurahashi Yumiko (see chapter 4) later published a collection of essays titled *Dokuyaku to shite no bungaku* (Literature as poison, 1999), using "poison" to discuss her difficult relationship with writing as a woman. Another woman writer, Ogino Anna, had taken up this topic in a parodic work of "fiction-cum-literary-criticism" (Aoyama, "Love That Poisons" 41) titled *Watashi no aidokusho* (1991), which puns *aidoku* (loving reading) with *doku* (poison) and is translated as *My Love-Hate Affair with Books* (Janet Ashby, ctd. in Aoyama, "Love That Poisons" 40). As Aoyama explains, Ogino's work engages in "close, intimate and pleasure-giving reading" as "inseparable" from critical, poisonous reading (41). Whereas Ogino's critical fiction, however, performs poisonous reading of canonical male-authored texts, Nonaka uses her postface to undertake a pleasurably intimate yet poisonous reading of fairy tales but also of her own novel.

Importantly, Nonaka pays more attention to the other half of the reading-as-eating metaphor: writing as preparing food. Nonaka plays with the figure of the female cook to insert herself into the text, positioning herself, as Mariko does, as the wicked queen in "Snow White" who offers the princess a poisoned apple. As Gilbert and Gubar write, the queen has internalized the voice of the patriarchy, but she is also an "artist" and a "plot-maker," as opposed to the passive, idealized Snow White (*Madwoman* 38). Perhaps Nonaka was familiar with this notion; certainly, many fictional works have been shown to interact with this influential piece of fairy tale criticism (see Joosen). Gilbert and Gubar argue that the queen's attempts to kill Snow White are in fact the queen's attempts to kill off the passive, feminine ideal within herself. Virginia Woolf had famously argued decades before that women must kill the meek, self-sacrificing angel within themselves before they can become authors. Nonaka may similarly be encouraging female readers to look into the mirror and see the Mariko within themselves and perhaps even to kill the naïve Mariko within themselves—or at least knock her off her feet and out of her beautiful, impractical high heels, as Nonaka does at the end of her story.

Nonaka's reframing move in her postface is, in Hutcheon's words, a distinctively postmodern "wholesale 'nudging' commitment to doubleness, or duplicity" (*Politics* 1). In the novel, the narrative is confined to Mariko's perspective, and Mariko is never fully aware of her own oppression. She is caught up in the gender roles she perceives in "Snow White." According to Bacchilega, in "Snow White," gender is naturalized through the device of "mirroring." A fairy tale presents itself as a mirror that reflects reality exactly. In consuming fairy tales, we do not always remember that the vision we see in the mirror is selected, bounded, and framed in some way (33). But postmodern transformations stress the existence of the frame, the act of framing itself, in order to expose and challenge ideas of the world and of gender that the fairy tale presents through its mirror as natural, unchanging, and normal (35–36). Nonaka, in her postface, as Bacchilega puts it, "challenges the authority of the mirror" through which Mariko accepts her gendered social role (36). Nonaka reveals that Mariko is trapped in her own fairy tale, confined to the two limiting roles of passive daughter and wicked queen. Nonaka herself, on the other hand, is not similarly confined but rather exhibits a playful sense of pleasure when she positions herself as a wicked witch lovingly preparing and feeding poisonous texts to innocent girl characters, girl readers, and other audiences. Nonaka reclaims awareness,[9] inserting herself back into the narrative process and naming herself to the reader as the agent who positions the mirror's frame and decides what it reflects. The postface shifts Mariko's story away from the

---

[9] Mary Daly had written in *Gyn/Ecology* that "the child who is fed tales such as Snow White is not told the tale itself is a poisonous apple, and the Wicked Queen (her mother/teacher), having herself been drugged by the same deadly diet through her lifetime, . . . is unaware of her venomous part in the patriarchal plot" (44).

nineteenth-century "Snow White" trajectory toward one of the many alternative versions that Gilbert and Gubar describe, in a chapter title for another work, as "The Further Adventures of Snow White" (*Letters* 359).

As a post–fairy tale, *Ningyo-hime no kutsu* is preoccupied with what happens after the happy ending. As a post-Andersen, postmodern text, the novel circles out beyond "The Little Mermaid" to transform a number of tales and engage with the fairy tale form itself. Like Max in *Dark Angel*, its heroine, Mariko, uses fairy tales to understand her own life but is left in a state of limbo rather than reaching any kind of concrete resolution. Though the novel might be described as feminist in its engagement with the objectification and limited roles offered to women, it is certainly not postfeminist in that it does not dismiss or even acknowledge feminist movements and relegate them to the past. However, if the postface is taken into account, the novel may be considered through a version of the "post"feminist theory that has been introduced to Japan by that feminist literary scholar Takemura Kazuko, in her volume *"Posuto"feminizumu* ("Post"feminism, 2003). Rather than viewing postfeminism as a persistent belief about the "finished" status of feminism and analyzing the way this belief manifests itself in cultural products, Takemura uses the term to describe a different kind of "undoing" of feminism. She argues that appending the word "post-" indicates a "self-referential, self-expanding approach" to feminism that does not define or confine the scope and depth of a preexisting notion of feminism (4). Certainly, Nonaka's critical look at women's experience of romance and family and their ambivalent pleasures incorporates a "self-referential, self-expanding approach" (4) to these feminist concerns.

The Mermaid and the City

A novel that is perhaps both more urban and more urbane than Nonaka's, *Sentō no ningyo-hime to majo no mori* (The little mermaid of the public bath and the witch's forest, 2008) nevertheless has several elements in common with other post–fairy tale transformations: an interest in fairy tale gender roles and in troubling conventional ideas of gender; a female protagonist dealing with her agency and her position as an artist; a plot that focuses on what happens after a happy couple is formed; and an extensive, self-conscious use of not only "The Little Mermaid" but multiple fairy tales and other texts.

The novel, attributed to the author D[di:], was serialized in *Bekkan bungei shunjū* (the bimonthly supplement to the general interest magazine *Bungei shunjū*) in March–September 2008 and published as a hardcover book in the same year. The second part of the author's penname, "[diː]," is the phonemic transcription of the pronunciation of the letter *d*, and on the novel's cover, the pronunciation *dī* is also printed above the name in *katakana* phonetic script. D[diː] appears as a young woman in the many photographs in the media, social media, and her official website but explains that she mainly chose her gender-neutral, anonymous alphabetical penname "in order to avoid preconceptions on the part of the reader based on the author's personal information (nationality, race, sex, age, etc)" (D[diː], online profile). According to her profile, D[diː] is active in creating novels and novelizations, children's books, manga, illustrations, fashion, and design. Her work has a dreamy, organic fairy tale aesthetic, and her debut illustrated story collection *Fantasutikku sairento* (Fantastic silent, 2000) was supported by the fairy tale film director Miyazaki Hayao of Studio Ghibli (D[diː], online profile).

Sentō no ningyo-hime is, like "Gill Girl" and *Ningyo-hime no kutsu*, preoccupied with women's beliefs about romance and with what happens beyond "happily ever after," which it expresses through uses of "The Little Mermaid" and other fairy tales. Narrated in the first person by a twenty-nine-year-old woman named Fū, the novel offers entertainment in the form of textual play, comic episodes, and intertextual images that Fū invites the reader to share with her. Like the mermaid protagonist of Jane Gardam's "The Pangs of Love" (see chapter 5), Fū is left unhappy by her combination of intelligent cynicism (expressed primarily through her knowledge of many different texts) and her desire for romance with a man who cannot give her what she wants (as expressed through her implicit identification with "The Little Mermaid"). This feeds into her fear that without a prince, she is doomed to grow into witch-like old age.

The story follows Fū's life as a freelance illustrator living in Tokyo, sharing with other texts in this chapter an interest in women's agency as artists. As well as many direct mentions of Andersen's fairy tale, several aspects of Fū's character may be implicit allusions to the mermaid. Like the mermaid, Fū has only sisters. Born and raised in the northern island Hokkaido, she feels out of her element in the national capital city, as Andersen's mermaid feels during her time on land. Fū's name means "wind," reflecting the mermaid's fate to become a "daughter of the air." The story begins with her happy relationship with her boyfriend and traces her journey to discovering that her boyfriend is a married man. Like the mermaid, then, the object of Fū's love is promised to another woman.

The postfeminist framework proves especially relevant to *Sentō no ningyo-hime* in its interest in femininity and aging as well as its urban setting. Fū captures the events of her narrative through the astrological concept of the "Saturn return," an eventful life-changing period at the age of twenty-nine and a half (17). The novel is, as Tasker and Negra describe postfeminist texts, "exceedingly precise about the age of their female protagonists" (11). Like *Ningyo-hime no kutsu*, it also exhibits a typically postfeminist fear of aging, which manifests itself in Fū's fear of becoming the classic fairy tale figure of the witch.

Fū's lifestyle seems to both embody and parody the urban experience portrayed in postfeminist texts. The postfeminist approach has developed in the Anglo-American context, and its products deny social diversity even within these locations: privileged white women are their standard heroines (Tasker and Negra 2). Representative television series such as *Sex and the City* from North America have as their protagonists an "upper-middle-class woman who is affluent, educated, and urban" and white (Leonard 104). A kind of equivalent is seen in Japanese series such as *Around 40*, in which protagonists are invariably female, heterosexual Japanese nationals (Freedman and Iwata-Weickgenannt 302). Fū matches these definitions in that she is involved in a circle of Tokyo fashion designers and other trendsetters. But rather than a wealthy or professional elite district or ordinary suburbia, she lives in a colorful *shitamachi*—a "low city" (see Seidensticker) or downtown backstreets area, associated with traditional urban lower classes and mass culture, inhabited by craftspeople and salespeople, and now often associated with creative types. By no means affluent, Fū is forced to recognize the precariousness of her freelance career when, late in the plot, she is injured by a passing motorbike and faces expensive hospital bills. The accident also underscores Fū's physical vulnerability, as well as her concern for her feminine appearance; when she is injured, she fears seeing her own face in the mirror (D[diː], *Sentō* 194). Later, she breaks up with her boyfriend, and we leave her questioning her identity and struggling to reinvent herself, a postfeminist subject of the self as a "project" to work on (Tasker and Negra 21).

Of Women and Witches

Fū's major concern in her own postfeminist construction of self is her gender and sexual identity. She expresses this concern through self-conscious storytelling and illustration, which form part of the novel's cocktail of intertextual allusions to fairy tales, fables, video games, film, television, and more. For instance, the chapter titles all involve wordplay on favorite fairy tale texts with girl protagonists:

1. 不思議の森の子栗鼠(コリス): "The baby squirrel in the strange forest" (*Fushigi no mori no korisu*), a play on *Alice in Wonderland* (*Fushigi no kuni no arisu*)
2. 百舌鳥(モズ)の魔法使い: "The butcher bird wizard" (*Mozu no mahō tsukai*), a play on *The Wizard of Oz* (*Ozu no mahō tsukai*)
3. 眠れる森の老女: "Sleeping old woman in the forest" (*Nemureru mori no rōjo*), a play on "Sleeping Beauty" (*Nemureru mori no bijo*)
4. 銭湯の人魚姫: "The little mermaid of the bath-house" (*Sentō no ningyo-hime*), a play on "The Little Mermaid" (*Ningyo-hime*)

Illustrations by D[di:] found on the book's cover and chapter title pages also form another type of fairy tale play, functioning as paratexts that give supplementary information about Fū. These illustrations are reportedly drawn by the fictional narrator and are described within the story. For example, Fū tells another character about an illustration (seen on page 5) of a prairie dog wearing a headband with three bunny ears attached to it. The story behind the picture, she explains, is a parody of both herself and of Aesop's "Town Mouse and Country Mouse": a country prairie dog wears playboy bunny ears to impress her city cousin but misguidedly adds an extra ear to improve them. Here the narrator seems to be explaining to the reader her delight in self-parody and play with traditional tales.

Fū also articulates her ambivalence toward gender norms in an informal, humorous style that often emulates oral storytelling. At the opening of the novel, she explains that she is a woman who chooses to refer to herself using the rough masculine pronoun *ore*:

> Warning. Or, attention please.
> 　Or then again, ※.
> 　I want to establish firstly that "*ore*" [I, masculine] am a woman....
> 　The reason I use "*ore*" is that this is how "*watashi*" [I, neutral] am inside my heart, so I would like to request your understanding on this one. (D[di:], *Sentō* 6)

Later, we learn that Fū refers to herself with the girlish *atashi* when speaking out loud to others; she explains she is confident (masculine) only on the inside but shy on the outside (12). The gap between Fū's inner and outer voices implies a mismatch between her sense of self and the social expectations she feels are placed on her.

Figure 6.2. D[di:] prairie dog illustration featured on the cover of *Sentō no ningyo-hime to majo no mori*.

This eloquent protagonist describes her sexuality to the reader in a similarly direct manner. She discusses her attraction to her boyfriend and also explains that she has had lesbian experiences and feels desire for women. Another character, Fū's friend Tsubaki-chan, is a self-styled *okama* (42), which here means a woman-identified gay man. Fū explains that "those women—or at least Tsubaki-chan—whose real sex is not female, but who cannot live if they don't pretend they are women, are more sensitive than anyone else about 'femininity'" (43). Although the idea of "real sex" does not reflect Judith Butler's theory that gender itself is a fiction, Fū does view gender as a performative, lived identity. She mentions elsewhere that she finds women frightening (20); she finds the company of Tsubaki-chan more relaxing, suggesting that she feels connected by their shared conscious engagement with gender norms, just as Max and the mermaid were connected by their hybrid feminine bodies in "Gill Girl."

Although there are far more female-identifying characters in the work, Fū's sensitivity to gender and sexuality extends to her view of male characters. Fū's beloved boyfriend, Kenji, is almost exaggeratedly physical. He is characterized by his insomnia; his addiction to sleeping tablets; his smoking, drinking, and excessive sweating; and also his size—Fū nicknames him the "green giant" (22). Unlike the two-dimensional handsome prince of Andersen's fairy tale, then, Kenji is unsettled and real.

Fu's anxious engagements with gender and sexual identities extend to her struggles in her role as an artist, which she often sketches through textual play. One entertaining example is a description of her dreamy piano-playing as "自分に酔っぱらい" (122). This is a clever use of the practice of *rubi*, which is the smaller text printed above the main text that usually provides the phonetic reading for the Chinese characters. Here the main text reads "Drunk on oneself" (*jibun ni yopparai*), but the smaller text above reads "poetic" in the loanword from English, *poetikku*. Equating drunkenness with being poetic captures Kanai's notion of creative work as "the experience of being controlled by one's passions" ("Anderusen no ashi" 281); however, in this case, the mermaid's drastic, painful punishment for this loss of control is mitigated by the smaller text that injects the artist's self-deprecating, comic acknowledgment of her self-indulgent reverie.

D[di:] often overlays the main text with *rubi* loanwords, or words with slightly different meanings, rather than phonetic readings. This smaller-font text beside the main text is a complex literary strategy that creates discrepancies in meaning and multiplies meanings in engaging ways for readers (Ariga 320). The use of *rubi* to open up the meaning of a word is not restricted to recent writing (see Ariga), but D[di:]'s technique here may be described as a postmodernist self-conscious play. Other textual play includes frequent use of the *katakana* alphabet; use of foreign alphabets and words, such as the English onomatopoeia "Ha-ha-ha!" (65); use of nontext such as the map icon for hot springs ♨ (50); and asterisked footnotes (65). As with the asterisked explanations in Joanna Russ's "Russalka" story (see chapter 5), the wordplay invites laughter as well as creating a kind of intimacy between the author and the reader as they share in this textual play.

However, this young, playful artist is depicted through fairy tale imagery as vulnerable. An older woman, Sonoda, employs Fū to make designs for her fashion label. Sonoda's young assistants begin as "fairies" (92) who view Sonoda as their "godmother," but later Fū comes to see Sonoda as a "cruel witch" (178) with her assistant "goblins" (174). Sonoda denies Fū's agency as an artist when she uses Fū's designs in her clothing line without paying for them. Sonoda is, as Gilbert and Gubar describe the wicked queen of "Snow White," "a plotter, a plot-maker, a schemer" (*Madwoman* 38) who takes advantage of younger women. Fū is disempowered by this witch character and attempts to regain control of the situation, but eventually she must accept her passive Snow White role, when a more experienced designer advises her that she has no power to retaliate.

Sonoda is one of a parade of characters who represent Fū's fairy tale fear of aging and of elderly women. Somewhat similarly to Mariko in *Ningyohime no kutsu*, Fū frames female aging as "becoming a witch"; at one point, Fū even provides specific examples of witchy women and then lists criteria to aid in identifying them (111). This fear that aging means shifting from fairy tale heroine to antagonist is cemented by the novel's title, "The little mermaid of the public bath and the witch's forest," which links the tragic young romantic mermaid with the wicked elderly witch, as both refer to a single character in the novel, another elderly woman named Hoshino.

Fū encounters Hoshino when she begins to use the local public bath, after the hot-water system in her apartment breaks. Apart from the public bath, Hoshino is associated with water in that she is a survivor of the World War II mass suicide in Saipan in 1944, an actual event in which many Japanese civilians jumped off cliffs to escape U.S. forces; in other words, like Andersen's mermaid, she attempted suicide by diving into the ocean. Moreover, the suicide attempt left her crippled so that walking causes her terrible pain. Hoshino is a mermaid figure whose stories of her innocent youthful love affair with a young Japanese soldier in Saipan are framed as romantic and tragic. The light and entertaining events of Fū's life are intertwined with Hoshino's anecdotes about her time in Saipan, as well as Fū's and other characters' thoughts on Japan's role in the war and the cruelty of war in general.

This elderly woman is also very strongly associated with fairy tale witches in anything from Ghibli animations (60) to the more traditional dark forest (58). Thus, both the subjects of the novel's title—the little mermaid and the witch—seem to refer to Hoshino's different life stages and Fū's fear that she will reenact them. Yet it is also Fū's friendship with Hoshino that helps her to mitigate her identity crisis. In a slightly mystical episode at the close of the novel, Fū dreams through Hoshino's eyes. Fū experiences Hoshino jumping off the cliff in Saipan and then her mermaid-like survival in the ocean, followed by her decision—unlike that of Andersen's mermaid—to live on (244). The dream connects the two women through their mermaid identities: this gives Fū the strength to ignore her fears of aging alone and becoming a witch, at least long enough for her to find the strength to leave her boyfriend, Kenji, after she has discovered he has betrayed her.

After suffering a traffic accident and breaking up with Kenji, Fū moves out of her apartment and leaves her downtown neighborhood in a continued search for self. In the final words, an English-speaking child mistakes her name Fū for the word *who*; Fū develops the bilingual wordplay to conclude that she is still "not who/not anybody" (251). This is by no means a concrete happy ending; it is emphatically non–fairy tale. The question cements Fū as an urban postfeminist protagonist on a journey of reinvention in which she sees herself in the postfeminist process of "self as project" (Tasker and Negra 21). Like *Dark Angel*'s Max and like Mariko in *Ningyo-hime no kutsu*, she draws on "The Little Mermaid" and an ever-broadening spectrum of other fairy tales in her struggle to establish a stable identity. And like both Max and Mariko, we leave her in a state of in-betweenness.

For these postfeminist Japanese and Anglophone transformations of "The Little Mermaid," depicting heroines searching for fairy tale models for their lives, Gilbert and Gubar's use of "Snow White" as a metaphor for Victorian women writers seems to hold a good deal of appeal. In their chapter titled "The Further Adventures of Snow White," Gilbert and Gubar muse on the experience of engaging with fairy tales for the contemporary woman writer: "Storyteller though she is, she might even be obliged to meditate on current ideas about the artifice of identity. In spite of her best efforts to achieve narrative closure, moreover, she would probably find herself entangled in multiple endings, confused and bemused by cultural pluralism that makes definitive definitions virtually inconceivable" (*Letters* 261). Their prediction captures many of the issues that occupy these post–fairy tale works. First, perhaps inspired by the little mermaid's hybrid body, her otherness, and her performance of beauty—graceful dancing—that hides her physical pain, all works "meditate" on "the artifice of identity." Female protagonists question their identities and their own control over them through their roles as artists and performers. "Gill Girl" and *Ningyo-hime no kutsu* use sites of performance to imply the performativity of gender: both Max's strip-club deception and Mariko's circus act expose these performers to an objectifying male gaze and measure their control over the situation. Whereas Mariko is quite unaware of her objectification, in the *Dark Angel* episode, the visual medium encourages viewers to simultaneously empathize with and objectify Max as she competently performs femininity and sexuality. Gender is also figured as performative in D[di:]'s novel, particularly through the narrator's self-conscious use of gendered personal pronouns to articulate her identity and the discussion of a female-identified male character. The protagonist, Fū, loses control over her agency as an artist when she is exploited by the type of "witchy" older woman she is afraid of becoming.

The female protagonists of these works also experience ambivalent relationships with their own physical changes. Nonaka's protagonist, Mariko, and D[di:]'s protagonist, Fū, attempt to understand the gendered, physical process of aging through fairy tales. They seem to echo Gilbert and Gubar's original reading of "Snow White" (*Madwoman*) when they view women's lives as divided into the two roles of youthful, desirable princess and the cunning older queen. Using imagery of "The Little Mermaid," male bodies are also "troubled," but in different ways—through hybridity and scientific experimentation, as well as medical problems such as disability, allergies, and injury.

As post–fairy tales, all the texts in the chapter address the problem of "narrative closure" that Gilbert and Gubar predict. In situating their tales "beyond happily ever after," the texts challenge the idea that a fairy tale wedding—happy or otherwise—is an "ending" at all. They also address the difficulty of achieving the concrete, tidy conclusion that is characteristic of fairy tales. They finish instead with "multiple endings": the *Dark Angel* episode sets a Disney-style happy ending in competition with the other genres at play in the overall series, *Ningyo-hime no kutsu* concludes with the protagonist realizing that she will forever be waiting, and D[di:]'s novel closes with its protagonist moving away from her home and questioning her identity.

However, the postfeminist stance of the post–fairy tales discussed in this chapter sets them apart from the more "radical" fairy tale retellings that Gilbert and Gubar analyze. The postfeminist approach (McRobbie; Tasker and Negra) explains the attempts that these works or their characters make to reconcile contradictory images of empowerment with sexual objectification and conservative gender roles. *Dark Angel* manifests unease about body and gender in its portrayal of hybridity. D[di:]'s work uses textual play and frequent allusions to other texts to invite in-group laughter from "knowing" audiences. This play produces a constant multiplicity of meanings that perhaps contributes to Fū's lack of certainty about who she is, which leads to her postfeminist quest for self-discovery.

On the other hand, the protagonist of Nonaka's novel, Mariko, might be viewed as pre- rather than postfeminist; she never understands the sexist nature of her own society or acknowledges feminism. In the postface, however, Nonaka rereads her own novel, offering a more pleasurable and empowered vision of the fairy tale role of the wicked queen, opening up its meanings in a way that is "post"feminist in Takemura's use of the term. Each of these post–fairy tales, despite their different versions of postfeminism, invites the reader to share with the protagonist the experience of negotiating the pleasures and discomforts of being a conscious reader of "The Little Mermaid." This process of conscious reading can never be limited to Andersen's story but inevitably extends to multiple fairy tales, as well as to the gender roles that, collectively, these fairy tales present.

Conclusion

Hans Christian Andersen's touching, imaginative story "The Little Mermaid" has inspired endless transformations. The fairy tale conveys a deep, dramatic sense of yearning and emotional suffering imagined through descriptions of muteness and terrible pain. It evokes experiences of girlhood and growing up through imagery of physical metamorphosis and upward movement through different environments. The mermaid's movement across different realms and her experience as an outsider on land is echoed in the journeys that the tale itself has made across cultures and into different shapes. The complex images of female experience in Andersen's tale, in the mermaid's metamorphosis, her romantic desire, and her spiritual quest, make these transformations particularly suitable for an analysis of the construction of gender. Here I have undertaken an examination of the journey of Andersen's Danish fairy tale into English and Japanese, believing that such a cross-cultural approach contributes a more global outlook to the field of Anglophone fairy tale studies. I have argued that the framework of "pleasure" is valuable in this endeavor because it can draw together a hugely diverse range of transformations and also because it can provide insight into the fairy tale's continued prosperity as a creative form.

Andersen's tale—or any European fairy tale—has not simply made a one-way trip from the West into Japan. Its path has branched out, doubled back, twisted and turned as the story transmutates. In Japan, the confluence of Western, local, and other traditions continues to provide fertile ground for popular culture in particular. Examples of mermaid stories that draw on the "fairy tale web" include Takahashi Rumiko's *Mermaid Saga* manga and animated adaptations, which are based on the legend of the special life-prolonging powers of mermaid meat. They stretch to collections such as Watanabe Peco's manga *Tales of Metamorphosis*, in which characters in modern-day Japan demonstrate their familiarity with Andersen's "The Little Mermaid" as they reenact its plot.

This kind of cross-cultural appropriation and transformation of Japanese and foreign mermaid and fairy tale traditions is not confined to the borders of Japan. I mentioned in chapter 1 the way the mermaid mummies of Edo-period Japan broke through the country's "closed" national borders to arrive in the United Kingdom and the United States in the nineteenth century. I also commented, for instance, in chapter 6 on ways the Japanese figure of the "beautiful fighting girl" and the Japanese cyberpunk aesthetic inform Anglophone texts. I add here that in recent decades, manga and anime especially are increasingly spreading outside Japan through official releases as well as online fan publications, and their narrative worlds are expanded in different cultures through practices such as cosplay (costume play) and community events.[1] Fantastical, mythological, and fairy tale themes are central to these multiplying imaginative worlds. The flow of popular-culture fairy tale transformations from Japan into the world through these channels offers further opportunity for research that overturns Orientalist understandings of the West as the dominant cultural creator and center.

However, as Mayako Murai has observed with reference to Cécile Sakai, "non-Western cultural products circulate globally as culturally marked" (*From Dog Bridegroom* 145); that is, what is perceived as the unique Japaneseness of such texts motivates their selection for translation and their marketing and presentation and therefore also shapes the commentary that emerges in response. This means that concurrent to analyzing Japanese fairy tale transformations as they appear in translation, scholarship that engages with the Japanese-language texts and academic study (and of course with other non-English, non-Western language texts and research) is vital to understanding the fairy tale within the global arena.

In my work on the fairy tale's cross-cultural movement, I have aimed not to perpetuate Orientalist critiques that view the West as subject and the East as other or *Nihonjinron* perspectives (see chapter 1) that hold up a unique, homogeneous Japan against an essentialized West. As such, I have not made generalizing comparisons of the Japanese and English stories as a whole or attempted to identify particular cultural elements that the tales might represent. Rather, I set out to scrutinize a diverse collection of stories from across different time periods, languages, and national borders through the lens of "pleasure." We might say that pleasure is so often at the heart of the act of writing, reading, and analyzing, but it is not always explicitly addressed in critical work. The notion of pleasure has helped to

---

[1] The international success of Japanese popular culture is the subject of a great deal of research, and the Japanese government has shown a strong interest in the "soft power" potential of what has been dubbed "cool Japan." See, for example, Napier's *From Impressionism to Anime* (2008) and Iwabuchi's work on Japanese popular culture in Asia, such as *Recentering Globalization* (2002).

identify and examine some of the intricate links among gender, genre, medium, and transformation mode in these retellings of Andersen's fairy tale.

Pleasure itself is a tricky concept to pin down. Since this book is not an investigation of reader responses but rather a textual analysis, it does not examine what real readers and authors report to have enjoyed; rather, it infers the types of pleasures that these texts might invite from their readers, such as laughter, as well as vicarious pleasure in the experiences of sympathetic characters. In fairy tale transformations, these kinds of pleasures can easily be offered to "unknowing audiences," not requiring any particular understanding of Andersen's tale or of the fairy tale form. What has emerged as a particularly interesting aspect of many of the works is their "knowing," self-reflexive portrayals of pleasure: the tendency for transformations to incorporate metatextual commentary on the construction of particular gendered identities in relation to the processes of fairy tale reading and reimagining.

Many of the transformations I have discussed present images of characters enjoying pleasures that simulate reading or characters actually reading fairy tales and other texts. These are somewhat divided along gender lines. Some male characters more readily throw themselves into wholesale enchantment with the mermaid and the fairy tale form, such as Wilde's Fisherman and Tanizaki's nobleman. Within this quite limited sample set, female characters such as Kawakami's narrator and Nonaka's Mariko are equally fascinated with fairy tales but more wary. Their hesitancy might demonstrate an awareness on the part of female characters (and authors and readers) of the fairy tale's work as Bacchilega describes it: "By showcasing 'women' and making them disappear at the same time, the fairy tale thus transforms us/them into man-made constructs of 'Woman'" (*Postmodern Fairy Tales* 9). On the other hand, Allen's Aquamarine, *Dark Angel*'s Max, and D[di:]'s Fū are more aware of multiple versions of "The Little Mermaid" and other fairy tales, though they struggle against them only to varying degrees of success.

The depiction of troubled women readers may indicate that women have a more uncomfortable relationship with fairy tales than men do. Certainly, ongoing debates around gender in fairy tales have centered on their depiction of women. The belief that fairy tales might socialize women into oppressive social roles has often been countered with the recommendation that fairy tales can be used to inculcate more progressive values in young readers. As I argued in chapter 5, both sides of this influential debate assume a passive mode of unquestioning absorption on the part of readers. This image is contested by the very awareness of the fairy tale that female characters demonstrate in these transformations of "The Little Mermaid."

In fact, in keeping with traditions of simple characterization and binaries of good and evil, the male protagonists of many classic fairy tales do not seem to fare much better than the female ones do: male characters such as Andersen's prince are neither complex nor three-dimensional. However, instead of being "showcased" and simultaneously "disappeared," the male protagonist is often simply overlooked. In Andersen's tale, in contrast to the prince's flatness, the mermaid character is endowed with subjectivity and complex motivation. Taking issue with the prince's comparatively undeveloped personality and his ironic lack of a "voice" in "The Little Mermaid," some transformations, such as Wilde's, Tanizaki's, and Abe's, redesign the prince character to justify or understand his actions. Others, such as Ogawa's tale, reinscribe the presence of mermen into the story realm. As such, the complex attitude to fairy tales expressed by female characters in the transformations may be a response less to the fairy tale's flattening of women characters and more to the complex hybridity and multiple possibilities that Andersen's tale presents through the mermaid—in contrast to the merely overlooked prince. Again, this suggests a more involved approach to fairy tales than is implied by the debates about whether they are socializing devices or tools for gender rebellion.

For most of the transformations discussed here (excepting Matsumoto's overtly feminist revision), affirming or subverting a specific construction of gender or traditional fairy tale role is not the main point. What brings together these transformations and their conflicting notions of gender and reading is their shared obsessive engagement with fairy tale, a need either way to continue to think these stories through. The reason authors continue to transform fairy tales is less to take an ideological stand and more to enjoy some of the intellectual, intertextual, and communal pleasures of the transforming process. These pleasures can be experienced through radical transformations that, as Roland Barthes puts it, "discomfort" and "unsettle" the reader but also through those that are "comfortable" and "do not break with [culture]" (14). Critique of fairy tale transformations, then, should similarly engage with texts that offer both types of reading pleasure.

Further insight into the pleasures of the fairy tale is offered by authors themselves in the form of paratexts such as postfaces. Authors' metatextual commentary on this topic often presents a different view from fairy tale scholarship. For example, feminist fairy tale studies approaches tend to value feminist works that expose and transform sexist gender norms in the classic fairy tales, as well as works that revive buried female fairy tale traditions. In some cases, this admirable emphasis on feminism means that texts with more conservative models of gender or more commercial leanings are not considered as worthy of discussion or analysis. Jack Zipes, for instance, writes on film adaptations of Andersen's tales that "the morals of American fairy tale films tend to be clear and easy to grasp, and there can never be real tragedy or exploration of sexuality and politics"; he prefers to discuss the work of a few European directors who "add complex philosophical and ideological aspects" (*Enchanted Screen* 259).

While Zipes's comparison is undoubtedly valid, this book aims to show—in the vein of recent work by Cristina Bacchilega and others—that gender ideology in "commercial" transformations of "The Little Mermaid" of any cultural origin can be read in equally complex ways. The authors' paratextual messages indicate that it is not necessary to draw lines between the conservative and the subversive in order to critique images of gender and the pleasures of fairy tale transformations. Using characters as well as paratexts such as postfaces, authors frame the pleasure of the fairy tale transformation as the wonder of engaging with the fairy tale world and the privilege of reinterpreting it as they please. Some authors suggest critical approaches to their own fairy tales, and others even invite readers to join in their transformative work, projecting connections between "knowing" readers and writers—such as within the girls' community of readers—who share their enjoyment and criticism of a text.

This discussion of the portrayal of reading in transformations seems to have directed our attention away from "The Little Mermaid." Reading is not depicted at all in Andersen's tale, yet in its transformations, we find many images of male and female readers and enchanted princes. Furthermore, in paratexts, some authors articulate their ideas and give advice about ways to read fairy tales. In the texts themselves as well as in these paratexts, images of readers are constructed with close attention to ideas about gender; in the transformations examined here, male readers are more able to throw themselves into the wondrous pleasure of the fairy tale, whereas female readers are more ambivalent in their approaches. In short, these fairy tale transformations present a great array of ideas about the ways fairy tales can be read, reread, and transformed, and they take infinite pleasure in these ever-changing processes.

For Andersen's little mermaid, metamorphosis is an unpleasant means to achieve her desires. Yet for many of these transformations, metamorphosis itself constitutes both the pleasure of the text and its end goal: that is, the intertextual, critical pleasure itself of knowing texts well, changing them, and "oscillating" between their different incarnations and different constructions of gender. It is this very intertextual pleasure that makes even the apparently superficial, simple fairy tale transformations so complex and so captivating.

Works Cited

Aarne, Antti Amatus. *The Types of the Folk-Tale: A Classification and Bibliography*. Trans. and enlarged Stith Thompson. 2nd rev. Helsinki: Soumalainen Tiedeakatemia Academia Scientiarum Fennica, 1961.

Abe Kōbō. "Ningyo-den." 1962. *Abe Kōbō zensakuhin*, vol. 8. Tokyo: Shinchōsha, 1972. 237–74.

Allen, Elizabeth, dir. *Aquamarine*. Twentieth Century Fox, 2006. DVD. Fox, 2007.

Allen, Virginia M. *The Femme Fatale: Erotic Icon*. Troy, NY: Whitston, 1983.

Andersen, Hans Christian. *The Stories of Hans Christian Andersen: A New Translation from the Danish*. Trans. Diana Crone Frank and Jeffrey Frank. Durham, NC: Duke University Press, 2005.

"Anderusen hen." *Zusetsu jidōbungaku hon'yaku daijiten*. Ed. Jidōbungaku hon'yaku daijiten henshū iinkai. Vol. 1. Tokyo: Ōzorasha, 2007. 56–112.

Aoyama, Tomoko. "The Genealogy of the 'Girl' Critic Reading Girl." *Girl Reading Girl in Japan*. Ed. Tomoko Aoyama and Barbara Hartley. New York: Routledge, 2010. 38–49.

———. "The Love That Poisons: Japanese Parody and the New Literacy." *Japan Forum* 6.1 (1994): 35–46.

———. *Reading Food in Modern Japanese Literature*. Honolulu: University of Hawai'i Press, 2008.

———. "Transgendering *Shōjo Shōsetsu*: Girls' Inter-text/sex-uality." *Genders, Transgenders and Sexualities in Japan*. Ed. Mark McLelland and Romit Dasgupta. New York: Routledge, 2005.

Aoyama, Tomoko and Barbara Hartley. Introduction. *Girl Reading Girl in Japan*. Ed. Tomoko Aoyama and Barbara Hartley. New York: Routledge, 2010. 1–14.

Araki, James T. "Otogi-zōshi and Nara-ehon: A Field of Study in Flux." *Monumenta Nipponica* 32.1 (Spring 1981): 1–20.

Ariès, Philippe. *Centuries of Childhood: A Social History of Family Life*. Trans. Robert Baldick. Harmondsworth, UK: Penguin, 1973.

Ariga, Chieko M. "The Playful Gloss: *Rubi* in Japanese Literature." *Monumenta Nipponica* 44.3 (Autumn 1989): 309–35.

Ashliman, D. L. "The Mermaid Wife." *Folktexts: A Library of Folktales, Folklore, Fairy Tales, and Mythology*. 7 Apr. 2011. 1 Dec. 2015. http://www.pitt.edu/

dash/type4080.html. Original source: C.J.T. *Folk-Lore and Legends: Scotland*. London: W. W. Gibbings, 1889. 86–88.

Ayame Hiroharu. *Ogawa Yōko: Mienai sekai o mitsumete*. Tokyo: Bensei shuppan, 2009.

Bacchilega, Cristina. *Fairy Tales Transformed? Twenty-First-Century Adaptations and the Politics of Wonder*. Detroit: Wayne State University Press, 2013.

———. *Postmodern Fairy Tales: Gender and Narrative Strategies*. Philadelphia: University of Pennsylvania Press, 1997.

———. "'Writing' and 'Voice': The Articulations of Gender in Folklore and Literature." Ed. Cathy Lynn Preston. *Folklore, Literature, and Cultural Theory: Collected Essays*. New York: Garland, 1995. 83–101.

Bachelard, Gaston. *Water and Dreams: An Essay on the Imagination of Matter*. 1942. Trans. Edith R. Farrell. Dallas: Pegasus Foundation, 1983.

Badia, Janet. "'One of Those People Like Anne Sexton or Sylvia Plath': The Pathologized Woman Reader in Literary and Popular Culture." *Reading Women: Literary Figures and Cultural Icons from the Victorian Age to the Present*. Ed. Janet Badia and Jennifer Phegley. Toronto: University of Toronto Press, 2005. 236–55.

Bakhtin, Mikhail. *Rabelais and His World*. Trans. Hélène Iswolsky. Bloomington: Indiana University Press, 1984.

Banerjee, Jacqueline. "Hans Christian Andersen and His Victorian Translators." 2008. *The Victorian Web* 24 Nov. 2008. 1 Dec. 2015. http://www.victorianweb.org/genre/childlit/fairytales2.html.

Barthes, Roland. *The Pleasure of the Text*. Trans. Richard Miller. New York: Hill and Wang, 1975.

Basile, Giambattista. "Sun, Moon, and Talia." Rev. trans. D. L. Ashliman. From *The Pentameron of Giambattista Basile*, trans. Richard F. Burton, 1983. "Sleeping Beauty." *Folktexts: A Library of Folktales, Folklore, Fairy tales, and Mythology* 7 June 2013. 10 Dec. 2015. http://www.pitt.edu/dash/type0410.html.

Bell, Elizabeth. "Somatexts at the Disney Shop: Constructing the Pentimentos of Women's Animated Bodies." *From Mouse to Mermaid: The Politics of Film, Gender, and Culture*. Ed. Elizabeth Bell, Lynda Haas, and Laura Sells. Bloomington: Indiana University Press, 1995. 107–24.

Bendix, Regina. "Seashell Bra and Happy End: Disney's Transformations of 'The Little Mermaid.'" *Fabula* 34.3–4 (1993): 280–90.

Benson, Stephen. Introduction. *Contemporary Fiction and the Fairy Tale*. Ed. Stephen Benson. Detroit: Wayne State University Press, 2008. 1–19.

Bettelheim, Bruno. *The Uses of Enchantment: The Meaning and Importance of Fairy Tales*. 1976. New York: Vintage Books, 1977.

Böcklin, Arnold. *Naiad*. 1887. Museum Syndicate. 10 July 2012. http://www.museumsyndicate.com.

Bode, Lisa. "Transitional Tastes: Teen Girls and Genre in the Critical Reception of *Twilight*." *Continuum Journal of Media & Cultural Studies* 24.5 (Oct. 2010): 707–19.

Borgen, Robert, and Marian Ury. "Readable Japanese Mythology: Selections from *Nihon shoki* and *Kojiki*." *Journal of the Association of Teachers of Japanese* 24.1 (Apr. 1990): 61–97.

Botticelli, Sandro. *The Birth of Venus*. 1486. Uffizi Gallery, Florence. Wikipedia. 28 Dec. 2012. http://en.wikipedia.org/wiki/The_Birth_of_Venus_(Botticelli).

Bottigheimer, Ruth. *Grimms' Bad Girls and Bold Boys: The Moral and Social Vision of the Tales*. New Haven, CT: Yale University Press, 1987.

Bredsdorff, Elias. *Hans Christian Andersen: The Story of His Life and Work 1805–75*. New York: Scribner, 1975.

Briggs, Julia. "A Liberating Imagination: Andersen in England." *Marvels & Tales: Journal of Fairy-Tale Studies* 20.2 (2006): 179–92.

Brockus, Susan. "Where Magic Lives™: Disney's Cultivation, Co-creation, and Control of America's Cultural Objects." *Popular Communication* 2.4 (2004): 191–211.

Buck, Chris, and Jennifer Lee, dir. *Frozen*. Walt Disney Studios, 2013. DVD. Walt Disney Home Entertainment, 2014.

Bullock, Julia C. *The Other Women's Lib: Gender and Body in Japanese Women's Fiction*. Honolulu: University of Hawaiʻi Press, 2010.

Butler, Judith. *Gender Trouble: Feminism and the Subversion of Identity*. 10th anniversary ed. New York: Routledge, 1999.

Cameron, James, dir. *Aliens*. Twentieth Century Fox, 1986. DVD. Twentieth Century Fox, 2010.

———, writ., prod. *Dark Angel: Complete Season One Collection*. First aired Fox network, United States, 2000–2001. DVD. Twentieth Century Fox Home Entertainment, 2006.

———, writ., prod. *Dark Angel: Complete Season Two Collection*. First aired Fox network, U.S.A, 2001–2. DVD. Twentieth Century Fox, 2006.

———, dir., writ. *The Terminator*. Orion Pictures, 1984. DVD. Twentieth Century Fox, 2004.

Carroll, Lewis. *Alice's Adventures in Wonderland and Through the Looking-Glass*. Oxford World's Classics. Oxford: Oxford University Press, 1971.

Carter, Angela. *The Bloody Chamber*. London: Vintage Books, 2006.

———. Introduction. *The Virago Book of Fairy Tales*. Ed. Angela Carter. London: Virago, 1990. ix–xii.

Chiba Shunji. "'Ningyo no nageki' ni tsuite." Special issue, "Tanizaki Jun'ichirō." *Yurīka* 35.8 (2003): 144–50.

———. "Tanizaki Jun'ichirō kenkyūshi taigai." *Gunzō Nihon no sakka*, vol. 8. Ed. Tanizaki Akio. Tokyo: Shōgakukan, 1991.

Cixous, Hélène. "The Laugh of the Medusa." Trans. Keith Cohen and Paula Cohen. *Signs* 1.4 (Summer 1976): 875–93.

Clements, Ron, and John Musker, dir. *The Little Mermaid*. Walt Disney Studios, 1989. Platinum Edition DVD. Buena Vista Home Entertainment, 2006.

Collins, Emily. "Nabokov's 'Lolita' and Andersen's 'The Little Mermaid.'" *Nabokov Studies* 9 (2005): 77–100.

Copeland, Rebecca, ed. *Woman Critiqued: Translated Essays on Japanese Women's Writing*. Honolulu: University of Hawai'i Press, 2006.

Dahlerup, Pil. "Splash! Six Views of 'The Little Mermaid.'" *Scandinavian Studies* 63.2 (1991): 141–63.

Daly, Mary. *Gyn/ecology: The Metaethics of Radical Feminism*. Boston: Beacon, 1978.

d'Arras, Jean. *Melusine; or, The Noble History of Lusignan*. Ed. and trans. Donald Maddox and Sara Sturm-Maddox. University Park: Pennsylvania State University Press, 2012.

D[di:]. *Fantasutikku sairento*. Tokyo: Besuto serāzu, 2000.

———. *Sentō no ningyo-hime to majo no mori*. Tokyo: Bungei shunjū, 2008.

———. Online profile. 2010. 12 Dec. 2015. http://deeth.net/gallery/profile/.

Demers, Patricia, and Gordon Moyles, eds. *From Instruction to Delight: An Anthology of Children's Literature to 1850*. Toronto: Oxford University Press, 1982.

Dijkstra, Bram. *Idols of Perversity: Fantasies of Feminine Evil in Fin-de-Siècle Culture*. New York: Oxford University Press, 1986.

Dinnerstein, Dorothy. "'The Little Mermaid' and the Situation of the Girl." *Contemporary Psychoanalysis* 3 (1967): 104–12.

Donder, Vic de. *Ningyo densetsu*. Trans. Togashi Yōko. Osaka: Kangensha, 1993.

Dollase, Hiromi Tsuchiya. "Early Twentieth Century Japanese Girls' Magazine Stories: Examining Shōjo Voice in *Hanamonogatari* (Flower Tales)." *Journal of Popular Culture* 36.4 (Spring 2003): 724–55.

———. "Ribbons Undone: The Shōjo Story Debates in Prewar Japan." *Girl Reading Girl in Japan*. Ed. Tomoko Aoyama and Barbara Hartley. New York: Routledge, 2010. 80–91.

———. "Shōfujin (Little Women): Recreating Jo for the Girls of Meiji Japan." *Japanese Studies* 30.2 (2010): 247–62.

Driscoll, Catherine. *Girls: Feminine Adolescence in Popular Culture and Cultural Theory*. New York: Columbia University Press, 2002.

Duffy, John Charles. "Gay-Related Themes in the Fairy Tales of Oscar Wilde." *Victorian Literature and Culture* 29.2 (2001): 327–49.

Duncker, Patricia. "Re-imagining the Fairy Tales: Angela Carter's Bloody Chambers." *Literature and History* 10.1 (Spring 1984): 3–14.

Easterlin, Nancy. "Hans Christian Andersen's Fish out of Water." *Philosophy and Literature* 25 (2001): 251–77.

"Fairy tale." *Oxford English Dictionary*. 3rd ed.; online ed. Oxford: Oxford University Press, 2015. 19 Nov. 2015. http://www.oxfordreference.com/view/10.1093/acref/9780199571123.001.0001.

Fass, Barbara F. "The Little Mermaid and the Artist's Quest for a Soul." *Comparative Literature Studies* 9 (1972): 291–302.

Finley, Erin. "One of These Days These Boots Are Gonna Walk All Over You: An Examination of the Femme Fatale's Evolution." *Beauty and the Abject: Interdisciplinary Perspectives*. Ed. Leslie Boldt-Irons, Corrado Federici, and Ernesto Virgulti. New York: Peter Lang, 2007. 211–24.

Fiske, John. *Reading the Popular*. 2nd ed. New York: Routledge, 2011.

Flaubert, Gustave. *Madame Bovary*. Trans. Merloyd Lawrence. Boston: Houghton Mifflin, 1969.

Flint, Kate. *The Woman Reader, 1837–1914*. New York: Oxford University Press, 1993.

Fouqué, Friedrich de la Motte. "Undine." *Romantic Fairy Tales*. Ed. Carol Tully. London: Penguin Books, 2000. 55–125.

Frank, Diana Crone, and Jeffrey Frank. "On Translating H. C. Andersen." *Marvels & Tales: Journal of Fairy-Tale Studies* 20.2 (2006): 155–65.

Fraser, Lucy. "An Unsuitable Job for a Girl: Violence and the Girl in Two Novels by Sakuraba Kazuki." *Intersections: Gender and Sexuality in Asia and the Pacific* 28 (Mar. 2012). 6 Jan. 2012. http://intersections.anu.edu.au/issue28/fraser.htm.

———. "Reading and Retelling Girls across Cultures: Mermaid Tales in Japanese and English." *Japan Forum* 26.2 (June 2014): 246–64.

Frederick, Sarah. *Turning Pages: Reading and Writing Women's Magazines in Interwar Japan*. Honolulu: University of Hawai'i Press, 2006.

Freedman, Alisa, and Kristina Iwata-Weickgenannt. "'Count What You Have Now. Don't Count What You Don't Have': The Japanese Television Drama *Around 40* and the Politics of Women's Happiness." *Asian Studies Review* 35 (Sept. 2011): 295–313.

Fujimoto Yoshitaka, dir. *Māmeido merodī pichi pichi pitchi*. First aired TV Aichi, Japan, 2003–4.

Fukawa Gen'ichirō. "Andersusen dōwa to Gurimu dōwa no hon hōhatsuyaku wo megutte—Meiji shoki no kodomo yomimono to kyōiku no setten." *Bungaku* 9.4 (July–Aug. 2008): 140–51.

Fukuda Kiyoto. "Dōwa." *Jidō bungaku jiten*. Ed. Namekawa Michio. Tokyo: Tokyo shoseki, 1988. 512.

Gardam, Jane. "The Pangs of Love." 1983. *The Pangs of Love*. London: Abacus, 1997. 35–46.

Garner, James Finn. *Once upon a More Enlightened Time: More Politically Correct Bedtime Stories*. New York: Macmillan, 1995.

Genette, Gérard. *The Architext: An Introduction*. Trans. Jane E. Lewin. Berkeley: University of California Press, 1992.

———. *Palimpsests: Literature in the Second Degree*. Trans. Channa Newman and Claude Doubinsky. Lincoln: University of Nebraska Press, 1997.

———. *Paratexts, Thresholds of Interpretation*. Trans. Jane E. Lewin. Cambridge: Cambridge University Press, 1997.

Genz, Stéphanie, and Benjamin A. Brabon. *Postfeminism: Cultural Texts and Theories*. Edinburgh: Edinburgh University Press, 2009.

Gilbert, Sandra M., and Susan Gubar. *Letters from the Front*. Vol. 3 of *No Man's Land: The Place of the Woman Writer in the Twentieth Century*. New Haven, CT: Yale University Press, 1988.

———. *The Madwoman in the Attic: The Woman Writer and the Nineteenth-Century Literary Imagination*. 2nd ed. New Haven, CT: Yale Nota Bene, Yale University Press, 2000.

Gloag, Isobel Lilian. *The Kiss of the Enchantress*. 1850. Wikipedia. 10 July 2012. http://en.wikipedia.org/wiki/File:The_knight_and_the_mermaid.jpg.

Grimm, Jacob, and Wilhelm Grimm. *The Brothers Grimm: The Complete Fairy Tales*. Hertfordshire, UK: Wordsworth Editions, 1997.

Grosz, Elizabeth. *Jacques Lacan: A Feminist Introduction*. Sydney: Allen and Unwin, 1990.

Haase, Donald. "Feminist Fairy-Tale Scholarship." *Fairy Tales and Feminism: New Approaches*. Ed. Donald Haase. Detroit: Wayne State University Press, 2004. 1–36.

Hand, David, dir. *Snow White and the Seven Dwarves*. Walt Disney Studios, 1937. DVD. Buena Vista Home Entertainment, 2009.

Hardwicke, Catherine, dir. *Twilight*. Summit Entertainment, 2008. DVD. Sony Pictures Home Entertainment Australia, 2009.

Harries, Elizabeth Wanning. *Twice upon a Time: Women Writers and the History of the Fairy Tale*. Princeton, NJ: Princeton University Press, 2003.

Harris, Peter, trans. *A Record of Cambodia: The Land and Its People*. By Zhou Daguan. 2nd ed. Chiang Mai, Thailand: Silkworm Books, 2007.

Hayashi Kōhei. "'Ningyo-den' kō: Abe Kōbō bungaku ni okeru dentō to sōzō." *Nihon bungakushi no shinkenkyū*. Ed. Usuda Jingorō. Tokyo: Miyai shoten, 1984. 319–30.

Hibbett, Howard. *The Chrysanthemum and the Fish: Japanese Humor since the Age of the Shoguns*. Tokyo: Kodansha International, 2002.

Hirabayashi Hirondo. *Anderusen no kenkyū*. Tokyo: Tokai University Press, 1967.

Hoban, Russell. "Wilde Pomegranates: The Ghost of a Room and the Soul of a Story." *Children's Literature in Education* 28.1 (1997): 19–29.

Hoffman, Alice. *Water Tales: Aquamarine & Indigo*. New York: Scholastic, 2003.

Homer. *The Odyssey*. Trans. E. V. Rieu, rev. trans. D. C. H. Rieu. London: Penguin Books, 1991.

Honda Masuko. "The Genealogy of *Hirahira*: Liminality and the Girl." Trans. Tomoko Aoyama and Barbara Hartley. *Girl Reading Girl in Japan*. Ed. Tomoko Aoyama and Barbara Hartley. New York: Routledge, 2010. 19–37.

———. *Ibunka to shite no kodomo*. Tokyo: Chikuma shobō, 1992.

———. "The Invalidation of Gender in Girls' Manga Today, with a Special Focus on Nodame Cantabile." Trans. Lucy Fraser and Tomoko Aoyama. *US-Japan Women's Journal* 38 (2010): 12–24.

———. *Ofiria no keifu: Aruiwa, shi to otome no tawamure*. Tokyo: Kōbundō, 1989.

Horlacher, Stephen. "A Short Introduction to Theories of Humour, the Comic, and Laughter." *Gender and Laughter: Comic Affirmation and Subversion in Traditional and Modern Media*. Ed. Gaby Pailer, Andreas Böhn, Stefan Horlacher, and Ulrich Scheck. Amsterdam: Rodopi, 2009. 17–47.

Howard, Ron, dir. *Splash*. Touchstone Pictures, 1984. DVD. Buena Vista Home Entertainment, 2003.

Hutcheon, Linda. *The Politics of Postmodernism*. 2nd ed. New York: Routledge, 2002.

———. *A Theory of Adaptation*. New York: Routledge, 2006.

———. *A Theory of Parody: The Teachings of Twentieth-Century Art Forms*. New York: Methuen, 1985.

Huyssen, Andreas. "Mass Culture as Woman: Modernism's Other." *Studies in Entertainment: Critical Approaches to Mass Culture*. Ed. Tania Modleski. Bloomington: Indiana University Press, 1986. 188–207.

Ikeda, Hiroko. *A Type and Motif Index of Japanese Folk-Literature*. Helsinki: Soumalainen Tiedeakatemia Academia Scientiarum Fennica, 1971.

Ikoma Natsumi. *Yokubō suru bungaku: Odoru kyōjo de yomitoku nichiei jendā hihyō*. Tokyo: Eihosha, 2007.

Inada Kōji. "Dōwa." *Nihon mukashibanashi jiten*. Ed. Inada Kōji, Kawabata Toyohiko, Mihara Yukihisa, Ōshima Tatehiko, and Fukuda Akira. Tokyo: Kōbundō, 1994. 641–43.

———. *Nihon mukashibanashi tsūkan*. Tokyo: Dōhōsha, 1998.

Inoue Miyako. *Vicarious Language: Gender and Linguistic Modernity in Japan.* Berkeley: University of California Press, 2006.

Ingwersen, Faith, and Niels Ingwersen. "A Folktale/Disney Approach." "Splash! Six Views of 'The Little Mermaid.'" By Pil Dahlerup. *Scandinavian Studies* 63.2 (1991): 149–52.

Ito, Ken. *Visions of Desire: Tanizaki's Fictional Worlds.* Stanford, CA: Stanford University Press, 1991.

Iwabuchi, Kōichi. *Recentering Globalization: Popular Culture and Japanese Transnationalism.* Durham, NC: Duke University Press, 2002.

"Japan Box Office Index." *Box Office Mojo* 7 July 2009. http://boxofficemojo.com/intl/japan/?yr=2008&p=.htm.

Jiburi kenkyūkai. *Miyazaki Hayao anime wa sugoi! "Gake no ue no Ponyo" made subete no sakuhin o yomitoku.* Tokyo: Rokusaisha, 2008.

Johansen, Jørgen Dines. "The Mask of Maidenhood: Andersen's 'The Little Mermaid.'" *Semiotica* 128.3 (2000): 349–57.

Jones, Diana Wynne. *Howl's Moving Castle.* New York: HarperCollins, 1986.

Jones, Mark A. *Children as Treasures: Childhood and the Middle Class in Early Twentieth Century Japan.* Cambridge, MA: Harvard University Asia Center, 2010.

Joosen, Vanessa. *Critical and Creative Perspectives on Fairy Tales: An Intertextual Dialogue between Fairy-Tale Scholarship and Postmodern Retellings.* Detroit: Wayne State University Press, 2011.

Jowett, Lorna. "To the Max: Embodying Intersections in *Dark Angel.*" *Reconstruction: Studies in Contemporary Culture* 5.4 (Fall 2005). 12 Dec. 2015. http://reconstruction.eserver.org/Issues/054/jowett.shtml.

Jung, Carl G. *Archetypes and the Collective Unconscious. The Collected Works of C.G. Jung.* Trans. R. F. C. Hull. Vol. 9, part 1. Princeton, NJ: Princeton University Press, 1959.

Kabat, Adam. "Tōyō to seiyō no ningyo no chigai." *Sōshi* 1.16 (Apr. 2004): 46–52.

Kan Satoko and Fujimoto Megumi. "'Shōjo shōsetsu' no rekishi o furikaeru." *<Shōjo shōsetsu> wandārando / Girls' Novels Wonderland.* Ed. Kan Satoko. Tokyo: Meiji shoin, 2008. 5–23.

Kanai Mieko. "Anderusen no ashi to chinmoku." *Kaku koto no hajimari ni mukatte.* Tokyo: Chūō kōron, 1981. 274–82.

———. "Anderusen no shitsū." *Soine no akumu, gosui no yume.* Tokyo: Chūō kōron, 1979. 46–52.

Karatani Kōjin. *Origins of Modern Japanese Literature.* Trans. Brett de Bary. Durham, NC: Duke University Press, 1993.

Kawai Hayao. *The Japanese Psyche: Major Motifs in the Fairy Tales of Japan.* 1982. Trans. Kawai Hayao and Sachiko Reece. Dallas: Spring, 1988.

Kawakami Hiromi. "Hanasanai." *Kami-sama.* Tokyo: Chūō kōron shinsha, 2001. 149–72.

Kawasaki Kenko. "The Climate of the Girl in Yoshimoto Banana: ♥?♥!♥!?" Trans. Tomoko Aoyama and Barbara Hartley. *Girl Reading Girl in Japan.* Ed. Tomoko Aoyama and Barbara Hartley. New York: Routledge, 2010. 50–63.

Kawato Michiaki. "Meijiki no Anderusen—deai kara hon'yaku sakuhin no shutsugen made." *Meiji Anderusen dōwa hon'yaku shūsei.* Ed. Kawato Michiaki and Sakakibara Takanori. Vol. 5. Tokyo: Nada shuppan sentā, 1999. 237–76.

Kawato Michiaki and Sakakibara Takanori, eds. *Hokubei/nanbei.* Vol. 5 of *Jidōbungaku: Hon'yaku sakuhin sōran: Meiji Taishō Shōwa Heisei no 135nen hon'yaku mokuroku.* Tokyo: Daikūsha, Nada shuppan sentā, 2005.

Kearney, Mary Celeste. "Coalescing: The Development of Girls' Studies." *NWSA Journal* 21.1 (2009): 1–28.

———. "Girlfriends and Girl Power: Female Adolescence in Contemporary U.S. Cinema." *Sugar, Spice, and Everything Nice: Cinemas of Girlhood.* Ed. Frances Gateward and Murray Pomerance. Detroit: Wayne State University Press, 2002. 125–44.

Killeen, Jarlath. *The Fairy Tales of Oscar Wilde.* Burlington, VT: Ashgate, 2007.

Kimura Sayo. "Ogawa Mimei 'Akai rōsoku to ningyo' to sono shūhen." *Fukui Kenritsu Daigaku ronshū* 29 (July 2007): 236–66.

Kinsella, Sharon. "Cuties in Japan." *Women, Media and Consumption in Japan.* Ed. Brian Moeran and Lise Skov. New York: Routledge, 2013. 220–54.

Kiryū Misao. *Hontō wa osoroshii Gurimu dōwa.* 3 vols. Tokyo: KK Besuto serāzu, 1998–2005.

Kleeman, Faye Yuan. "Sexual Politics and Sexual Poetics in Kurahashi Yumiko's *Cruel Fairy Tales for Adults*." *Constructions and Confrontations: Changing Representations of Women and Feminisms, East and West.* Ed. Cristina Bacchilega and Cornelia N. Moore. Honolulu: College of Languages, Linguistics and Literature, University of Hawai'i, 1996. 150–58.

Kobayashi, Fumihiko. *Japanese Animal-Wife Tales: Narrating Gender Reality in Japanese Folktale Tradition.* New York: Peter Lang, 2015.

Kondō Hiroko. "Yoshimoto Banana." *Nihon josei bungaku daijiten.* Ed. Ichiko Natsuo and Kan Satoko. Tokyo: Nihon tosho sentā, 2006. 334–35.

Kristeva, Julia. "Word, Dialogue, and Novel." Trans. Alice Jardine, Thomas Gora, and Léon S. Roudiez. *The Kristeva Reader.* Ed. Toril Moi. New York: Columbia University Press, 1986. 35–61.

Kurahashi Yumiko. *Dokuyaku to shite no bungaku*. Tokyo: Kōdansha, 1999.

———. *Otona no tame no zankoku dōwa*. Tokyo: Shinchōsha, 1984.

Kuzumi Kazuo. "Edo-jidai izen no 'ningyo' zō." *Fukushima Daigaku ningen hattatsu bunka gakurui ronshū* 2 (Dec. 2005): 49–59.

———. "Taishō-jidai no 'ningyo' zō (1)." *Fukushima Daigaku ningen hattatsu bunka gakurui ronshū* 6 (June 2007): 49–59.

Lacan, Jacques. *Écrits: The First Complete Edition in English*. Trans. Bruce Fink. New York: Norton, 2006.

LaMarre, Thomas, trans. "The Mermaid's Lament." By Tanizaki Jun'ichirō. *Shadows on the Screen: Tanizaki Jun'ichirō on Cinema and "Oriental" Aesthetics*. Ann Arbor: University of Michigan Press, 2005. 34–53.

———. *Shadows on the Screen: Tanizaki Jun'ichirō on Cinema and "Oriental" Aesthetics*. Ann Arbor: University of Michigan Press, 2005.

Lederer, Wolfgang. *The Kiss of the Snow Queen: Hans Christian Andersen and Man's Redemption by Woman*. Berkeley: University of California Press, 1986.

Leonard, Suzanne. "'I Hate My Job, I Hate Everybody Here': Adultery, Boredom, and the 'Working Girl' in Twenty-First-Century American Cinema." *Interrogating Postfeminism: Gender and the Politics of Popular Culture*. Ed. Yvonne Tasker and Diane Negra. Durham, NC: Duke University Press, 2007. 100–131.

Levy, Indra. *Sirens of the Western Shore: The Westernesque Femme Fatale, Translation, and Vernacular Style in Modern Japanese Literature*. New York: Columbia University Press, 2006.

Lieberman, Marcia R. "'Some Day My Prince Will Come': Female Acculturation through the Fairy Tale." *College English* 34.3 (Dec. 1972): 383–95.

Long, Tom. "Tweens Will Learn a Few Good Lessons in *Aquamarine*." *Detroit News* 3 Mar. 2006.

Loomba, Ania. *Colonialism/Postcolonialism*. New York: Routledge, 1998.

Lurie, Alison. *Don't Tell the Grown-Ups: Subversive Children's Literature*. Boston: Little, Brown, 1990.

Lüthi, Max. *Once upon a Time: On the Nature of Fairy Tales*. Trans. Lee Chadeayne and Paul Gottwald. New York: Frederick Ungar, 1970.

Maeda Ai. "Kodomo-tachi no hen'yō: Kindai bungakushi no naka." *Kokubungaku* 30.12 (Oct. 1985): 32–41.

———. *Text and the City: Essays on Japanese Modernity*. Ed. James A. Fujii. Durham, NC: Duke University Press, 2004.

Magritte, René. *L'invention collective*. 1934. Kunstsammlung Nordrhein-Westfalen, Düsseldorf. *WikiPaintings* 1 Dec. 2015. http://www.wikipaintings.org/en/rene-magritte/collective-invention-1934.

Marin, Louis. *Food for Thought*. 1986. Trans. Mette Hjort. Baltimore: John Hopkins University Press, 1989.

Markus, Andrew L. "The Carnival of Edo: Misemono Spectacles from Contemporary Accounts." *Harvard Journal of Asiatic Studies* 45.2 (1985): 499–541.

Matsumoto Yūko. *Akage no An no kyō ga shiawase in naru kotoba*. Tokyo: Shufu to seikatsusha, 2001.

———. *Kyoshokushō no akenai yoake*. Tokyo: Shūeisha, 1991.

———. *Romantikku na tabi e—Amerika hen*. Tokyo: Gentōsha, 1997.

———. *Shokubutsusei ren'ai*. 1988. Tokyo: Shūeisha, 1991.

———. *Tsumibukai hime no otogibanashi*. Tokyo: Kadokawa shoten, 1996.

———. "Yūko Matsumoto Homepage." 1 Dec. 2015. http://homepage3.nifty.com/office-matsumoto/profile_e.htm#essays.

McClintock, Anne. *Imperial Leather: Race, Gender, and Sexuality in the Colonial Contest*. New York: Routledge, 1995.

McConnell, Kathleen. "*Dark Angel*: A Recombinant Pygmalion for the Twenty-First Century." *Gothic Studies* 4.2 (2002): 178–90.

McGray, Douglas. "Japan's Gross National Cool." *Foreign Policy: The Magazine of Global Politics, Economics, and Ideas* 1 May 2002. 12 Dec. 2015. http://homes.chass.utoronto.ca/ikalmar/illustex/japfpmcgray.htm.

McKeon, Midori. "Ogino Anna's Gargantuan Play in *Tales of Peaches*." *The Father-Daughter Plot: Japanese Literary Women and the Law of the Father*. Ed. Rebecca L. Copeland and Esperanza Ramirez-Christensen. Honolulu: University of Hawai'i Press, 2001. 327–67.

McRobbie, Angela. "Postfeminism and Popular Culture: Bridget Jones and the New Gender Regime." *Interrogating Postfeminism: Gender and the Politics of Popular Culture*. Ed. Yvonne Tasker and Diane Negra. Durham, NC: Duke University Press, 2007. 27–39.

McRobbie, Angela, and Jenny Garber. "Girls and Subcultures." 1976. *Feminism and Youth Culture*. 2nd ed. By Angela McRobbie. Basingstoke, UK: Macmillan, 2000. 12–25.

"Mermaid." *Oxford English Dictionary*. 3rd ed.; online ed. Oxford: Oxford University Press, 2012. 9 July 2012. http://www.oed.com/view/Entry/116826.

Meyer, Stephenie. *Twilight*. 2005. New York: Little, Brown, 2006.

Miyazaki Hayao, dir. *Gake no ue no Ponyo / Ponyo on the Cliff by the Sea*. Studio Ghibli, 2008. DVD. Walt Disney Studio Home Entertainment, 2009.

———, dir. *Sen to Chihiro no kamikakushi / Spirited Away*. Studio Ghibli, 2001. DVD. Madman Entertainment, 2003.

———, dir. *Tonari no Totoro / My Neighbor Totoro*. Studio Ghibli, 1988. DVD. Madman Entertainment, 2006.

Mizuno Junko. *Ningyo-hime-den*. Tokyo: Bunkasha, 2002.

Mizuta Noriko. *Feminizumu no kanata: Josei hyōgen no shinsō*. Tokyo: Kōdansha, 1991.

Mizuta Noriko and Kitada Sachie, eds. *Yamambatachi no monogatari: Josei no genkei to katarinaoshi*. Tokyo: Gakugei shorin, 2002.

Montgomery, L. M. *Anne of Green Gables: Authoritative Text, Backgrounds, Criticism*. Ed. Mary Henley Rubio and Elizabeth Waterston. New York: Norton, 2007.

Morgan, Robin. *The Mer-Child: A Legend for Children and Other Adults*. New York: Feminist Press, 1991.

Morreall, John. *Comic Relief: A Comprehensive Philosophy of Humor*. Chichester, UK: Wiley-Blackwell, 2009.

Mouer, Ross, and Yoshio Sugimoto. "Nihonjinron at the End of the Twentieth Century: A Multicultural Perspective." La Trobe Asian Studies Papers. Bundoora, Austral.: School of Asian Studies, Latrobe University, 1995.

Mulvey, Laura. *Visual and Other Pleasures*. London: Macmillan, 1989.

Murai, Mayako. *From Dog Bridegroom to Wolf Girl: Contemporary Japanese Fairy-Tale Adaptations in Conversation with the West*. Detroit: Wayne State University Press, 2015.

———. "Re-envisioning of Fairy Tales in Contemporary Japanese Art. The Post-Feminist Aesthetics of the Grotesque-Cute Guro-Kawaii." *Postmodern Reinterpretations of Fairy Tales: How Applying New Methods Generates New Meanings*. Ed. Anna Kérchy. Lewiston, NY: Edwin Mellen, 2011. 145–62.

———. "The Translation and Reception of Angela Carter's Work in Japan." *Angela Carter traductrice—Angela Carter en traduction*. Ed. Martine Henard Dutheil de la Rochere. Lausanne: Centre de Traduction Littéraire, 2014. 39–55.

Murphy, Patrick D. "'The Whole Wide World Was Scrubbed Clean': The Androcentric Animation of Denatured Disney." *From Mouse to Mermaid: The Politics of Film, Gender and Culture*. Ed. Elizabeth Bell, Lynda Haas, and Laura Sells. Bloomington: Indiana University Press, 1995. 125–36.

Murray, Isobel. Introduction. *The Complete Shorter Fiction of Oscar Wilde*. Ed. Isobel Murray. Oxford: Oxford University Press, 1979. 1–18.

Mylius, Johan de. "The Life of Hans Christian Andersen, Day by Day." The Hans Christian Andersen Center. 1998. 1 Dec. 2015. http://andersen.sdu.dk/liv/tidstavle/index_e.html.

———. "The Voice of Nature in Hans Christian Andersen's Fairy Tales." Notre Dame Seishin University, Okayama. 1989.

Nagashima, Yoichi. "Hans Christian Andersen Remade in Japan: Mori Ōgai's Translation of 'Improvisatoren.'" *Hans Christian Andersen, a Poet in Time:*

Papers from the Second International Hans Christian Andersen Conference, 29 July to 2 August 1996. Ed. Johan de Mylius, Aage Jørgensen, and Viggo Hjørnager Pedersen. Odense: Hans Christian Andersen Center, Odense University, 1999. 397–406.

Nakagawa Masafumi. "Otogibanashi." *Nihon mukashibanashi jiten*. Ed. Kawabata Toyohiko et al. Tokyo: Kōbundō, 1994. 160–61.

Namekawa Michio. "Otogibanashi." *Jidōbungaku jiten*. Ed. Namekawa Michio. Tokyo: Tokyo shoseki, 1988. 135.

Napier, Susan. *From Impressionism to Anime: Japan as Fantasy and Fan Cult in the Mind of the West*. New York: Palgrave Macmillan, 2008.

Nassar, Christopher S. "Andersen's 'The Shadow' and Wilde's 'The Fisherman and His Soul': A Case of Influence." *Nineteenth-Century Literature* 50.2 (1995): 217–24.

Nicol, Bran. *The Cambridge Introduction to Postmodern Fiction*. Cambridge: Cambridge University Press, 2009.

Nishihara Daisuke. *Tanizaki Jun'ichirō to orientarizumu: Taishō Nihon no Chūgoku gensō*. Tokyo: Chūō kōron, 2003.

Nishimoto Keisuke. "Yōseiteki ningyo to yōkaiteki ningyo: Sekai no densetsu, meruhen o megutte." *Gakuen: Shōwa Joshi Daigaku* 613 (1990): 1–13.

Nonaka Hiiragi. *Ningyo-hime no kutsu*. 1994. Tokyo: Shinchō bunko, 1998.

———. *Yomogi aisu*. 1991. Tokyo: Shūeisha, 1997.

Nünning, Ansgar F. "Reconceptualizing Unreliable Narration: Synthesizing Cognitive and Rhetorical Approaches." *A Companion to Narrative Theory*. Ed. James Phelan and Peter J. Rabinowitz. Malden, MA: Blackwell, 2005. 89–107.

Ogawa Mimei. *Akai rōsoku to ningyo*. 1921. Tokyo: Ten'yūsha hakkō, 1978.

———. "Shin dōwa ron." *Dōwa to zuihitsu*. Tokyo: Nihon dōwa kyōkai shuppanbu, 1934. *Aozora bunko* 12 Apr. 2016. http://www.aozora.gr.jp/cards/001475/files/51802_46584.html.

Ogawa Yōko. *Chinmoku hakubutsukan*. Tokyo: Chikuma shobō, 2000.

———. "Daibingu pūru." 1989. *Samenai kōcha*. Tokyo: Fukutake bunko, 1993. 93–181.

———. "Domitorī." 1990. *Ninshin karendā*. Tokyo: Bungei shunju, 1994. 75–148.

———. *Hoteru Airisu*. Tokyo: Gentōsha, 1998.

———. "Kusuriyubi no hyōhon." 1992. *Kusuriyubi no hyōhon*. Tokyo: Shinchō, 1994. 9–90.

———. *Ogawa Yōko taiwashū*. Tokyo: Gentōsha, 2007.

———. *Otogibanashi no wasuremono*. Illus. Higami Kumiko. Tokyo: Shūeisha, 2006.

———. *Umi*. Tokyo: Shinchōsha, 2006.

"Ogawa Yōko." Special issue, *Bungei* 48 (2009).
"Ogawa Yōko." Special issue, *Yurīka* 36.2, no. 489 (2004).
Ogino Anna. *Watashi no aidokusho*. 1991. Tokyo: Fukutake shoten, 1994.
Ong, Walter J. *Orality and Literacy: The Technologizing of the Word*. London: Methuen, 1982.
Orbaugh, Sharalyn. "Busty Battlin' Babes: The Evolution of the *Shōjo* in 1990s Visual Culture." *Gender and Power in the Japanese Visual Field*. Ed. Joshua S. Mostow, Norman Bryson, and Maribeth Graybill. Honolulu: University of Hawai'i Press, 2003. 200–228.
———. "The Debate over Pure Literature." *The Columbia Companion to Modern East Asian Literature*. Ed. Joshua Mostow. New York: Columbia University Press, 2003. 132–36.
———. "Shōjo." *Encyclopedia of Contemporary Japanese Culture*. Ed. Sandra Buckley. New York: Routledge, 2002. 458–59.
Orbaugh, Sharalyn, and Joshua S. Mostow. Editors' preface. *Proceedings for the Association for Japanese Literary Studies: Parody* 10 (Summer 2009): iv–vi.
Oriental Land Group. "About Tokyo Disney Resort: Guest Statistics." 28 Oct. 2015. http://www.olc.co.jp/en/tdr/guest/.
Ōsawa Chieko. "Anderusen dōwa ni okeru ikyō e no shōkei: Chiisai ningyo-hime no ai to tensei." *Ikai no kōsaku*. Ed. Hosoda Ayako and Watanabe Kazuko. Tokyo: Lithon, 2006. 237–62.
Ōtsuka Eiji. *Shōjo minzokugaku*. Tokyo: Kōbunsha, 1989.
———. "Yoshimoto Banana ron: Katsudon o daite hashiru shōjo." *Subaru* (Nov. 1989): 202–31.
Ōtsuka Hikari. *Busu ron*. Tokyo: Chikuma shobō, 2005.
Ozawa Toshio. *Mukashibanashi no kosumorojī: Hito to dōbutsu to no konintan*. Kawasaki City, Japan: Ozawa mukashibanashi kenkyusho, 2014.
Pailer, Gaby, Andreas Böhn, Stefan Horlacher, and Ulrich Scheck, eds. *Gender and Laughter: Comic Affirmation and Subversion in Traditional and Modern Media*. Amsterdam: Rodopi, 2009.
Patessio, Mara. "Readers and Writers: Japanese Women and Magazines in the Late Nineteenth Century." *The Female as Subject: Reading and Writing in Early Modern Japan*. Ed. P. F. Kornicki, Mara Patessio, and G. G. Rowley. Ann Arbor, MI: Center for Japanese Studies, 2010. 191–213.
Pedersen, Tara E. *Mermaids and the Production of Knowledge in Early Modern England*. Burlington, VT: Ashgate, 2015.
Pinnington, Adrian. "'Foreign Bodies': 'Race,' Gender and Orientalism in Tanizaki Jun'ichirō's 'The Mermaid's Lament.'" *Representing the Other in Modern Japanese Literature: A Critical Approach*. Ed. Rachel Hutchinson and Mark Williams. New York: Routledge, 2007. 75–95.

Posadas, Baryon Tensor. "Double Fictions and Double Visions of Japanese Modernity." Ph.D. diss., University of Toronto, 2010. 26 Mar. 2012. https://tspace.library.utoronto.ca/bitstream/1807/26225/3/posadas_baryon_tensor_s_201011_PhD_thesis.pdf.

Propp, Vladimir. *Morphology of the Folktale*. 1928. Trans. Lawrence Scott, rev. Alan Dundes. Austin: University of Texas Press, 1968.

Prough, Jennifer. *Straight from the Heart: Gender, Intimacy, and the Cultural Production of Shojo Manga*. Honolulu: University of Hawai'i Press, 2011.

Ramirez-Christensen, Esperanza. Introduction. *The Father-Daughter Plot: Japanese Literary Women and the Law of the Father*. Ed. Rebecca Copeland and Esperanza Ramirez-Christensen. Honolulu: University of Hawai'i Press, 2001. 1–23.

Rich, Adrienne. "When We Dead Awaken: Writing as Re-vision." *On Lies, Secrets, and Silence: Selected Prose, 1966–1978*. New York: Norton, 1979. 35–49.

Robertson, Jennifer. *Takarazuka: Sexual Politics and Popular Culture in Modern Japan*. Berkeley: University of California Press, 1998.

Rowe, Karen E. "To Spin a Yarn: The Female Voice in Folklore and Fairy Tale." *Fairy Tales and Society: Illusion, Allusion, and Paradigm*. Ed. Ruth B. Bottigheimer. Philadelphia: University of Pennsylvania Press, 1986. 53–74.

Rubin, Jay. *Injurious to Public Morals: Writers in the Meiji State*. Seattle: University of Washington Press, 1984.

"Rusalka." *The Oxford Companion to World Mythology*. Ed. David Leeming. Oxford Reference Online, Oxford University Press, 2004. 1 Apr. 2011. http://www.oxfordreference.com/views/ENTRY.html?subview=Main&entry=t208.e1372.

Russ, Joanna. *How to Suppress Women's Writing*. Austin: University of Texas Press, 1983.

———. *Kittatinny: A Tale of Magic*. New York: Daughters, 1978.

Said, Edward W. *Orientalism*. 1978. London: Penguin Books, 2003.

Saitō Minako. 2006. "Yoshimoto Banana and Girl Culture." Trans. Eiji Sekine. *Woman Critiqued: Translated Essays on Japanese Women's Writing*. Ed. Rebecca Copeland. Honolulu: University of Hawai'i Press. 176–85.

Saitō Tamaki. *Beautiful Fighting Girl*. Trans. J. Keith Vincent and Dawn Lawson. Minneapolis: University of Minnesota Press, 2011.

Sakaki, Atsuko. "Kurahashi Yumiko's Negotiations with the Fathers." *The Father-Daughter Plot: Japanese Literary Women and the Law of the Father*. Ed. Rebecca Copeland and Esperanza Ramirez-Christensen. Honolulu: University of Hawai'i Press, 2001. 292–26.

———. *Obsessions with the Sino-Japanese Polarity in Japanese Literature*. Honolulu: University of Hawai'i Press, 2006.

———. *Recontextualizing Texts: Narrative Performance in Modern Japanese Fiction.* Cambridge, MA: Harvard University Asia Center, 1999.

———. "'Watashi' to 'kare' no aida—Kurahashi Yumiko ni miru 'tasha' gainen no tawamure." *Nihon bungaku ni okeru <tasha>.* Ed. Tsuruta Kin'ya. Tokyo: Shin'yōsha, 1994. 342–63.

Sakuraba Kazuki. *Akakuchibake no densetsu.* 2006. Tokyo: Sōgensha, 2010.

———. "Intabyū Sakuraba Kazuki kuronikuru: 2006–2012." Ed. Enomoto Masaki. *Dōtoku to iu na no shōnen.* Tokyo: Kadokawa bunko, 2013. 77–157.

———. "Sakka no dokushomichi: No. 54." 28 Apr. 2006. *Web hon no hanashi* 30 June 2010. http://www.webdoku.jp/rensai/sakka/michi54.html.

———. *Satōgashi no dangan wa uchinukenai / A Lollypop or a Bullet.* Tokyo: Kadokawa shoten, 2009.

———. *Seinen no tame no dokusho kurabu.* Tokyo: Shinchōsha, 2007.

———. *Shōjo ni wa mukanai shokugyō / An Unsuitable Job for a Girl.* Tokyo: Sōgensha, 2007.

———. *Watashi no otoko.* Tokyo: Bunshun bunko, 2007.

Sarra, Edith. *Fictions of Femininity: Literary Inventions of Gender in Japanese Court Women's Memoirs.* Stanford, CA: Stanford University Press, 1999.

Sasama Yoshihiko. *Ningyo no keifu: Itoshiki umi no jūnintachi.* Tokyo: Gogatsu shobō, 1999.

Sax, Boria. "The Mermaid and Her Sisters: From Archaic Goddess to Consumer Society." *ISLE: Interdisciplinary Studies in Literature and Environment* 7.2 (2000): 43–54.

Schaffert, Timothy. "The Mermaid in the Tree." *My Mother She Killed Me, My Father He Ate Me: Forty New Fairy Tales.* Ed. Kate Bernheimer. London: Penguin Books, 2010. 171–99.

Schalow, Gordon, and Janet A. Walker, eds. *The Woman's Hand: Gender and Theory in Japanese Women's Writing.* Stanford, CA: Stanford University Press, 1996.

Schilling, Mark. "It's Kids' Play for Anime King: Director Hayao Miyazaki ('Spirited Away') Delivers Another Classic." *Japan Times* 11 July 2008. 5 Nov. 2008. http://search.japantimes.co.jp/cgi-bin/ff20080711a1.html.

Sebastian-Jones, Marc, and Tateya Koichi, trans. "Two Tales from *Cruel Fairy Tales for Adults*" by Kurahashi Yumiko. *Marvels and Tales: Journal of Fairy-Tale Studies* 22.1 (2008): 171–82.

Seidensticker, Edward. *Low City, High City: Tokyo from Edo to the Earthquake: How the Shogun's Ancient Capital Became a Great Modern City, 1867–1923.* San Francisco: Donald S. Ellis, 1985.

Seki Keigo. *Nihon mukashibanashi shūsei.* 6 vols. Tokyo: Kadokawa shoten, 1950–61.

———. *Nihon mukashibanashi taisei.* 11 vols. Tokyo: Kadokawa shoten, 1987–90.

———. *Nihon no mukashibanashi: Hikaku kenkyū josetsu*. Tokyo: Nihon hōsō shuppan kyōkai, 1977.
Sells, Laura. "Where Do the Mermaids Stand? Voice and Body in The Little Mermaid." *From Mouse to Mermaid: The Politics of Film, Gender, and Culture*. Ed. Elizabeth Bell, Lynda Haas, and Laura Sells. Bloomington: Indiana University Press, 1995. 175–92.
Shamoon, Deborah. *Passionate Friendship: The Aesthetics of Girls' Culture in Japan*. Honolulu: University of Hawai'i Press, 2011.
Sherif, Ann. "Japanese without Apology: Yoshimoto Banana and Healing." *Ōe and Beyond: Fiction in Contemporary Japan*. Ed. Stephen Snyder and Philip Gabriel. Honolulu: University of Hawai'i Press, 1999. 278–302.
Shibusawa Tatsuhiko. *Erotishizumu*. 1967. Tokyo: Tōgensha, 1977.
Shida Moto. "Yaobikuni." *Nihon mukashibanashi jiten*. Ed. Inada Kōji, Kawabata Toyohiko, Mihara Yukihisa, Ōshima Tatehiko, and Fukuda Akira. Tokyo: Kōbundō, 1994. 964.
Shiff, Jonathan M, writ., prod. *H20 Just Add Water: The Complete First Series*. Dir. Jeffrey Walker and Colin Budds. First aired Network Ten, Australia, 2006. DVD. Magna, 2009.
———. writ., prod. *H20 Just Add Water: The Complete Second Series*. Dir. Jeffrey Walker and Colin Budds. First aired Network Ten, Australia, 2007–8. DVD. Magna, 2009.
Shimizu Reiko. *Tsuki no ko*. Serialized in *LaLa*, 1988–92. 13 vols. Tokyo: Hakusensha, 1989–93.
Shimizu Yoshikazu. "H. Anderusen to Terayama Shūji no 'Ningyo-hime' kara J. Jirodu no 'Ondīnu' o hete B. Barutōku to Terayama Shūji no 'Aohige-kō no shiro' ni arawareru yōsei." *Aichi Gakuin Daigaku kyōyōbu kiyō* 55.2 (2007): 49–77.
Sickafoose, Munro. "Knives." *The Armless Maiden and Other Tales for Childhood's Survivors*. Ed. Terry Windling. New York: Tom Doherty Associates, 1995. 155–71.
Smith, Janet S. "Women in Charge: Politeness and Directives in the Speech of Japanese Women." *Language in Society* 21 (1992): 59–82.
Smith, Kevin Paul. *The Postmodern Fairytale: Folkloric Intertexts in Contemporary Fiction*. New York: Palgrave Macmillan, 2007.
Soracco, Sabrina. "A Psychoanalytic Approach." "Splash! Six Views of 'The Little Mermaid.'" By Pil Dahlerup. *Scandinavian Studies* 63.2 (1991): 145–49.
"Special Features." *The Little Mermaid*. Walt Disney Studios, 1989. Platinum Edition DVD. Buena Vista Home Entertainment, 2006.
Spivak, Gayatri Chakravorty. "Can the Subaltern Speak?" *Marxism and the Interpretation of Culture*. Ed. Lawrence Grossberg and Cary Nelson. London: Macmillan Education, 1988. 271–313.

Studio Ghibli. "Sakuhin no naiyō no kaisetsu." *Gake no ue no Ponyo* 16 Feb. 2010. http://www.ghibli.jp/ponyo.

Sudo, Yoko. "'Frozen' Ranks as Third-Biggest Hit in Japan." *Wall Street Journal* 4 June 2014. 12 Apr. 2016. http://blogs.wsj.com/japanrealtime/2014/06/04/frozen-ranks-as-third-biggest-hit-in-japan/.

Takahara Eiri. "The Consciousness of the Girl: Freedom and Arrogance." Trans. Tomoko Aoyama and Barbara Hartley. *Woman Critiqued: Translated Essays on Japanese Women's Writing*. Ed. Rebecca Copeland. Honolulu: University of Hawai'i Press, 2006. 185–93.

———. *Shōjo ryōiki*. Tokyo: Kokushokankokai, 1999.

Takahashi Rumiko. *Mermaid Saga*. 4 vols. San Francisco: VIZ Media, 2004.

———. *Ningyo shirīzu*. 3 vols. Tokyo: Shōgakukan, 2003.

Takanezawa Noriko, ed. *Ogawa Yōko*. Tokyo: Kanae shobō, 2005.

Takase Ryō. *Orenji poketto*. Tokyo: KC Nakayoshi, 1990.

———. "Otogibanashi no gogatsu." 1989. *Buraddi Marī*. Tokyo: KC Nakayoshi, 1990.

Takemura Kazuko. "Naze 'posuto'feminizumu na no ka?" *"Posuto"feminizumu*. Ed. Takemura Kazuko. Tokyo: Sakuhinsha, 2003. 1–4.

Tanabe Satoru. *Ningyo*. Tokyo: Hōsei Daigaku shuppan kyoku, 2008.

Tanizaki Jun'ichirō. *Chijin no ai*. 1924. Tokyo: Shinchōsha, 1947.

———. "Jōzetsu." *Tanizaki Jun'ichirō zenshū*, vol. 20. Tokyo: Chūō kōronsha, 1983. 69–166.

———. *Naomi*. 1924. Trans. Anthony H. Chambers. New York: Knopf, 1985.

———. *Ningyo no nageki / Majutsushi*. Tokyo: Chūō bunko, 1978.

———. *A Portrait of Shunkin*. Trans. Howard S. Hibbett. Tokyo: Hara shobō, 1965.

———. Preface. "Uindamīya fujin no ougi." *Tanizaki Jun'ichirō zenshū*, vol. 24. Tokyo: Chūō kōronsha, 1983. 157–58.

———. *Shunkinshō*. 1933. Aozora bunko. 29 Sept. 2016 http://www.aozora.gr.jp/cards/001383/files/56866_58169.html.

Tasker, Yvonne, and Diane Negra. "Introduction: Feminist Politics and Postfeminist Culture." *Interrogating Postfeminism: Gender and the Politics of Popular Culture*. Ed. Yvonne Tasker and Diane Negra. Durham, NC: Duke University Press, 2007. 2–25.

Tatar, Maria. *Off with Their Heads: Fairy Tales and the Culture of Childhood*. Princeton, NJ: Princeton University Press, 1992.

Tatsumi, Takayuki. *Full Metal Apache: Transactions between Cyberpunk Japan and Avant-Pop America*. Durham, NC: Duke University Press, 2006.

Tattersall, Carol. "An Immodest Proposal: Rereading Oscar Wilde's 'Fairy Tales.'" *Wascana Review* 26.1–2 (1991): 128–39.

Terayama Shūji. "Ningyo-hime." 1968. *Terayama Shūji zenshū*. Vol. 8. Tokyo: Magajin hausu, 1994.
Thomsen, Ulla. "A Structuralist Approach." "Splash! Six Views of 'The Little Mermaid.'" By Pil Dahlerup. *Scandinavian Studies* 63.2 (1991): 141–45.
Thwaite, Mary F. *From Primer to Pleasure in Reading*. Boston: Horn Book, 1972.
Tiffin, Jessica. *Marvelous Geometry: Narrative and Metafiction in Modern Fairy Tale*. Detroit: Wayne State University Press, 2009.
Todorov, Tzvetan. *The Fantastic: A Structural Approach to a Literary Genre*. Trans. Richard Howard. Cleveland: Press of Case Western Reserve University, 1973.
Toro, Guillermo del, dir. *Pan's Labyrinth*. Warner Bros, 2006. DVD. 20th Century Fox, 2010.
Treat, John Whittier. "Yoshimoto Banana Writes Home: *Shōjo* Culture and the Nostalgic Subject." *Journal for Japanese Studies* 19.2 (Summer 1993): 353–87.
Tseëlon, Efrat. "*The Little Mermaid*: An Icon of Woman's Condition in Patriarchy, and the Human Condition of Castration." *International Journal of Psycho-Analysis* 76 (1995): 1017–30.
Touponce, William F. "Children's Literature and the Pleasures of the Text." *Children's Literature Association Quarterly* 20.4 (Winter 1995): 175–82.
Uchiyama, Akiko. "Meeting the New Anne Shirley: Matsumoto Yūko's Translation of *Anne of Green Gables*." Paper presented at Ninth International Women in Asia Conference: Transition and Interchange, University of Queensland, Brisbane, Australia, 29 Sept. 2008.
——. "*Akage no An* in Japanese Girl Culture." *Japan Forum* 26.2 (June 2014): 209–23.
Viswanathan, Meera. "In Pursuit of Yamamba: The Question of Female Resistance." *The Woman's Hand: Gender and Theory in Japanese Women's Writing*. Ed. Paul Gordon Schalow and Janet A. Walker. Stanford, CA: Stanford University Press, 1996. 239–61.
Wagner, Richard. "The Ride of the Valkyries." Perf. Berlin Philharmonic. CD. *The Berlin Philharmonic on EMI*. EMI Classics, 2007.
——. *Der Ring des Nibelungen*. *Richard Wagner, Der Ring des Nibelungen: A Companion Volume*. By Rudolph Sabor. London: Phaidon, 1997.
"Wairudo hen." *Zusetsu jidōbungaku hon'yaku daijiten*. Ed. Jidōbungaku hon'yaku daijiten henshū iinkai. Vol. 3. Tokyo: Ōzorasha, 2007. 855–80.
Waki Akiko. "Dansō no ningyo-hime to Yao bikuni: Seiō to Nihon no ningyo-tachi." *Yurīka* 25.1 (1993): 183–91.
Walker, Barbara G. *Feminist Fairy Tales*. New York: Harper, 1996.
Warner, Marina. *From the Beast to the Blonde: On Fairy Tales and Their Tellers*. 1996 ed. New York: Farrar, Straus and Giroux, 1994.

———. *Once upon a Time: A Short History of Fairy Tale*. Oxford: Oxford University Press, 2014. Kindle e-book.

Wasko, Janet. "Is It a Small World, After All?" *Dazzled by Disney? The Global Disney Audiences Project*. Ed. Janet Wasko, Mark Philips, and Eileen R. Meehan. Leicester, UK: Leicester University Press, 2001. 3–30.

Watanabe Peco. *Henshin monogatari*. Tokyo: Akita Shoten, 2008.

Waterhouse, John William. *A Mermaid*. 1900. Royal Academy of Arts, London. *Wikipedia Commons*. 6 Nov. 2010. http://commons.wikimedia.org/wiki/File:John_William_Waterhouse_-_Mermaid.JPG.

Wavehill, Ronnie. "Karukany (Mermaids)." Trans. Erika Charola and Ronnie Wavehill. *Yijarni: True Stories from Gurindji Country*. Ed. Erika Charola and Felicity Meakins. Canberra, Austral.: Aboriginal Studies Press, 2016. 13–20.

Wells, Paul. "Thou Art Translated: Analysing Animated Adaptation." *Adaptations: From Text to Screen, Screen to Text*. Ed. Deborah Cartmell and Imelda Wheelan. New York: Routledge, 1999. 199–213.

Whitley, David. *The Idea of Nature in Disney Animation*. Aldershot, UK: Ashgate, 2008.

Wilde, Jane. *Poems by Speranza*. Dublin: James Duffy, 1864. *Internet Archive* 2013. 1 Dec. 2015. https://archive.org/details/poems00wild_0.

Wilde, Oscar. *The Happy Prince and Other Tales*. 1888. Stilwell, KS: Digireads. com, 2006.

———. *A House of Pomegranates*. 1891. Stilwell, KS: Digireads.com, 2006. 43–82.

———. *The Picture of Dorian Gray*. 1890. London: Vintage Books, 2007.

Williams, Christy. "Mermaid Tales on Screen: *Splash*, *The Little Mermaid*, and *Aquamarine*." *Beyond Adaptation: Essays on Radical Transformations of Original Work*. Ed. Phyllis Frus and Christy Williams. Jefferson, NC: McFarland, 2010. 194–205.

Wilson, Michiko N. "Ōba Minako the Raconteur: Refashioning a Yamauba Tale." *Marvels & Tales: Journal of Fairy-Tale Studies* 27.2 (2013): 218–33.

Woolf, Virginia. "Professions for Women." *Collected Essays of Virginia Woolf*. Ed. Leonard Woolf. Vol. 2. London: Chatto and Windus, 1966. 284–89.

Works Design Group. "Brand Stories: The Evolution of Starbucks." 25 Feb. 2015. 1 Dec. 2015. http://worksdesigngroup.com/brand-redesign-evolution-starbucks/.

Yamada Fumiko. "Nihon ni okeru Gurimu, meruhen hen'yō." *Keio-Germanistik Jahresschrift* 21 (2004): 60–82. 27 Dec. 2012. http://ci.nii.ac.jp/naid/110007354534.

Yamamuro Shizuka. *Yamamuro Shizuka no kōen to hon'yaku mokuroku*. Tokyo: Kokuritsu kokkai toshokan, jidōsho no kai, 1971.

Yanagita Kunio. *Kōshō bungeishi kō.* Vol. 6 of *Teihon Yanagita Kunio shū.* Tokyo: Chikuma shobō, 1963.

Yokote Michiko and Hanamori Pinku. *Māmeido merodī pichi pichi pitchi.* Serialized in *Nakayoshi,* 2002–5. 7 vols. Tokyo: Kodansha, 2003–5.

Yolen, Jane. *The Mermaid's Three Wisdoms.* Cleveland: Collins + World, 1978.

Yolen, Jane, and Shulamith Oppenheim. *The Fish Prince and Other Stories: Mermen Folk Tales.* New York: Interlink Books, 2001.

Yoshimi, Shunya. "Japan: America in Japan / Japan in Disneyfication: The Disney Image and the Transformation of 'America' in Contemporary Japan." *The Global Disney Audiences Project: Dazzled by Disney?* Ed. Janet Wasko, Mark Philips, and Eileen R. Meehan. London: Leicester University Press, 2001. 160–81.

Yoshimoto Banana. *Kitchin.* 1989. Tokyo: Kadokawa shoten, 1998.

———. *Utakata/Sankuchuari.* Tokyo: Shincho bunko, 2002.

Yoshimoto, Mitsuhiro. "Images of Empire: Tokyo Disneyland and Japanese Cultural Imperialism." *Disney Discourse: Producing the Magic Kingdom.* Ed. Eric Smoodin. New York: Routledge, 1994. 181–99.

Yoshiya Nobuko. *Hanamonogatari.* 1920–21. Tokyo: Kawade shobō, 2009.

Zipes, Jack, ed. *Don't Bet on the Prince: Contemporary Feminist Fairy Tales in North America and England.* Aldershot, UK: Gower, 1986.

———. *The Enchanted Screen: The Unknown History of Fairy-Tale Films.* New York: Routledge, 2011.

———. *Fairy Tale as Myth / Myth as Fairy Tale.* Lexington: University Press of Kentucky, 1994.

———. *Fairy Tales and the Art of Subversion: The Classical Genre for Children and the Process of Civilization.* 2nd ed. New York: Routledge, 2006.

———. *Hans Christian Andersen: The Misunderstood Storyteller.* New York: Routledge, 2005.

———. Introduction. *Don't Bet on the Prince: Contemporary Feminist Fairy Tales in North America and England.* Aldershot, UK: Gower, 1986. 1–38.

———. *Relentless Progress: The Reconfiguration of Children's Literature, Fairy Tales, and Storytelling.* Hoboken, NJ: Taylor and Francis, 2008.

———. *Why Fairy Tales Stick: The Evolution and Relevance of a Genre.* New York: Routledge, 2006.

Zornado, Joseph L. *Inventing the Child: Culture, Ideology, and the Story of Childhood.* New York: Routledge, 2006.

Zuk, Rhoda. "The Little Mermaid: Three Political Fables." *Children's Literature Quarterly* 22.4 (1997–98): 166–74.

Index

Abe Kōbō: biography, 86; "Ningyo-den" (Legend of a mermaid), 72, 86–94, 112, 159
adaptation, 31, 42–43, 188; as transformation across media, 43, 50n10, 61. *See also* fairy tale transformation
agency: creative, 158–59, 176, 182; feminist, 165; girl, 54, 111, 153, 155
aging, 176, 181
Akai rōsoku to ningyo (The red candles and the mermaid) (Ogawa), 50–51
Alice's Adventure's in Wonderland (Carroll), 32, 115, 151, 170, 178
Allen, Elizabeth, *Aquamarine* (film), 144–48, 154, 186
Andersen, Hans Christian: biography, 24–25, 28, 40; tales by, 45, 128, 188, 146; "The Little Mermaid", 25–29; writing techniques, 73
Anderson, Benedict, 130
animation: bodies in motion in, 39, 46–49, 54; fairy tale transformations in, 39, 42–43; metamorphosis in, 43, 49, 52, 56–57; music in, 49–50, 61–65, 67–69. *See also* Disney; *Little Mermaid, The* (film); *Ponyo on the Cliff by the Sea*; Studio Ghibli
Anne of Green Gables (Montgomery), 98, 128, 129
Aoyama, Tomoko: girls' intertextuality, 38, 130, 134; new literacy, 13, 96, 106; on Ogino Anna, 173; *shōjo*, 133–34, 140, 147
Aoyama, Tomoko and Hartley, Barbara, 131, 133

Aquamarine (film) (Allen), 144–48, 154, 186
Aquamarine (novel) (Hoffman), 144–48
Arabian Nights, 82
architexts: Andersen's "The Little Mermaid" as, 145, 161–63; animation studio as, 43–46, 68, 163; fairy tale, 71–72, 81, 85, 88, 92–94; mermaid, 92. *See also* fairy tale transformation.
Ayame Hiroharu, 114, 125

Bacchilega, Cristina: "fairy tale web," 15, 71, 184; mirroring, 174; narrators, 76, 121, 172; transformation, 7–8, 13, 104, 188; women, 10, 117, 186
Bachelard, Gaston, 27, 130
Bakhtin, Mikhail: carnival, 9, 11, 66, 41, 90; logic, 7, 113
Barthes, Roland, 9, 13, 77, 123–24, 187
beautiful fighting girl (*sentō bishōjo*), 161, 164
Benson, Stephen, 106
Bettelheim, Bruno, 41–42, 61
Birth of Venus (Botticelli), 17
Bonaparte, Marie, 102
Botticelli, Sandro, *Birth of Venus*, 17
boy. *See* patriarchy; prince; "reading boy"
Brothers Grimm: The Complete Fairy Tales, The (Grimm and Grimm): in Japan, 30, 35, 37, 40, 128; tales, 89, 108, 115, 117. *See also* Grimm Boom
Buck, Chris and Lee, Jennifer, *Frozen*, 45, 146
busu, 110–11
Butler, Judith, 8, 66, 119, 179

Cameron, James, *Dark Angel* (producer), 160–69, 175–76, 179, 182–83, 186
candy, 122, 124, 149, 154–55, 170. *See also* food
Carter, Angela, 104–6, 114, 173
cathartic pleasure, 41, 69, 124. *See also* pleasure
Carroll, Lewis, *Alice's Adventure's in Wonderland*, 32, 115, 151, 170, 178
Chiba Shunji, 75n3, 76n4
children: as audience, 24, 40, 46, 53, 58, 68–69; as a construct, 50–52, 67; socialization of, 40–42, 58, 63, 74. *See also* children's literature; *shōjo*.
children's literature: and education, 29–31, 40; trends, 29, 30–32, 35, 41
China: Japan's relations with, 30; literary depictions of, 75, 77–78, 82, 84–85, 90, 105; mermaid stories from, 20, 112
Christian: Church, 17; ideology, 32, 47, 53–54, 60; influence, 28–29, 99, 104; Devil, 66n16, 72n1, 73, 83. *See also* souls
Cixous, Hélène, "The Laugh of Medusa", 9–10, 60, 111
Clements, Ron and Musker, John, 61. *See also The Little Mermaid* (film).
comedy. *See* laughter
consumerism, 55n13, 137–40, 147, 163–64
cyberpunk, 161, 164, 166–67. *See also* postmodern

D[di:]: biography, 176; *Sentō no ningyo-hime to majo no mori* (The little mermaid of the public bath and the witch's forest), 175–82
Daly, Mary, 174n9
Dark Angel (Cameron), 160–69, 175–6, 179, 182–83, 186
desire: blurred borders, 142–43; for food, 48; for freedom, 54, 56, 166n7; girl's, 48–49, 152–53; for mermaid or "other", 75, 82, 83, 84–85, 150; mermaid's, 25, 28, 48–49, 53–56; and pain, 71, 85–86, 124, 142–43; same-sex, 83, 92, 137, 179; sexual, 82–83, 89–91, 109–11, 179; for souls 16–18, 25, 32, 109
disability, 151, 166, 166n7
Disney: as architext, 43–45, 64, 161–63, 165, 168; dominance of, 36, 47–48, 67; traits, 57, 59, 146. *See also Frozen*; *Little Mermaid, The* (film)
dissemination, 143. *See also* girl consciousness
dōwa, 35, 50, 102–3, 106. *See also* children's literature
Driscoll, Catherine, 138n9, 139n10, 147
Duncker, Patricia, 104

eternal girl, 27, 151, 170. *See also* Honda Etō Jun, 113

fairy tale: architext, 71–72, 81, 85–86, 88, 92–94, 96; "canon," 13, 102, 113–14, 125; definition of, 11–13, 36n26, 108–9; endings in, 22, 29, 36–37, 83; ideologies of romance, 135, 137, 146; and the marvelous, 8, 74, 76–77, 83, 88, 109; narrative formulas, 34, 71, 76, 85, 121, 141; post-, 159, 169, 172, 182–83; studies, 7–8, 12, 15, 41, 102, 132, 174. *See also* folklore; folktale; *mukashibanashi*; *otogibanashi*
fairy tale transformation, 7–8, 113, 174. *See also* adaptation; architexts; girls' intertextuality; intertextuality; metafiction metamorphosis; metatexts; (magical and physical); paratexts; parody; plagiarism; post–fairy tale transformation; revision; sequels; translation; transtextuality
family: absent maternal figures and, 50, 62, 64; abuse in the, 152–53; depiction of fathers, 58, 64, 153; evil maternal figures, 62, 64, 66–67; father-daughter conflicts, 49–50, 57–58, 61, 140, 145; positive maternal figures, 58, 62, 68–69; and siblings, 49, 46, 132, 135,

142–43, 150; unconventional, 140, 142–43, 150
femininity: constructions of, 26–27, 68, 152, 155, 161, 164; feminine power, 56–57, 62; as nature, 99–100; performance of, 65–66, 68, 119, 165
feminism: in fairy tale studies 27, 89, 101–2; 175; messages of, 96–97, 104–5. *See also* postfeminism
"Fisherman and His Soul, The" (Wilde), 72–75, 77, 79–85, 91–94, 121, 124
Fiske, John, 147
folklore, 15, 34–35, 150. *See also* folktale
folktale: animal-wives in, 21–23, 22n13, 36, 48, 87; indexes, 34n24; traditions, 17, 34.
food: desire for, 48; imagery, 170, 173–74; sweet foods, 115, 122, 124, 154–55
Fouqué, Friedrich de la Motte, *Undine*, 18, 24, 26, 28, 72, 104–5
Frozen (Buck and Lee), 45, 146
Fukawa Gen'ichirō, 31n19

Gake no ue no Ponyo (*Ponyo on the Cliff by the Sea*) (Miyazaki), 46–62, 67–69
Gardam, Jane, "The Pangs of Love," 134–35
Garner, James Finn, "Little Mer-persun, The," 101–2, 104
gay. *See* sexuality
gaze: desiring, 110–11, objectifying, 28, 84, 164–65, 167, 169; as taboo, 23, 87, 110, 142
genbun itchi, 76
gender: binaries, 99–100, 104–5; identity, 66, 152, 166, 177, 179, 182; order, 58, 60, 62–63, 69; as performative, 8, 65–66, 119, 177–79, 182; role inversion, 116–19; roles, 57–58, 62–64, 89, 91, 170–71, 175
Genette, Gérard; architexts, 71–72, 85, 88, 163; intertextuality, 113; paratexts, 97–98, 172
Gilbert, Sandra and Gubar, Susan: on patriarchy, 63, 65–66, 171, 174; on Snow White, 79, 117n16, 170, 180; and story telling, 182–83
"Gill Girl" (dir. Spicer, writ. David), *Dark Angel* (Cameron): 160–69, 175–76, 179, 182–83, 186
girl. *See shōjo*. *See also* girl consciousness, girls' intertextuality
girl consciousness, 48–49, 126–28, 131, 141, 143. *See also* Takahara; *shōjo*
girls' intertextuality, 38, 130, 134. *See also* Aoyama; fairy tale transformation
Gloag, Isobel Lilian, *The Kiss of the Enchantress*, 18–19
Grimm boom, 37, 96, 102, 125. *See also Brothers Grimm Fairy Tales, The*
Grimm brothers. *See Brothers Grimm Fairy Tales, The*
Grimm, Jacob and Grimm, Wilhelm, *Brothers Grimm Fairy Tales, The*
Gurimu būmu, 37, 96, 102, 125. *See also Brothers Grimm Fairy Tales, The*

H20 Just Add Water (Shiff), 162n4
hair: and beauty, 92, 117; combing, 19, 55n13, 59, 145, 147; length and styling, 21, 58, 64, 65, 92, 116, 117; red, 17, 47, 56, 68, 81, 83
"Hanasanai" ("I won't let go") (Kawakami), 71–72, 92–94, 186
"Happyaku bikuni," 20–21, 23, 87–88, 170
Harries, Elizabeth Wanning, 7
Henshin monogatari (Tales of metamorphosis) (Watanabe), 157, 159, 184
heterosexuality. *See* sexuality
Higami Kumiko: and Matsumoto, 99–100, 123; and Ogawa, 96–97, 112, 115, 117–18, 123–24; style of, 115, 154
hikikomori, 150
hirahira, 130, 152. *See also* Honda
Hisaishi Jō, 46, 49
Hoffman, Alice, *Aquamarine* (novel), 144–48
Homer, *The Odyssey*, 16, 49n9
homosexuality. *See* sexuality

Honda Masuko: *shōjo*, 26–27, 128–31, 141, 151–52; children's culture, 52, 67; girls' sphere, 130, 137, 151
Hontō wa osoroshii Gurimu dōwa (The Grimms' tales that are actually terrifying) (Kiryū), 102–3, 113
Howard, Ron, *Splash*, 44, 56, 145n12, 145–46, 162n4
humor. *See* laughter
Hutcheon, Linda: knowing audience, 12–13; adaptation, 13, 42–43, 105; transcoding, 43, 61; intertextuality, 43, 68, 78, 105; parody, 96, 104; postmodernism, 162, 174
hybrid: bodies, 25, 52, 71, 108–9, 163; postfeminist, 161, 164, 166–68, 182

identity: gender and, 8, 59, 66, 152, 166, 177, 179, 182; Lacan, 26–27, self and, 93, 109, 150–55; sexual, 26, 169–70, 177–79; stereotyped, 63
Ikoma Natsumi, 171–72
illustrations: in children's literature, 32, 129; by Higami, 97, 99–100, 115, 117–18, 123; by Mizushima, 75, 78–79; as textual play, 178–79; tradition, 23–24. *See also* Higami; Mizushima
implied author, 120–22
intertextuality: definitions, 7, 113; musical, 49–50, 68; and plagiarism, 113; as play, 159, 176–77. *See also* fairy tale transformation; pleasure: intertextual
inversions: 10–11, 96–97, 108–9, 113–14, 116–17
Iwaya Sazanami, 30, 34
Izanami and Izanagi, 110

Jung, Carl, 22, 62, 102

Kanai Mieko, 158–59, 180
Karatani Kōjin, 50–51
Kawai Hayao, 15, 22–23, 23n13
kawaii, 88n9, 138–39, 155. See also *shōjo*

Kawakami Hiromi, "Hanasanai" (I won't let go), 71–72, 92–94, 186
Kawasaki Kenko, 131, 140–43
Kiryū Misao, *Hontō wa osoroshii Gurimu dōwa* (The Grimms' tales that are actually terrifying), 102–3, 113
Kittatinny: A Tale of Magic (Russ), 132, 135–37, 143
Kiss of the Enchantress, The (Gloag), 18–19
"Knives" (Sickafoose), 151n13
knowing audience, 12–13, 38, 59, 72, 186. *See also* Hutcheon
Kobayashi, Fumihiko, 22n13
Kojiki, 110
Kristeva, Julia, 7
Kurahashi Yumiko: as an author, 13, 95, 105–6, 113, 153, 173; biography, 106; *Dokuyaku to shite no bungaku* (Literature as poison) 173; "Ningyo no namida" (The mermaid's tears), 107–14; *Otona no tame no zankoku dōwa* (Cruel fairy tales for adults), 96, 106, 108, 113, 116

Lacan, Jacques, 26–27, 58–60
language: as authority, 59–61, 66; gendered, 68, 76, 122, 152, 178; in literature, 121; onomatopoeia, 67. *See also* fairy tale, silence, voices, wordplay
"The Laugh of Medusa" (Cixous), 9–10, 60, 111
laughter: affirming stereotypes, 59–61, 63; challenging stereotypes, 88, 113, 90–91, 106, 113; comic texts, 90, 145, 166, 178, 180, 108, 108n9; theories of, 10n2, 10–11, 91, 96n1, 113. *See also* parody, pleasure
Lederer, Wolfgang, 64
lesbian. *See* sexuality
Levy, Indra, 84n7
Lieberman, Marcia R., 132
Little Mermaid, The (film) (Clements and Musker): analysis, 43–48, 53–67,

145–46, 153; making of, 43–44, 46, 56–58, 61–62, 65; in *Dark Angel*, 161–62, 165, 168; Japanese release 44–45, 54, 63
"Little Mermaid, The" (Hans Christian Andersen story): analysis, 25–29; as architext, 145, 161–63; and Christianity, 25, 28–29, 32, 40, 53, 60 (*see also* Christian; souls); feminist critiques of, 27, 101–2, 126; girlhood in, 26–27, 32, 36, 144–45 (*See also* girls; *shōjo*); major plot elements, 86–87, 100, 107–8, 115–16, 145, 167; influences on, 18, 23–24; influential themes from, 42, 75, 81, 125, 140, 144, 170–71; pain in, 28, 38, 53, 63, 126, 159; publishing history, 24–25, 29–32, 40, 74–75
"Little Mer-persun, The" (Garner), 101–2, 104
Lolita (Nabokov), 44n4
Lollypop or a Bullet, A (*Satōgashi no gandan wa uchinukenai*) (Sakuraba): analysis, 148–55; and *Pan's Labyrinth*, 151–52
Loomba, Ania, 82
Lurie, Alison, 132
Lüthi, Max, 70, 73, 76–77, 112

Maeda Ai, 51–52, 60–61
Miyoshi, Masao 140
masculinity: types of, 63–64, 75, 147–48, 179–80; and the body, 157, 166–67, 170, 183
matriarchy, 62, 68–69, 99–100, 104–5, 116–17, 119
Matsumoto Yūko: approach, 95, 97, 102–3, 105; biography, 96, 98–99, 102; "Otoko no kuni e itte shinda ningyo-hime" (The little mermaid went to the man's country and died), 99–105; *Shokubutsu ren'ai*, 102–3; *Tsumibukai hime no otogibanashi* (Fairy tales of sinful princesses), 99, 103, 105, 123
matsu onna, 171

McGray, Douglas, 161
Mer-Child, The (Morgan), 101, 104
mermaids: in art, 17, 19, 22, 24, 32–33, 108n; association with death, 17, 23, 26–27, 81; brides, 18, 22; and Christianity, 17, 28, 32 (*see also* soul); illustrations of, 23–24, 32, 75, 78–79, 97, 117; in Japan, 20–23, 32, 35, 150; mummies, 23, 87, 162; as objects, 79–81, 84, 86, 90, 150, 159 (*see also* other); and reproduction, 18, 117, 166–67; sacrifice, 29, 53–54, 177; sexualized, 17, 21, 56, 90, 163; sex with, 21, 90, 109–10, 112; in the West, 16–20, 29. *See also* hybrid, mermen
mermen, 116–17, 119–20, 124–25, 166–67
metafiction, 88, 132, 134. *See also* fairy tale transformation
metamorphosis (magical and physical), 7, 43, 47, 49, 52, 56–57, 66, 83, 125. *See also* fairy tale transformation
metatexts, 186–87. *See also* fairy tale transformation; paratexts
Miyazaki Hayao: *Gake no ue no Ponyo* (Ponyo on the Cliff by the Sea) 46–62, 67–69; role of, 45–46, 176
Mizuno Junko, *Ningyo-hime-den* (Princess mermaid) (manga), 88n9
Mizushima Niou, 75, 78–79
monogatari. See folktale, folklore, *mukashibanashi*
Montgomery, L. M., *Anne of Green Gables*, 98, 128, 129
Morgan, Robin, *The Mer-Child*, 101, 104
Morreall, John, 91
Mori Ōgai, 31
mother. *See* family
mukashibanashi, 21–22, 34–35, 76, 141. *See also* folktales
Mulvey, Laura, 164–65
Murai, Mayako, 3, 14–16, 35, 37, 88n9, 114, 139, 185
music, 49–50, 61–65, 67–69
musume, 131. *See also* family

Nabokov, Vladimir, *Lolita*, 44n4
narrator: first-person, 88–89, 92, 178, 182; girl as, 140–41, 143; third-person, 73, 76, 121, 135–36, 172; unreliable, 120–22, 125
nature: children and, 52; climate and, 141–42; depictions of, 108; femininity and 51, 56–58, 69, 99–100; girls and, 51, 100, 130, 151. *See also* ocean
Nihonjinron, 15, 23n14, 185
"Ningyo-den" (Legend of a mermaid) (Abe), 72, 86–94, 112, 159
ningyo-hime. *See* "The Little Mermaid"
"Ningyo-hime" ("The Little Mermaid") (puppet-play) (Terayama), 35, 50
Ningyo-hime no kutsu (The little mermaid's shoes) (Nonaka): allusions to "Snow White" in, 170–71, 173–74; analysis, 168–75, 177, 183
Ningyo-hime-den (Princess mermaid) (manga) (Mizuno), 88n9
"Ningyo hōseki shokunin no isshō" (The life of a mermaid's jeweler) (Y. Ogawa), 115–25, 166–67. *See also* Higami
ningyo no miira, 23, 87, 162
"Ningyo no nageki" (The mermaid's lament) (Tanizaki), 74–86, 88–93, 112, 124
"Ningyo no namida" (The mermaid's tears) (Kurahashi), 107–14
Ningyo shirīzu (Mermaid Saga) (Takahashi), 21, 184
Nonaka Hiiragi: biography, 169; *Ningyo-hime no kutsu* (The little mermaid's shoes), 168–75, 177, 183; use of postface, 172–75

objectifying: gaze, 164–66, pleasure in, 79, 81; sexual, 56, 90, 150, 159, 183
ocean: drowning or becoming sea foam, 112, 112n12, 123–24, 149, 151, 181; as imagination, 51n12; women and 27, 56–57, 68, 99–100, 104, 141–42. *See also* nature
Odyssey, The (Homer), 16, 49n9

Ogawa Mimei: *Akai rōsoku to ningyo* (The red candles and the mermaid) 50–51; and children, 35, 39–40, 50–52
Ogawa Yōko: biography, 114–15; "Ningyo hōseki shokunin no isshō" (The life of a mermaid's jeweler), 115–25, 166–67; *Otogibanashi no wasuremono* (Lost property fairy tales) 114–15, 121–25, 155, 173
Ogino Anna, 173
okama, 179
Ong, Walter, 7
ongaeshi, 21, 87
Orbaugh, Sharalyn, 138, 161n3
Orientalism, 14–15, 38, 78, 82–84, 105, 185
other: foreign lands and people as 82, 84; laughter and, 63; mermaid as 5, 79, 81–82, 159, 161, 167, 182. *See also* objectification, Orientalism
otogibanashi, 34–35. *See also mukashibanashi*
Otogibanashi no wasuremono (Lost property fairy tales) (Ogawa), 114–15, 121–25, 173
otogizōshi, 34–35
"Otoko no kuni e itte shinda ningyo-hime" (The little mermaid went to the man's country and died) (Matsumoto), 96–105
Otona no tame no zankoku dōwa (Cruel fairy tales for adults) (Kurahashi), 96, 106, 108, 113, 116
Ōtsuka Eiji, 138, 141

pain: Andersen's use of, 28, 38, 63, 126; and artistic creation, 28, 158; desire and, 71, 85–86, 124, 142–43; endurance of, 158–59, 170–71, 181; erasure of, 49, 53–54, 111, 146; transformed, 150, 155
"Pangs of Love, The" (Gardam), 134–35
Pan's Labyrinth (Toro), 151–52
paratexts: bibliography, 103, 113, 115; frame story, 122–23; postface, 105,

108–9, 113, 124, 170, 174; use of, 47, 97–98, 172, 178. *See also* fairy tale transformation; Genette
parody: gender as, 8, 66; in literature, 13, 22, 96, 101–2, 104, 108. *See also* fairy tale transformation
patriarchy: challenging, 64–67, 99–100, 104, 111, 155; internalized, 171, 174; in literary establishments, 131, 140, 153; minipatriarchs, 59–60; socialization into the, 58–61, 89
plagiarism, 102, 113
pleasure: ambivalent, 159, 164–65, 168–69; of audience, 58–59, 105, 166, 168; in critical reading, 147, 135; definition of, 9, 11; and fairy tales, 71, 74, 77, 79, 188; intertextual, 12, 68, 78, 97, 105; and laughter, 9, 58–60, 88, 91, 180; in reading, 93, 123–25, 135, 147–48, 173; in text as object 77–78, 115; in transformation, 8–9, 12–13, 98, 105, 94, 98; visual, 164–65, 168
political correctness, 101–2, 103, 104
Ponyo on the Cliff by the Sea (*Gake no ue no Ponyo*) (Miyazaki), 46–62, 67–69
postface, 170, 172, 174. *See also* paratexts
post-fairy tale transformation, 158–161, 183. *See also* fairy tale transformation; postfeminism
postfeminism, 161–62, 164–65, 171–72, 175–77, 183
postmodernism, 106, 113, 158–59, 161–62, 174–75
precious objects, 64, 70–71, 77, 81, 84
prince: and patriarchy, 56, 58–61, 69, 147; as protagonist, 70–71, 88, 91–92, 187; role of, 28, 48, 53–55, 88, 134, 142, 152
psychological growth, 41–42. *See also* children
Pygmalion, 28, 55

queer. *See* sexuality

reading: boys and, 147; communities, 124, 127, 130–31, 146–48; conscious reading, 183; girls and, 98, 127, 130–33, 135–36, 137, 144, 147, 155; women and, 94, 132–34, 155. *See also* pleasure
"reading boy," 147. *See also* patriarchy; reading
"reading girl," 133, 147. *See also* reading
retelling. *See* fairy tale transformation; *shōjo* (girl)
revision, 96–98, 104–5, 115–16, 119, 140. *See also* fairy tale transformation
Rich, Adrienne, 97, 116
Rītoru māmeido (*Little Mermaid, The*) (Japanese release of Disney film): 44–45, 54, 63
Russ, Joanna: biography, 135; *Kittatinny: A Tale of Magic*, 132, 135–37, 143

Saitō Minako, 140, 149
Saitō Tamaki, 161n3
Sakaki, Atsuko, 76, 106
Sakuraba Kazuki: biography, 149; *Satōgashi no gandan wa uchinukenai* (*Lollypop or a Bullet, A*), 148–55
Satōgashi no gandan wa uchinukenai (*A Lollypop or a Bullet*) (Sakuraba) 148–55
Sax, Boria, 55n13
sea. *See* ocean
Seki Keigo, 22n13, 23n14, 34n24
Sells, Laura, 54–55, 65
sentō bishōjo, 161, 164
Sentō no ningyo-hime to majo no mori (little mermaid of the public bath and the witch's forest, The), (D[di:]), 175–82
sequels, 101, 104. *See also* fairy tale transformation
sexuality: and development, 26, 54–55; heterosexual romance and relationships, 56, 92, 145–46, 152–53; heterosexual sex and reproduction, 69, 105, 117; homosexuality, 83, 92, 137, 172, 179. *See also* identity
Shiff, Jonathan, *H20 Just Add Water*, 162n4

shitamachi, 177
shōjo (girl): association with candy, 115, 124, 145, 154–55; aesthetic, 32, 130, 152–53; as audience, 132–33, 137, 139, 144, 148; critical capacity, 147, 153; culture, 32, 128–29, 138–39, 144–47, 155; friendship, 130, 145–46, 152–54; girl consciousness, 48–49, 126–28, 130–31, 141, 143; and girlhood, 26–27, 36, 115, 127, 152, 170; growing up, 26–27, 58, 61, 126, 155, 157; history of, 128–30; manga, 32–34, 128–30; as protagonist, 58, 108, 135, 139–40, 149, 153–55; retelling tales, 127, 148–56; sphere, 130–31, 151–53; studies, 38, 48–49, 127, 129–32, 139–40. *See also* eternal girl, reading
Shokubutsu ren'ai (Matsumoto), 102–3. *See also* Sleeping Beauty.
shōsetsu, 76
Sickafoose, Munro, "Knives," 151n13, 153n15
silence: and authorship, 63, 158; feminist responses to, 27, 27n17, 63, 101, 135, 137, 153; as mermaid's tragedy, 59, 65, 135, 136–37; and power, 65–66, 68, 91–93, 125
Sleeping Beauty: as a trope, 103, 110, 130, 141, 172, 178; Kurahashi, 109–10; Matsumoto's, 99, 102–3
Snow White: evil queen, 65, 117n16, 170–71, 174, 180; as a trope, 79, 99, 103, 110, 172–74, 182
souls: deals with, 53, 66, 73, 111; desire for, 16–18, 25, 32, 109; as a reward, 28–29, 60; symbols and, 55n13, 135
Spivak, Gayatri Chakravorty, 120
Splash (Howard), 44, 56, 145n12, 145–46, 162n4
Studio Ghibli: and adaptation, 45–48; approach, 43, 57, 61–62, 67–68, 69, 181

Takahara Eiri, 48–49, 115, 126–27, 131, 141

Takahashi Rumiko, *Ningyo shirīzu* (Mermaid Saga), 21, 184
Takemura Kazuko, 175, 183
Tales of metamorphosis (*Henshin monogatari*) (Watanabe), 157, 159, 184
Tanizaki Jun'ichirō: biography, 74–75; "Ningyo no nageki" (The mermaid's lament), 74–86, 88–93, 112, 124; and Wilde, 74–75
Tatar, Maria, 41, 58
Terayama Shūji, "Little Mermaid, The" (Ningyo-hime) (puppet-play), 35, 50
textual play, 177–78, 180–81. *See also* wordplay
Tiffin, Jessica, 12, 36, 86
Todorov, Tzvetan, 88
Toro, Guillermo del, *Pan's Labyrinth*, 151–52
transformation. *See* fairy tale transformation; metamorphosis (magical and physical)
translation, 29, 30–32, 122, 128
transtextuality, 113n13. *See also* fairy tale transformation
treasure. *See* precious objects
Tsumibukai hime no otogibanashi (Fairy tales of sinful princesses) (Matsumoto), 99, 103, 105, 123

Uchiyama, Akiko 98
ugliness, 110-1
Undine (Motte Fouquè), 18, 24, 26, 28, 72, 104–5
unreliable narrator, 120–22, 125
urban, 161, 176–77, 181–82
Utakata (Bubbles) (Yoshimoto), 138–43, 147

voices, 63–66. *See also* silence

Wagner, Richard, *Die Walküre* (The Valkyrie) in *Der Ring des Nibelungen* (The Ring of the Nibelung), 50, 50n10, 68
Waki Akiko, 23

Warner, Marina, 5–6, 8, 17, 27n17, 54
Watanabe Peco, *Henshin monogatari* (Tales of metamorphosis), 157, 159, 184
water. *See* ocean
Wilde, Oscar: "Fisherman and His Soul, The," 72–75, 77, 79–85, 91–94, 121, 124; techniques, 72–74, 85
witch: aging woman as, 176–77, 180–82; author as, 174; in classic fairy tales, 64, 177; and Queen in Snow White, 65, 170–71, 180; scientist as, 136; *yamauba* (mountain witch), 10
women: as readers, 94, 132–34, 155; association with nature, 57–58, 99–100, 104, 108, 141–42; association with water, 27, 56, 181; as protagonists, 158–59, 169, 172, 175, 177; who wait, 171. *See also* femininity
Woolf, Virginia, 174
wordplay, 60, 68, 99–100, 177–78, 180–81
writing, 9–10, 136, 143, 147, 159, 173

yamauba, 10
Yanagita Kunio, 34, 34n24, 87n8
"Yao bikuni," 20–21, 23, 87–88, 170
Yoshimoto Banana: biography, 139, 150; reception of, 127, 131, 138–40; *Utakata* (Bubbles), 138–43, 147

Zipes, Jack: approaches to fairy tales, 2, 7, 137, 158, 188; on utopia, 32, 52–53; on revision, 97, 132

www.ingramcontent.com/pod-product-compliance
Lightning Source LLC
Chambersburg PA
CBHW070315240426
43661CB00057B/2653